laneman
publishing

Gravel Pit Carp

the definitive guide to fishing for gravel pit carp

by Jim Gibbinson

Gravel Pit Carp - a limited edition book.
Published in 1999 by Laneman Publishing
5 Lyons Court, Dorking, Surrey RH4 1AB

British Library Cataloguing in Publication Data

A catalogue record for this book is available from the British Library.

ISBN 1-901717-06-2

Design and production by Lane Design.
Telephone: 01306 875154

Printed in Great Britain.

Contents

Acknowledgements

My thanks go to Tim Paisley (Carpworld, Crafty Carper and Carp-Talk), Bob Roberts (Advanced Carp Fishing), Jim Foster (Catchmore Carp), Simon Roff and Stuart Dexter (Coarse Fisherman) for approving the use of extracts from articles of mine which first appeared in their magazines.

I am an admirer of Brian Atkins' clear and precise draughtsmanship, so I am grateful to him for agreeing to produce the illustrations.

Some of the photographs which appear in these pages have been taken by family, friends and acquaintances - I thank them for doing so, and I am appreciative of their expertise.

Finally, my love and gratitude to Maria for her unstinting support.

James Gibbinson
Kent
October 1999

Introduction

In this, my fifth book on carp fishing, I have focussed on my favourite waters, gravel pits. But no branch of carp fishing is completely divorced from other aspects so some of what I write will be applicable to estate lakes, meres, ponds, canals, dykes and even rivers.

In common with my previous books, its content is primarily technical. Regular readers of my articles in Carpworld, Carp-Talk, Crafty Carper, Catchmore Carp, Advanced Carp Fishing and Coarse Fisherman will doubtless find some of my rigs, baits and general views familiar. Only rarely have my tactics and opinions undergone sudden change - most of the time the process is one of refinement rather than radical reappraisal.

Gravel Pit Carp is a very personal book in that it describes my own - some may say individualistic - approach. It makes no claims to be comprehensive. This results in omissions. You will not, for example, find more than the occasional passing mention of tactics to overcome silt because "ooze" is not a feature of the pits I fish. Nor will you find detailed information on stiff links, lead core links or braided main line - I do not use them, so know little or nothing about them.

I am not a "monster hunter", so only rarely do I fish high profile big fish waters. My dislike of crowds means that when a water's popularity reaches a certain threshold, I move somewhere else. This circumstance tends to accompany carp attaining newsworthy size and - one of my aversions - acquiring names...!

In none of my trophy pictures will you find a carp's weight given. This is not to suggest that I consider a carp's size unimportant. On the contrary, I get as big a thrill as anyone else when a massive expanse of flank slides over the net - but I cannot empathise with the way a carp's weight has become elevated to the level where, in many anglers' minds, it is the only criterion which matters. You cannot - as I have said in my writings in the past - measure either merit or enjoyment in pounds and ounces.

That mention of pounds and ounces brings me to the next point - the seemingly schizoid way I vacillate between imperial and metric measurements! I refer to rod length, test curve, casting distance, bankside geography, water size, line breaking strain, lead mass and - where I deem it relevant - fish weight in imperial; but hooklink length, hair length, boilie size and bait quantity are all expressed in metric. In this regard I suspect my choices are fairly conventional - but I thought it as well to mention it in case some readers find it confusing!

I am not and have never been a session angler. I used to fish overnight, and occasionally strung two nights together, but even that mini session approach has been abandoned in favour of day trips. This has resulted in my having to hone my location and feeding skills because I cannot use time on the bank to rectify mistakes. The importance of these and related aspects is therefore a recurrent theme throughout the book.

With the exception of the occasional passing mention to illustrate a point, overseas' gravel pits do not feature in the text. The same applies to photographs. A small number of the action or "author fishing" pictures were taken on continental waters (where this is the case, it is indicated in the captions), but all the trophy pictures are of fish caught in England.

Some of the opinions I express go against the mainstream. They are not attempts to court controversy, but merely conclusions to which my experience has led me. Occasionally, when I feel strongly about something, words on the page can come across as somewhat arrogant. Were we to talk face to face you would readily distinguish between conviction and arrogance - but unfortunately it is difficult to convey tone of voice in print!

I have tried to ascribe credit where it is due, but no matter how conscientious I have been in this regard, there will inevitably be omissions and possibly errors - so if anyone feels that I have failed to acknowledge them, I hope they will accept my apologies, and my assurance that no slight was intended.

Finally, I would like to "state my interests" and say that whilst commercial products are mentioned by name, the only companies with whom I have a formal link are Simpson's of Turnford and Kevin Nash Tackle.

Avoiding the crowds.

Chapter one

Gravel Pits

Although gravel pits come in all shapes and sizes, there are three main types; the first sort were dug in the late 1940's and throughout the '50's to fulfil the need for aggregates to supply the post war building programme. Many of these pits are shallow - often averaging less than 10ft - because only the gravel which afforded easiest access was extracted.

Most of these first generation pits are characterised by islands, submerged ridges (bars), flat topped humps (plateaux) and mounds; all of which were created by the dumping of unwanted topsoil and spoil (fig 1).

Fig.1 GRAVEL PIT FEATURES

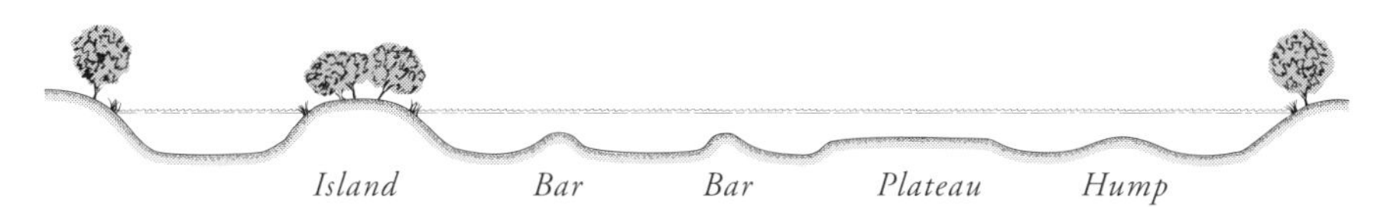

Bars usually run parallel - anything from 5-25 yards apart with channels of deeper water between; this being a consequence of the excavators having moved in just one direction. But in some pits, instead of unidirectional ridges, we find a sort of egg box configuration which is caused by the excavators working across the pit a second time, but at right angles to their original direction.

Second generation pits dug through the 1960's and early 1970's tend to have an average depth of about 15ft due to the development of improved digging techniques which made deeper excavation and the extraction of lower grade aggregates economically viable.

Whilst second generation pits often have islands and shallow plateaux, they are generally devoid of bars because post sixties legislation required that most of the spoil be used to backfill other pits in the vicinity.

Third generation gravel pits, which were created during and since the late 1970's, are deeper due to excavations going down to and sometimes below the greensand layer. They average 18-24ft deep, but may occasionally be more than 30ft.

A characteristic of third generation pits is the presence of one particularly deep

Aveley - parallel reed-topped bars can be clearly seen.

area - usually in a corner. Its purpose was to enable water to be drained away from the excavations. Gullies - along which the water was channelled - connect with this deep spot.

Only rarely are third generation pits uniformly deep; often they have substantial shallow areas, and occasionally islands too. Sometimes these were created by spoil dumping, but more usually by sediment produced during gravel washing. Initially these deposits are extremely soft - making them potentially dangerous because they are like quicksand - but in time they consolidate and become quite firm. Generally these sedimentary shallows are found in just one or two parts of the pit, and take the form of large expanses. Occasionally, however, sediment forms into long, thin promontories or ridges which closely resemble bars.

The age of a pit can usually be gauged from bankside vegetation. Old, first generation gravel pits will have taken on the appearance of natural lakes. They are likely to be skirted with full size mature trees, densely bushed areas, and have well established reedbeds. The newest pits - those dug in the '80's and early '90's - may have a somewhat barren appearance, with their treeless banks broken only by a few shrubs. Extensive reedbeds are unlikely, but there will probably be reeds in the margins. Many anglers dislike pits of this type, finding them somewhat inhospitable. I can understand their reaction, but when you become accustomed to open, "big sky" gravel pits, and develop an affinity for them, they appear beautiful rather than bleak.

As has already been stated, pits come in a range of sizes. The smallest might only cover an acre or two, while the largest might be in excess of 80 acres.

They vary in shape, too. Recently excavated pits are often more or less rectangular. Older pits - due to extensive spoil dumping - are usually somewhat amoeboid in appearance, with lots of bays, promontories, nooks and crannies.

A shape which is frequently encountered - particularly in second generation pits - is not dissimilar to an hourglass. It arises as a consequence of a new pit being dug very close to a previous excavation, with just a few yards of earth barrier between them. The purpose of this "wall" is to prevent water from the abandoned pit flooding the new one. Eventually, when the new diggings are completed and the pit is abandoned, it too will fill with water. Winter storms and wave erosion soon break through the barrier, thereby connecting the two pits via a relatively narrow "waist" - hence the characteristic hourglass shape. Occasionally the barrier collapses at each end but remains intact in the middle. This results in the creation of an island.

If water is pumped from a relatively deep pit over a period of several years, the water table in the immediate vicinity can be sufficiently lowered for adjacent, shallower excavations to remain dry. During this period, shrubs, bushes and even trees might become established. When, eventually, the pumping in the deep pit ceases, other pits in the vicinity will flood. Lots of gravel pits have snag areas as a consequence of this, while some are so overgrown with semi submerged willows and hawthorns that they resemble the Everglades rather than gravel pits!

Due to the nature of gravel pits, they tend to be found in clusters along river valleys. Examples which immediately spring to mind include such famous waters as Savay, Harrow and Harefield in the Colne Valley; Darenth, Sutton at Hone and Brooklands alongside the River Darenth; the Larkfield and Johnson's group of waters beside the River Medway; Linford Lakes in Buckinghamshire, which lie either side of the River Ouse; the Lee Valley Water Park just north of London; the A1 Pits adjacent to the River Trent in Nottinghamshire... and many, many more.

Some gravel pits, due to their large size and low stocks are lightly fished, making them ideal locations for anglers with a touch of Marco Polo in their personality. Many of the pits adjacent to the Thames and its tributaries are of this type.

RMC Angling's Sutton at Hone; a small pit which contains carp to over 40lb.

Other pits - particularly if available on a day ticket - can be horribly overcrowded. I remember visiting Horton Kirby - this was prior to it becoming a members' only club water - and finding the car park so congested that new arrivals had to leave their vehicles on the verge adjacent to the gate! Needless to say, I did not stay!

An increasing number of gravel pits are controlled by syndicates - membership is restricted and annual subscriptions are high. I know of two syndicates which charge £500 per annum, and plenty of others which have fees in the £200-£300 range. At the other end of the scale, one of the clubs to which I belong has access to a big coastal gravel pit, and they charge just £20 per annum.

The best value, though, has to be RMC Angling - a subsidiary of Ready Mixed Concrete - who control something like 100 pits spread over about 35 different sites. In 1998/99 you could fish most of them (plus, incidentally, about 25 stretches of river) for £100.

All features great and small...

With the sun high in the sky and behind you, it is sometimes possible to see where bars and plateaux are located, especially if they are weed-free when they show up as light patches against the darker, deeper water.

If the bars and plateaux lay deep, or the water is too turbid for them to be visible, the best option is a boat and an echo-sounder. I have mapped many of my waters by this means, and I augment the knowledge thus obtained by casting from the bank with a marker rod.

Another method which can be practiced from a boat involves using a long pole to prod the bottom. In addition to giving precise depth readings, it differentiates between hard gravel and soft mud.

Back in the high and far off days when I fished at Billing, I had an extraordinary experience while prodding. Billing was and is an extremely difficult water (the Beekay Guide rates it as "super-difficult"). In the year I fished it, just one carp was caught - and that a modest 11 pounder! Those of us who knew the water reckoned there were only about 15 carp in its 12 or so acres. They were reclusive as well as elusive, and weeks could pass without even seeing one. Imagine my amazement then, when I saw several massive carp appear alongside my boat while I was banging an oar on a hard gravel bottom! I stopped in mid-prod and looked in disbelief as approximately a third of the lake's carp population came so close I could see every scale and every fin ray. Presumably they had come to see what all

Fig.2 USING FAR BANK FEATURES AS DIRECTION MARKERS

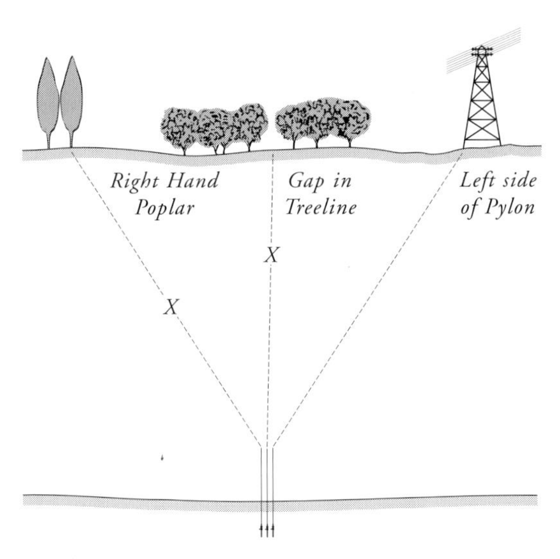

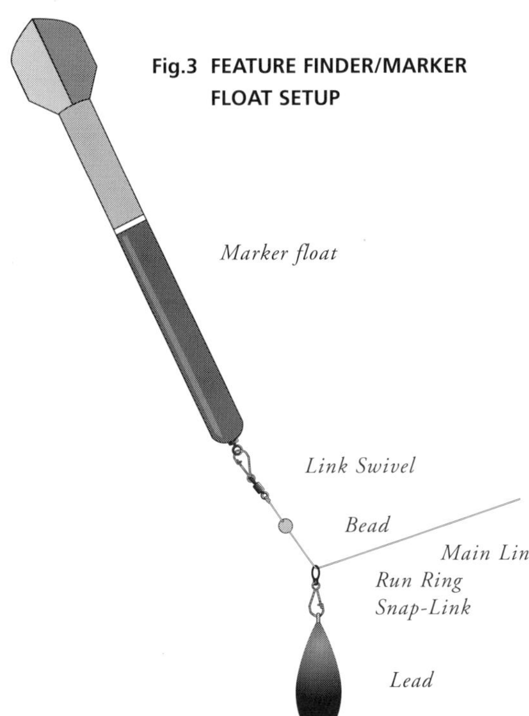

Fig.3 FEATURE FINDER/MARKER FLOAT SETUP

the noise was about!

It goes without saying that no one - not even if they are a strong swimmer - should go out in a boat without wearing a life jacket.

If, for whatever reason, a boat is not an option, you will have to rely entirely on a marker rod. This is the slowest method, but has the advantage that features can be lined up against permanent objects (trees, fence posts, pylons etc) on the far bank (fig 2), which enables those features to be located subsequently.

Marker rod setups vary in their detail, but they all work on the same principle. Mine (fig 3) comprises a large run-ring to which the lead is attached by means of a heavy duty snap-link. My main line is passed through the run-ring, through a bead, and then tied to a small link swivel to which the float is clipped.

For distances up to about 50yd I use a polyball float (approximately the size of a ping pong ball) in conjunction with a lead of 2oz. The float is painted black because I worry that a brightly coloured one might spook carp.

Feature finding setup - a telescopic rod is convenient to carry.

At longer range, visibility has to take precedence - alongside good aerodynamics - so I use a Nash fluorescent orange vaned model. It is more buoyant than the polyball so requires a heavier lead; 3oz will usually suffice, but occasionally I use 4oz.

After casting, the line is tightened. This pulls the float down to the lead. By paying out line in foot or yard increments until the float appears on the surface, the depth is easily established. All well and good. No difficulties so far...

If, however, you read articles on feature finding you will learn that it is possible to do far more than measure the depth. By "feeling" the lead as it is pulled gently along the bottom, information regarding the whereabouts of ridges, bars, troughs, gravel patches, mud and weed will all be revealed.

Or so we are told.

Now, I accept that I may lack the necessary interpretive skills - but I find it difficult to "read" the bottom the way others are apparently able to. I have studied articles and how-to-do-it picture strips, and seen in diagrams how my rod top will nod simultaneously with my feeling a distinct "tap, tap, tap" as my lead passes over gravel. From these informative features I have also learned that my lead will lock up as it climbs the far side of a bar, and suddenly feel weightless as it falls down the nearside slope. And as if all that was not enough, it will slide easily over firm sand, mud or clay - but will stick in silt. Finally, I am told, it will become snagged in weed.

Got it!

The weed one, I mean. I am definitely okay with weed. If my lead gets stuck in weed, I have no difficulty "reading" the situation. Usually, of course, when I retrieve my float and lead they are enveloped in the stuff - which is a bit of a giveaway! But no matter - if I have got a weedbed in front of me, I am confident I can find it. No problem at all!

I am able to locate hard bottomed places too. If I hook the line over my finger immediately the lead hits the water, I can feel a distinct "bump" if it lands on a hard bottom. If I then retrieve some line - fairly rapidly in order to lift the float and lead high in the water - I can repeat the procedure. But it is an imprecise method in that it only differentiates between a hard and soft bottom at the various points of impact - it gives no information regarding what lies between.

But as for the rest of it - all that locking up, "tap, tap, tapping" and sliding easily - I confess it causes me considerable confusion. How, for example, does "locking up" on the far side of a bar feel any different to "locking up" on a rock, or a lump of clay, or a sunken branch, or even someone else's lost tackle, for that matter? And what is the difference between "locking up" on a bar and sticking in silt? And when I feel "tap, tap, tap", how do I know it is gravel rather than mussels, bits of flint or ridged hard packed sand? And when my lead comes in with little resistance, how do I distinguish between the easy slie down the nearside of a bar, and that which occurs when it slips over hard mud or clay?

With encouragement from brothers Martin and Rick, I recently rigged my feature finding rod with non-stretch ultrafine braid (Gorilla Braid). Certainly it transmits far more information than does mono, and enables me to readily differentiate between rough and smooth areas of bottom. I feel "tap, tap, tapping" more distinctly than ever before, and I have found such patches where hitherto I was unaware of their existence - which is useful to know, of course - but accurate interpretation of the tactile signals is a skill which continues to elude me.

Notwithstanding its shortcomings, I would feel seriously handicapped were I to be deprived of the use of a feature finding rod - especially one equipped with braid. It may not do all that some writers claim, but it is an invaluable tool which, in addition to enabling me to measure the depth, feel for hard spots, find rough patches and locate weed, is frequently pressed into service as a tuftie scarer!

Talking of birds. . . If I am visiting a new water, one about which I have no prior knowledge, I watch where water birds are active. Coots, in particular, will often reveal the presence of bars and plateaux by diving down to feed - especially if other areas are relatively deep.

The final method I would recommend - assuming a fairly long term commitment is being made to a particular pit - is to obtain an aerial photograph.

This is not such an absurd suggestion as it might seem. It would, of course, be inordinately expensive to commission such a picture, but a number of companies are engaged in aerial photography (try Yellow Pages), and if they already have the photograph you require in their files you will be able to obtain a copy at reasonable cost. How distinctly shallow areas, bars, troughs and weedbeds show up depends on the depth of the water, its clarity and the position of the sun when the picture was taken. But you will be given the opportunity to examine a picture, and thereby evaluate its usefulness, before deciding to buy it. It is an avenue well worth investigating because the few aerial pictures I have seen have been excellent - and extremely informative.

Mapping

Whatever form your feature finding takes, I strongly recommend that maps which show the underwater topography be made. In addition to my water maps, I always carry a notebook in which I keep swim plans, details of where fish show, what times they show and in what weather conditions, what times takes occur, hotspots, clear spots, what far bank markers I should cast towards, at what range... and so on.

Memory is unreliable especially if, like me, you fish lots of different waters and the sheer volume of information becomes overwhelming. Sometimes details change of course; last year's clear spot might be this year's weedbed, for example. But most information remains relevant year after year. Many times I have returned to a swim after a long absence, consulted my notebook and read, "Right hand rod; gentle underarm lob towards left of pylon. Left hand rod; maximum maple pea distance towards bare patch on far bank" or something similar. "Gentle underarm lob" is self explanatory; "maximum maple pea" indicates the furthest distance I can catapult maple peas - in other words, further than hempseed, but not so far as chick peas... if you see what I mean. Some distances are more precise and involve an actual measurement. I carry a surveyor's tape in

A gorgeous big pit mirror.

the boot of my car for this purpose - it enables me to peg a prescribed distance along the bank, which I use to measure a length of line so I can attach a stop-knot marker. All this so I can gauge my range without having to disturb the swim with a marker rod. I believe that last point - not disturbing the swim - to be of tremendous importance. Frequently I see anglers thrashing the water to a foam by repeatedly casting their feature finding setup. Every few minutes there is another "spudoosh" as the heavy lead hits the surface. And what about down below? Is it not likely that the impact of the lead on the bottom creates a water borne "thud"? It might not matter - witness my Billing experience - but I would rather not take the chance.

These are my feature finding principles:

- **whenever possible, I do not use the marker rod, relying instead on information recorded in a notebook or on a water map**
- **if a marker rod is deemed essential, I use the smallest float and the lightest lead which will do the job**
- **the marker rod is cast as infrequently as possible - preferably only once.**

Important Waters

Gravel pits occupy an important place in carp fishing history by having contributed greatly to its development and popularity. They are an indispensable and integral part of carp fishing's present; and are an essential part of its future.

Some of the best known carp waters in the country are gravel pits - I have already mentioned Billing, Savay, Harefield, Harrow, Darenth and Sutton at Hone; to them can be added Horton, Wraysbury, Horseshoe, Orchid, Yateley, Conningbrook... the list could continue indefinitely.

To many carp anglers, myself included, gravel pits are the mainstay of our fishing. We might occasionally fish estate lakes, rivers, canals and dykes - but pits are where we feel happiest. They are and have always been my favourite waters (I recently did a mental audit and calculated that I have fished more than 50 different pits). I even dedicated one of my books (Big Water Carp) "to the anonymous entrepreneur who first thought of excavating sand and gravel from the ground"!

From which you will correctly conclude that I am not talking mere preference here, but passion!

I was taught at school that Marie Antoinette claimed her love of her country was so great, that were her heart to be examined they would find the word "France" engraved upon it. Were my heart to be subjected to the same scrutiny, I suspect they would find it full of stones and grit!

Chapter Two

Shallow Pits

The angler looked through narrowed eyes across the vastness of the pit. Then, with a smooth but powerful sweep over his shoulder, he sent his marker more than 150yd; just past the fourth bar. As he slowly retrieved he tested the depth at intervals, until a sudden decrease told him he had found the bar's far slope. The first of his three rods, all of which were baited in readiness, was cast so the end-tackle dropped alongside his marker float. He gave a quiet grunt of satisfaction.

Oh come on!

We have all read such accounts, but precision at distances of that magnitude is only possible on Zorgar or in the anorak world of Nintendo! It does not happen here on planet Earth. Have you noticed, incidentally - apropos of Zorgar - that names of sci-fi planets always seem to incorporate a "Z" and never consist of more than two syllables..?

Back to the subject in hand! In the real world there are practical issues with which to contend. First, weed. I have discussed weedy waters at length in Chapter Six, so at this juncture will merely say that many, if not most shallow pits are so heavily weeded that the identification of features is somewhat irrelevant. What we spend our time seeking are clear spots. If we find an area free of weed we count ourselves lucky, and do not worry too much about whether it is on the top, side or bottom of a bar. Clear spot; go for it! End of story.

Swans - I'm not a fan...

And swans. If you have access to a shallow pit which remains weedfree - or you find nice clear areas in an otherwise weedy water - you will discover that swans are capable of picking up baits from a depth of almost 5ft. Their normal range is nearer 4ft, but those which inhabit carp waters have discovered that by adopting a bobbing motion they can obtain an extra 25% on the downstroke!

The extent to which this poses a problem will depend primarily, of course, on how shallow your pit is. Also pertinent is the number of swans present. The worst case of swan trouble I ever encountered was on the Mid Kent Fisheries water at Chartham. It is a lovely water, about 15 acres I would guess, with sheep meadows going down to the water's edge. And the Chartham carp are some of the prettiest you will find anywhere. But the water is shallow. Very shallow. I doubt if more than 10% of the bottom is out of the swans' reach. Its shallowness, however, is only part of the problem. What puts Chartham in a league of its own is the number of swans present - last time I was there I counted more than 35! According to one of the regulars, this was a considerable improvement on a few months earlier when the population reached about 70! As we all know, two swans can be an unmitigated pain, four have the capability to induce hair tearing exasperation. Can you imagine fishing a water with 35 or even worse, 70 of the damn things? We are not talking mere loss of control here, but serious red mist apoplexy!

Chartham - and one of the few swims immune from swans!

There are, however, some shallow pits where - due to mysterious reasons which we cannot hope to understand but for which we should fall on our knees in gratitude - neither weed nor swans pose much of a problem. On these waters we look for features.

Gravel Bars

I suspect it was the late, great Jack Hilton who started it - putting baits on bars, that is. If memory serves me correct, Jack was fishing Brooklands, near Dartford, when he wrote about this approach. And Brooklands was - and may still be for all I know - a water where fishing the tops of bars was a reliable tactic. The A2 Point was one such place, with a sizable bar little more than a gentle lob from the bank. A freelined golfball-size lump of sausage meat would probably be taken sometime during the night, or more usually shortly after sunrise. The Bridge Swim had a bar even closer, while the adjoining Slaughterhouse Bay had several. Brooklands carp responded to baits fished on bars. Jack noted this fact, wrote about it, and was the

Late summer mirror.

unwitting cause of more thousands of wasted hours than he could possibly have imagined!

Herein lies a paradox. In some waters the tops of bars are good spots to fish; in others they are not. Indeed, I go further, and say that in most waters they are not.

The paradox does not end there, because even in waters where the tops of bars can be productive, it does not apply to all bars.

Were we to subject the productivity of the tops of bars to statistical analysis, I have little doubt that the overwhelming weight of evidence would point to their being a relatively poor bet. But folk memory is deeply ingrained, and when we find a tempting looking bar few of us can resist putting a bait on it!

What are the qualities which make a bar, in some waters at least, worth fishing? The best, in my opinion, are low bars; those which rise only a foot or two from the bottom.

High bars are okay providing they have at least 2ft of water over them. An additional requirement is that they should not undulate too much. Carp, I believe, prefer to swim at a particular level, so are unlikely to follow a bar which requires that they constantly change depth in order to follow its contours. My least favourite bars are those which almost reach the surface in places, and can give rise to the incongruous sight of a swan, far out in the pit, standing with water no higher than its knees! (Do swans have knees..?)

Ideally I like a bar to be at least 5ft wide, too.

"Designer" bars of that type are well worth a try, especially when the weather is warm, or when the morning sun first strikes the water. I have never found the tops of shallow bars productive in winter, but in "Tiger Bay" (Beekay, 1988) Rob Maylin described how he enjoyed an astonishing run of winter success from such spots in a Colne Valley pit. A far more consistent tactic than fishing the top of a high bar is to fish its base. Carp are natural "bank huggers", and the base of a bar is like a margin, but well out in the pit - if you see what I mean.

FIG.4 END OF BAR AND GAP IN BAR

The channels between bars can sometimes be good, especially if a wind blows lengthwise along them.

But while tops, bases and troughs all have their day, the best places of all are at the very ends of bars where they create underwater promontories. I like gaps too (Fig 4). Whether food accumulates in such places as is sometimes suggested, or they are simply good interception points I am not sure - although I suspect the latter.

Accurate location of a bar requires that a marker float be used. Most anglers use a separate marker rod to find their feature, and leave it in position while they cast their hookbait and put out freebies.

On waters where boats are allowed, many anglers use an inflatable to take out markers, freebies and sometimes even their hookbaits. Usually they leave their markers in place until they pack up - which not only poses a hazard when a fish is being played, but is appallingly naff! I recall a weekend on Johnson's Railway Lake when the surface was so littered with multi-coloured floats and squeegee bottles it looked as though preparations were being made for a jet-ski slalom race!

For relatively short distances - say, up to 50yd - bait placement when there is a marker float to aim for is not very difficult. It is important to note, however, that a lead does not sink vertically. It maintains its forward momentum and, depending on the depth of water, can hit bottom several feet further than its point of splashdown (Fig 5). I was unaware of this until I noticed how far from the centre of the spreading rings did bubbles - caused by the lead's impact on the bottom - appear. I try to make allowance for this by casting a little short of my target.

An alternative method is to feather the line just before it lands, and then trap it so the lead's forward momentum is arrested. Some anglers worry that this will cause the lead to swing-in; but in shallow water this does not happen and, for all practical purposes, it sinks vertically.

When I need to cast further than 50yd I prefer to use a technique which places less reliance on accuracy, and enables me to replicate the range easily. I am referring to clipping-up.

Fig.5 RIG MAINTAINS FORWARD MOMENTUM AFTER SPLASHDOWN

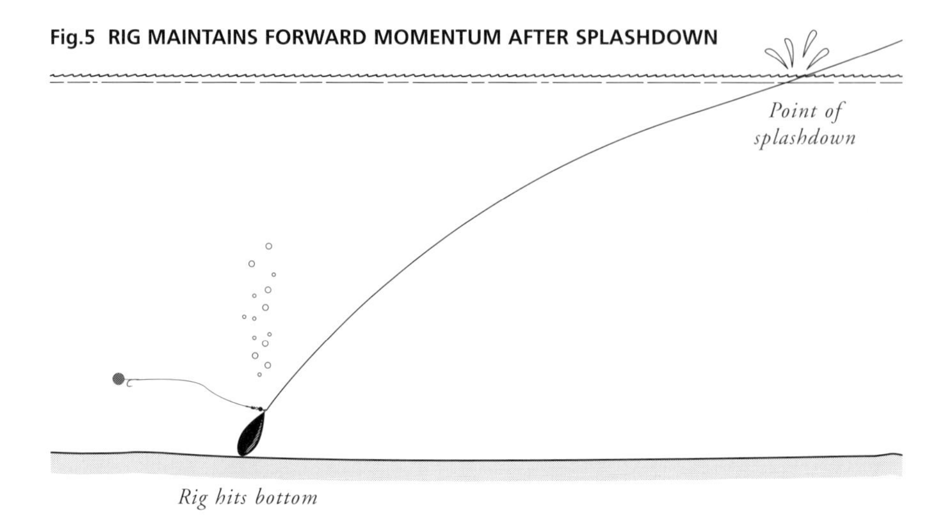

The problem with conventional clipping-up is that it damages the line - not a lot, but sufficient to result in slight loss of strength. Exactly what percentage of strength loss can be expected depends primarily on the model of reel in use (and hence the severity of its clip); also on the brand of line and its diameter. The use of thick line (0.37mm plus) reduces such weakening to the point where in most circumstances it probably does not matter. Such thick line would be a liability if long casting was required, but at distances up to about 80yd no significant range retarding penalty is incurred.

There is, however, a better method. In order to mitigate the pinching effect of the reel's line clip, I do not use it - not to hold the line anyway. What follows is one of those procedures which is utter simplicity in practice, but somewhat

Fig.6a "U" OF POWER GUM LAID ACROSS SPOOL

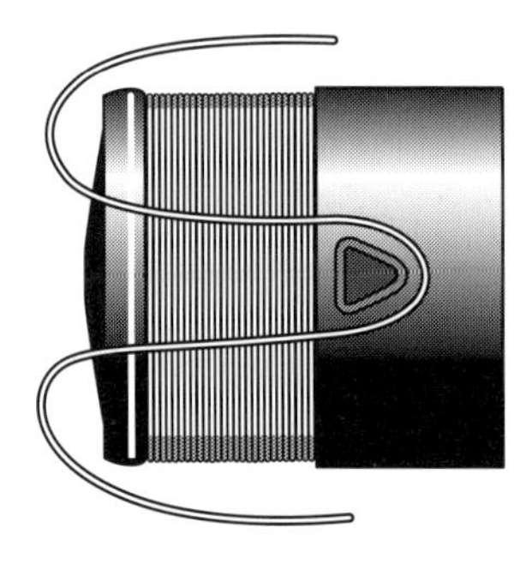

Fig.6b TAG ENDS OF POWER GUM DOUBLED BACK

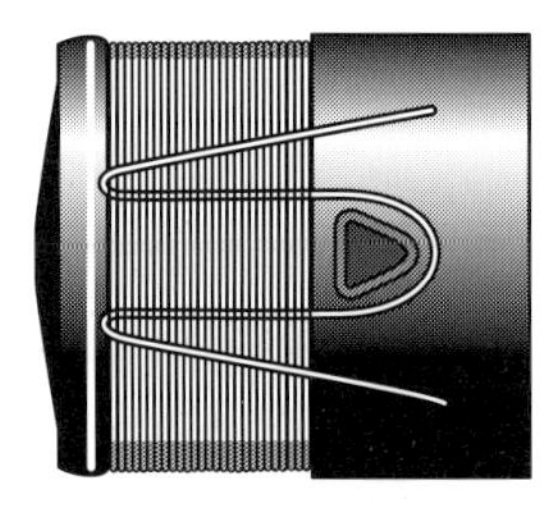

difficult to describe. The combination of text and drawings (Figs 6a and 6b)) should, however, make it clear.

- **A maxi range cast is made in order to empty the spool of as much line as possible.**
- **A long "U" of Power Gum is laid across the spool, with its closed end about 1cm behind the line clip.**
- **The Power Gum is held in position by wrapping with about 5yd of line (the first few turns are best done by hand).**
- **The tag ends of the Power Gum are doubled back so they protrude beyond the back of the spool - a few more turns of line are made by hand, then several yards retrieved in the normal way. This holds the Power Gum loop securely in place.**
- **The tag ends of Power Gum are trimmed off, and the remaining line is retrieved.**

The loop thus created is tucked beneath the clip when not in use to prevent it becoming buried by wraps of line.

Back to the fishing. My rod (normal fishing rod, not marker rod) is equipped with a marker setup. I then set about locating the feature to which I intend fishing. Having located it - be it the top of a bar, its base, or wherever - I put out my feed. This, incidentally, will be the last occasion on which I will have the benefit of a marker for the purpose - subsequent baiting has to be undertaken by estimation.

After making a mental note of the far bank marker towards which I need to cast, I tighten the line (which pulls the float down to the lead) and attach a stop-knot made from fine pole elastic (Fig 7) adjacent to the butt ring or the second ring along. It does not matter which, just so long as with the rod in the rests, the stop-knot is located beyond the indicator and the alarm, thereby eliminating the risk of it becoming tangled or jammed. The stop-knot will not be required for my first cast, but will be needed subsequently to enable me to duplicate the range.

Fig.7 POLE ELASTIC STOP KNOT (MINIMUM 5 TURNS ARE REQUIRED)

- **The line is hooked beneath the Power Gum loop (Fig 8), which acts like a harness. The marker setup is then retrieved.**
- **The marker setup is replaced with my terminal rig - which is then baited, and most likely equipped with a stringer. A cast towards my far bank marker will ensure the direction is accurate, while the line harness establishes the range. I lift the rod high just before splashdown, and allow it to be pulled down to the horizontal by the momentum of the lead.**

After the lead has sunk I remove the line from the harness (very important, that!), place the rod in its rests and tighten up.

I have used this method a lot, and the Power Gum harness is far more durable than you might expect. Even when Method fishing, which can result in casts pulling tight with considerable force, I rarely have a harness break. Normally, however, I play safe and replace it after a couple of trips.

Fig.8 LINE HOOKED BENEATH POWER GUM LOOP, WHICH IS THEN SECURED BENEATH LINE CLIP. POWER GUM THUS ACTS LIKE A HARNESS

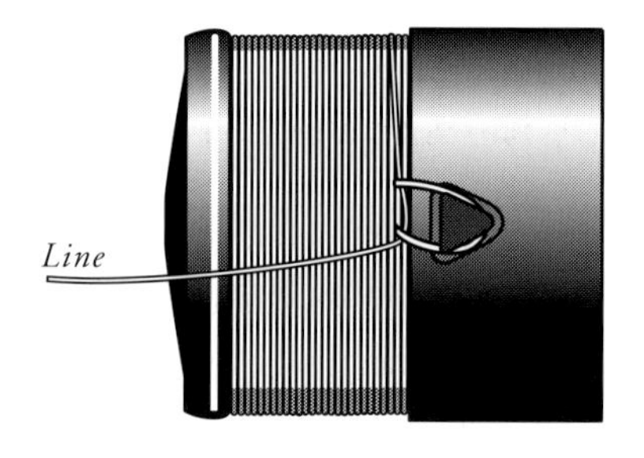

Before leaving the subject of clipping-up, may I make a plea? Although the use of a Power Gum harness leaves the line completely unmarked, it is a somewhat fiddly procedure - certainly less convenient than using a line clip in the usual way. What is required is a nylon clip with nice rounded edges. If spring loaded, it should hold the line in place with gentle, non-distorting tension. It does not have to be a clip though, it could be a simple bracket. Whatever form it takes, it should be compatible with popular Shimano and Daiwa models so it can replace the overly harsh clips with which they are equipped (although, in fairness, it has to be said that some recent models have versions which look to be more line-friendly).

Whether my suggestion is tenable, I do not know - but if someone of an inventive turn of mind could develop such an item, I am sure it would find a ready market.

At which point some readers are probably wondering why I place so much emphasis on accuracy - after all, if a cast goes wrong, it can be retrieved and recast. If that one goes wrong, it too can be recast... and so on. But if I have got my location right, carp will likely be in the area from the outset. The likelihood of their staying is severely reduced if I bombard them with leads. And where is the sense in striving for spot-on bait placement if there are no carp left to eat it?

Plateaux

Spoil dumping or gravel washing sometimes creates irregularly shaped high places which may be as small as the average suburban garden, or bigger than a football field; and every size between. Over the years these areas may consolidate and become eroded by wave action, whereupon they evolve into relatively flat topped plateaux. They are superb places for carp, especially in spring and early summer. If I could choose my perfect warm weather carp swim it would be a 5ft deep, tennis court size plateau within comfortable casting distance of the north-east corner of a big pit. With a mellow force three south-westerly blowing - what I call a T-shirt wind - I would expect a large proportion of the water's carp population to be on and around the plateau. I would place one bait in the middle of the plateau, another near its lip, and a third on the slope (Fig 9) or, if the plateau was no more than 6ft high, at its base.

Fig.9 BAIT PLACEMENT ON PLATEAU

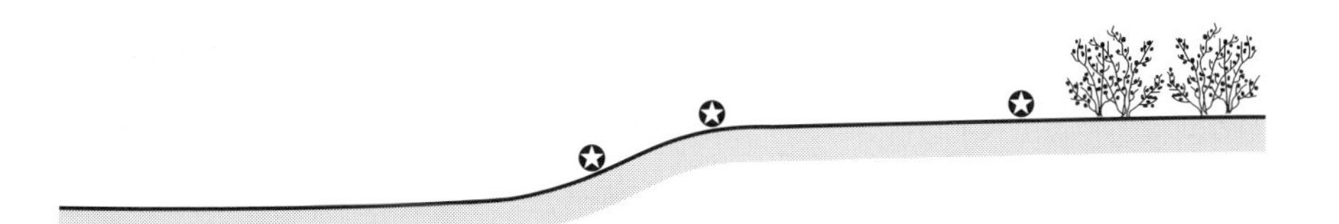

Humps and Bumps

Not all high places can be readily categorised as bars or plateaux - some are more like mounds. In my experience, they rarely live up to expectations. One such feature which immediately comes to mind is a table top size mound with 6ft of water over it, which rises from 10ft of weedy water in Johnson's Road Lake. Despite being quite close in, few anglers seem aware of its existence - probably because it is situated in such a position that casting is hampered by a large bush. When I discovered it I had one of those Meg Ryan moments - you know, "Yes! Yes! Yes!" But my excitement was misplaced because I have yet to take a fish from it; not even a tench.

If the tops of mounds are often disappointing, their sides are exactly the opposite. So weed permitting, a bait halfway down or at the base of a mound is a very good bet.

Fig.10 BAIT PLACEMENT IN GAP

Gaps and Ends

Gaps are good spots because carp use them to pass from one channel to another. Similarly the ends of bars. This, I suspect, is because carp like to swim at a constant depth, and they would rather go round or through a bar than over it.

If the gap is a wide one, I like to place one bait halfway down the slope one side, and one bait at the bottom of the slope the other side (Fig 10). If the gap is narrow, or the range too great for pinpoint precision, I would probably settle for just one bait, and would be happy for it to land anywhere in the gap.

The same circumstances apply to the end of a bar. If the incline is long and gentle, and the range no more than 60yd - thereby permitting accurate casting - I would place two baits down the slope (Fig 11).

Fig.11 BAIT PLACEMENT ON LONG GENTLE SLOPE

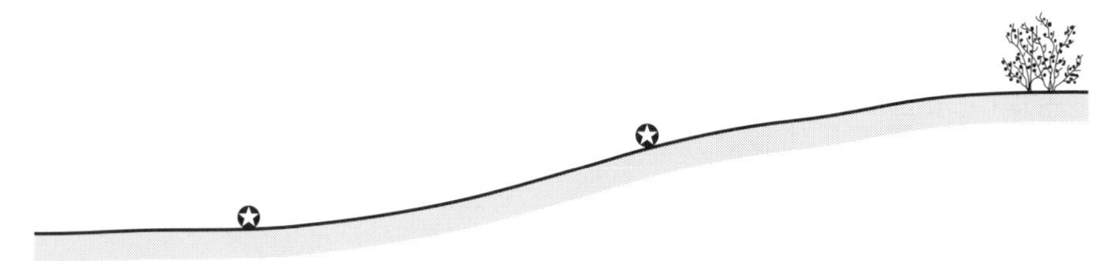

Islands

If a water is quiet, carp will spend a lot of time in the margins. Even in busy waters they will move in close if they can find quiet places such as a marshy, inaccessible stretch of bank, or an area overgrown with brambles. Or an island. An island, if out of bounds to anglers, offers quiet, undisturbed margins. That is their appeal.

Fig.12 BAIT PLACED CLOSE TO TIPS OF OVERHANGING BRANCHES

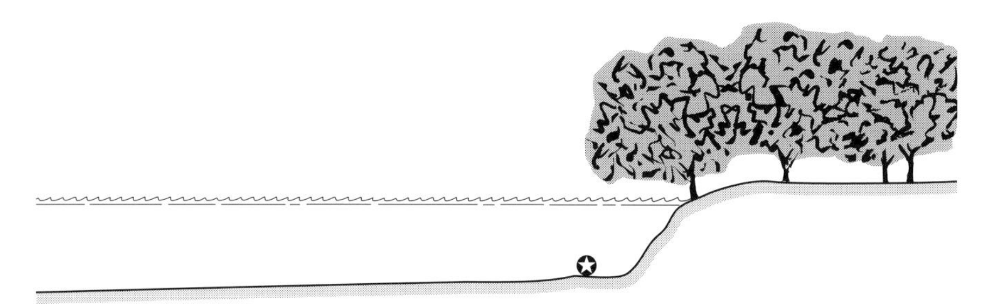

Most carp anglers know this, of course, so swims within casting range of islands tend to be popular. In time, they may become so hard fished that they lose their attraction. When this stage is reached it is worth casting well short of the island, rather than trying to tuck up close.

Let us, however, assume our water is one where carp still hug island margins. If the end of an island is overhung by trees, and there is at least 2ft of water, I would try to cast a bait as tight to the tips of the branches as possible (Fig 12).

When casting to an island which runs parallel to the bank, it is good policy to cast as close as is safe - assuming, as before, that there is at least 2ft of water. The best means of achieving this is to aim for gaps (Fig 13). This places baits within the outer edge of the treeline.

Clipping-up (by which I actually mean "harnessing-up" - but the term has too much of an equine ring about it!) is the safest means of casting to a treeline - but in this instance it is used in conjunction with a technique different to that described for bars. The first cast is a cautious one which we know will fall short. An estimate is made of how far short it fell, and sufficient line pulled from the reel to make up this shortfall. Well, not quite - it is wise to err on the conservative side. The line is then placed in the Power Gum harness and the tackle retrieved. The next cast - due to the extra line which was pulled from the reel - will land nearer

Fig.13 BAITS PLACED IN GAPS BETWEEN TREES (PLAN VIEW)

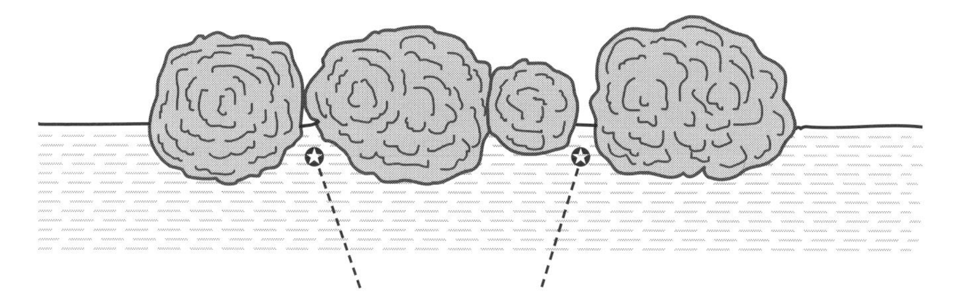

the island. The process of clipping-up, casting, feeding extra line, clipping-up and recasting is continued until the tackle drops just right. At which point the line is tightened, and a stop-knot tied as already explained.

I said earlier that I do not like having to cast repeatedly, but in the circumstance just described I know of no suitable alternative. If, however, the swim is fished regularly, spools can retain their pole elastic distance markers from one trip to the next, thereby obviating the need to re-establish the range on subsequent occasions.

Sanctuary!

Carp, like Notre Dame's hapless hunchback, yearn for sanctuary! Several of the pits I fish are also used for water sports. Anglers are not allowed to fish in the vicinity of launch ramps or the clubhouse, and the carp know it! Such places may be the busiest and noisiest on the pit, but from the carp's point of view they are the safest.

Nature reserves, private stretches of bank, gravel workings - these and other out of bounds areas will attract carp. Additionally, and as a consequence of the Law of Sod, the area from which you are excluded is almost certain to have the carpiest characteristics! One of the pits I occasionally fish is relatively featureless over most of its area save for a large bay which has a lovely sandy bottom and wide reed margins - the only reeds on the lake. As if that was not enough, it is located at the north-east corner which means that it receives the benefit of south-westerly winds. A prime area. But... Need I continue? Of course not because everyone knows, in principle at least, what comes next. But I shall tell you anyway! Those nice people from the R.S.P.B. have designated the bay and its environs a nesting site for the lesser spotted muckpicker - or some such - and declared the whole area closed to anglers. Not that I am complaining. Being confined to the unproductive end of the pit so a bird I have never seen can make its nest is, without doubt, a price well worth paying. A privilege, even!

On some big pits the sanctuary areas are not so much out of bounds as out of range. And this is where we enter controversial territory - literally as well as metaphorically. Where distance fishing is safe, there is no problem - those who acquire the necessary equipment and develop good casting technique will get within range of fish which are beyond the reach of everyone else. Nothing wrong with that. But what if there are intervening bars - possibly topped with flints or mussels? Is it legitimate to cast beyond bars where, if a fish is hooked, there is a high likelihood of being cut off? Lots of anglers think it is, because they do it. Some even seem to get perverse pleasure from relating how many fish they lose, thereby denoting a lack of concern for carp welfare which defies belief.

I am a realist and know that when fishing gravel pits it is impossible to guarantee 100% safety, but I think it is unacceptable to fish where the loss rate exceeds about one in ten. Many anglers, however, are unwilling to forego fishing areas where the risk of losses is high - so what do we do?

We cannot legislate for this sort of thing because to an extent it depends on the skill and experience of the angler, and how well equipped he is. But no club or syndicate could be run on the basis of some anglers being permitted to fish potentially dangerous areas, while others are not allowed to do so.

Some swims, however, are so dangerous that even well equipped, experienced anglers lose a high proportion of all fish they hook. We have all read accounts of carp being fished for in circumstances where losses in the order of two out of three are considered usual. What amazes me about such accounts is that while such losses are viewed with frustration, they seem to be regarded as acceptable.

The issue is irresolvable, so we each have to make a decision as regards where our personal boundary will be drawn. It is a difficult decision because it compels us to choose between altruism and conscience on the one hand, and our desire to succeed on the other.

The foregoing does not apply to what might be termed "normal risks". Even the most benign gravel pits have some hazards, but with common sense and suitable equipment these should rarely result in lost fish. A mistake many anglers make is

No sign of mouth damage - this is the sort of carp I like to catch.

to assume that mono lines which claim high abrasion resistance will cope with sharp topped gravel bars. They will not. What is required in this circumstance is resistance to shear, not abrasion. And no mono yet made embodies that quality. The only material I have used which copes with shear is Quicksilver. Its value as a shockleader for long casting is well known, but less commonly realised is the fact that it makes an excellent rubbing leader. I have caught numerous carp with the aid of Quicksilver which I am sure would otherwise have been lost.

Use of Quicksilver as a leader is discussed in detail in Chapter Five.

Backleads.

Backleads

References to being cut off brought the subject of backleads to mind. I use them a lot - mainly in situations where I think steeply angled lines might scare carp. They also help avoid line bites. But I only consider employing backleads if the bottom is free of flints and mussels - otherwise I rely on a slack line and a tiny roll of tungsten putty immediately above my anti-tangle tube.

Backleads are also useful in a tight swim because they reduce the risk of a second or third line being picked up when a fish is being played, but they become a liability if the bottom is very uneven because line held taut across a gully enables a hooked carp to get beneath it and set about constructing a "cat's cradle" of intertwined mono. Where no backlead is used, however, the offending line can usually be lifted clear and trouble avoided.

Another situation when I use backleads is if I need to keep the line below flotsam, troublesome water birds, wind surfers, jet-skiers, water skiers etc. Zenon Bojko may recall the time we fished adjacent pitches at Layer Pit during the course of a gale which resulted in numerous small branches drifting crossways through our respective swims. Without backleads we could not have coped, but with them we fished without difficulty and caught about 18 carp between us.

I rarely use backleads in weed due to the risk of my other line(s) being picked up while a fish is being played. The combination of weed and a powerful fish fouling a backleaded line (or two) is too awful to contemplate.

Before leaving the subject, I should mention auto-release backleads. A couple of years ago I lost a fish as a result of a hookpull after playing it back and forth through a backlead which had snagged.

Steve Edwards, on being told about the episode, suggested I make some auto-release backleads. These, he explained, incorporate plastic covered plant tie, which is obtainable from garden centres. I subsequently bought some - it is like a sandwich bag twist tie, but comes on a long reel.

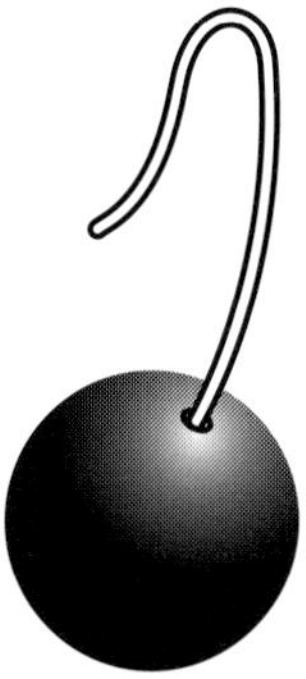

Fig.14 AUTO RELEASE BACKLEAD

I Superglued a short (5-7cm) length of plant tie into a drilled bullet lead (Fig 14), and to ensure it was line friendly covered it with PVC tubing.

The tie is bent to create an inverted "U", then hooked over the line and slid into position. Should the backlead become snagged, the tie will straighten and the line will "ping" free.

Since using Steve's auto-release backleads I have not been snagged, so I cannot cite an actual example of how they saved me from losing a carp. But the principle is foolproof, so I have no doubt that they will function exactly as Steve suggested.

Small Pits

Thus far the sort of pit I have had in mind has been one of 10 acres or more, but dotted around the country are many of only 1-3 acres. Some of these mini pits are perfect replicas of their big brothers and have all the usual gravel pit features such as spits, islands, humps and bars. Often several such waters are found in close proximity; they might even be interconnected. Others are found singly, and were probably dug to provide a source of ballast to bed a nearby road or railway line. Top quality aggregate is not required for this purpose, so such pits tend to be dug out completely, which renders them relatively featureless.

Although I am primarily a big water angler, I enjoy occasional trips to these small waters, providing I can have them to myself. I can cope with one other person being there, but if a second angler arrives I get very restless, and will likely pack up and go home. A third, and I will be on my way for sure. The reason for this apparently antisocial reaction is because carp in small waters are very easily spooked. Three or four anglers on a water of just 2-3 acres, no matter how quiet they are, will make the fish nervous. If the anglers are noisy, or wander along the bank, the situation is made worse.

But some small pits are quiet, and occasionally completely neglected, especially if they benefit from what I call the "sponge syndrome" - the proximity of a high profile water which "soaks up" most of the angling attention. One of the clubs to which I belong has two pits; they lay side by side - so close you could stand on the bank of one and throw baits into the other! The larger water produces carp to mid 30's; the smaller one holds relatively few fish, most of which are low doubles, with the biggest about 20lb. The first is fished hard, summer and winter; the other is invariably deserted.

I have caught virtually all the carp in the larger water - some several times - and magnificent beasts though they are, I have no wish to continue catching them so nowadays I rarely fish there. I do, however, enjoy occasional trips to its "Cinderella" neighbour, where I catch immaculate, hard fighting, previously uncaught commons.

All the small pits I have fished share the characteristic that carp come right into the edge when the weather is warm and sunny. Small pits are therefore excellent margin waters - leastways, they are until about mid-August when, for what reason I do not know, the margins become progressively less productive. This happens even if the weather remains warm; and interestingly is quite independent of angling pressure. So mid-August onwards I fish further out; and usually this is likely to be to plateaux, the ends of bars, gaps in bars, the sides of humps, clear spots in weed, snags etc. - standard stuff, in fact.

The main advantage of small waters is that carp can never be far away, so location is rarely very difficult. The downside, as I said earlier, is that they are readily spooked by the presence of other anglers.

As I wrote that last sentence, an image of Whelford Lakes flashed into my mind. I have never fished Whelford, but recently, while visiting relatives in the area, I thought I would have a reconnoitre. They are attractive enough little pits, notwithstanding the worn swims and the bare bankside paths. I was somewhat disconcerted to see that the site boasted a house, a lodge and what looked like a shop(!), but what really struck me was how crowded the pits were. As I wandered round I felt somehow depressed - not for myself, but for the anglers who were fishing there. Then I took stock of the situation and realised that my sympathy was wasted because the reason those anglers were not out exploring quiet, unexploited waters in

Brother Rick lands a carp from a small Essex pit.

what is probably one of the gravel pit heartlands of the country, is because such places would not be to their taste. They prefer busy waters. I nonetheless found it impossible to shake off my mood, and as I said to Rick when telling him about it later, "If that ever became the only sort of carp fishing available to me, I would quit."

Mind you, if I found Whelford excessively busy, what about Cuttle Mill? I admit that not only have I never fished Cuttle Mill, I have not even seen the place. But 22 swims (sorry, "pegs" - God, I hate that term!) on a water of about 4 acres. Oh come on! It isn't true, surely... And seemingly the swims have to be drawn for, prior to the commencement of the day's fishing! But best of all - and this I believe because no one could possibly invent anything so bizarre - each swim has its boundaries indicated by markers in the water!

It gets worse. Cuttle Mill's 22 "pegs" (I cannot bring myself to write the word without the disassociation afforded by quotation marks) on 4 acres is absurdly crowded by any standards; so how about 20 swims on one acre? And every 24 or 48 hours, or whatever, everyone has to change swims to ensure that hotspots(!) are not unfairly monopolised. That, implausible though it may seem, is the situation which purportedly applies on Warmwell, in Dorset.

Which, if true, goes way beyond bizarre. It is grotesque.

I realise, of course, that what I have written is likely to result in my receiving a permanent ban from Cuttle Mill and Warmwell.

Damn. There's my life in ruins..!

A big, windswept coastal pit.

Chapter Three

Deep Waters

Deep is a relative term. Most English gravel pits are quite shallow, so anywhere over 15ft is regarded as deep. But talk to anglers who fish the French barrages and the big alpine lakes of Italy, Austria and Switzerland, and you will get a very different picture. I have been told that Cassein carp are frequently caught at depths in excess of 40ft, and Rod Hutchinson told me he has caught them from 90ft! I cannot compete with those figures, but I have caught them down to 34ft in the West Warwick Reservoir at Walthamstow, and at 36ft in a gravel pit at Stonar, near Ramsgate. But such depths are extreme in the U.K., and for all practical purposes deep water tactics - or what I define as such - come into effect where there are significant areas over about 20ft.

Comfort Zone

Divers have told me that there is a tremendous temperature variation between the surface and the bottom. In high summer the surface may be quite warm - tepid even - but it gets considerably cooler as the depth increases. At 20ft it will feel cold.

Other factors which change with depth include pressure, dissolved oxygen, pH and light intensity.

Hardly surprising, then, that carp are very particular about where they want to be. My belief is that they choose a sort of optimum "comfort zone" - and once they have selected it, they are reluctant to move deeper or shallower.

Depth change is not a particularly easy matter for fish. Anyone who has caught pike or perch from deep water knows how distressed they can become. Some, sadly, do not recover. This problem is exercising the minds of Ken Crow's Bough Beech pike syndicate because the occasional deep water capture dies after release.

Fish cope with depth change by adjusting the gas content in their swim bladder - pike and perch can do this only slowly, relying on gas exchange with the blood via a capillary rich gland. Carp have a twin chamber swim bladder which is connected to the oesophagus by a tract. This enables them to more readily adjust to pressure change - in effect by gulping air or burping. I recall Brian Mills telling

Long range Essex mirror taken on an autumn day of strong southerlies, sunshine and showers.

The one-time Aveley record taken from the margins on a busy Bank Holiday weekend.

Fishing the margins in a big, deep pit which is still being worked.

Nicer than a dugout, surely?

A lovely summer south-westerly set the indicators flying.

A lovely linear and autumn's first leaf fall. . . I feel a poem coming on!

Correct feeding is tremendously important.

me how, when drawing carp up from deep water in Stonar he noticed bubbles appearing on the surface. He assumed this to have been caused by the expulsion of gas. After having it drawn to my attention I looked for it when I played carp from Stonar's deeps, and on calm days saw it exactly as Brian described.

This, incidentally, is possibly one of the reasons carp roll and head-and-shoulder. I said "one of the reasons" because I think there are probably a number of others. Carp spend a lot of their time at midwater - as anyone who has used an electronic fish finder will testify. So let us assume a group of fish are meandering around at a depth of 10ft in 20ft of water. They decide to feed, and the food is on the bottom 10ft below them, so is it not reasonable to suppose that they might roll or head-and-shoulder in order to gulp air into their swim bladder? This in preparation for making adjustments to cope with the increased water pressure they will encounter when they start feeding.

If true, it would explain why deep water carp often show on the surface over my feed prior to my getting a run.

It makes immaculate sense.

Unfortunately it does not explain why they do it in some deep waters, and not in others! But that minor flaw will not persuade me to reject the idea because it is far too elegant a notion for that!

Whilst carp can cope with rapid pressure increase or decrease, I doubt that they do so from choice. I think they select their comfort zone, and remain there until circumstances change, or - as just suggested - they need to alter their depth for feeding.

The Right Depth

The reason I am so totally convinced of the existence of a comfort zone is because I have found the identification of the right depth to be absolutely critical. I could cite numerous examples where a bait placed at, say, 12ft produced several fish, whereas one placed 3ft shallower or deeper produced nothing.

Unfortunately there is no universal critical depth. It is cyclic in that it is influenced by both season and time of day. It might also be modified by water conditions. What will not alter it, however, is bait. So often I have read something along the lines of, "I relied on the strength of my bait to pull them down". I am not sure what "bait strength" is, but whatever form this mysterious quality takes, I do know it will not "pull them down". It is essential to find the critical depth, and fish for them there.

Stonar - 50 acres and more than 50ft deep.

Trial and Error

While there are a few guiding principles - which I will discuss presently - there is no certain means by which the critical depth can be predicted. The only reliable method is by trial and error. I use what I call a "down the slope" approach - not the catchiest of labels I concede, but nonetheless apt for all its prosaic dullness!

Whilst some deep waters have the bars, humps and plateaux associated with shallower waters, their main depth gradation occurs in the margins. Margin fishing is discussed in detail in the next chapter, so at this juncture I will confine myself to a description of my "down the slope" process.

I shall assume that three rods are permitted - where only two are allowed it makes the establishment of the critical depth considerably more difficult. First I make what might be termed an "educated guess" - based on the weather, time of year and previous experience of that particular water as regards the depth at which I expect to find carp. Let us suppose I have judged it to be 12ft; I set a sliding float at precisely 12ft, and deliberately overcast a short way. The lead is sufficient to sink the float, so it immediately vanishes from sight. It is then inched back until its tip shows on the surface.

Typically this will not be very far out, so accuracy with the baited terminal rig is no problem. While the float is in position I use it as a marker for tight feeding.

The marker float is then retrieved, and the stop-knot set at 15ft - whereupon the casting and baiting process is repeated.

Finally, the float is set at 9ft - and the third rod placed in position.

By means of that procedure I have bracketed what I think will be the most likely feeding depth with one rod a bit deeper, and another slightly shallower (Fig 15). The reason I have varied them by just 3ft is because I doubt that carp deviate more than a foot or two either side of the critical depth. Baits placed 3ft apart therefore reduce the likelihood of there being a bait-free zone through which they can pass.

If the 12ft rod produces a take, I will continue to fish the other two rods at 9ft and 15ft - thereby enabling me to check if the carp was representative of how others are behaving, or just a one-off. If, however, a take comes to the rod fished at 15ft, I will dispense with the 9ft rod and recast it to 18ft. My new depth pattern becoming 12ft, 15ft and 18ft.

Conversely, if a take comes to the 9ft rod, I would relocate the 15ft bait at 6ft.

No doubt many anglers will regard all this "critical depth" business as far fetched, and will wonder if I have overstated its importance. I shall not try to convince those who think that way, merely suggest that they try the tactic before rejecting it.

I realise that my description of "down the slope" depth bracketing makes it sound like an extremely dull and soulless way of fishing. And I fully understand how anglers who prefer a more intuitive approach might find its clinical precision distinctly off-putting, intimidating even. One of my critics scornfully dismissed it as "mechanical" and "fishing by numbers". Which was somewhat hurtful - or would have been were I not a clinical, soulless automaton!

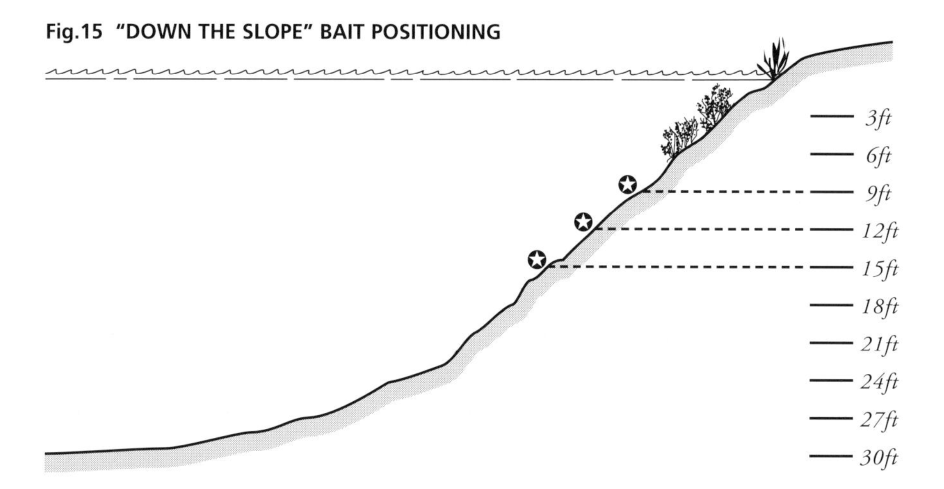

Fig.15 "DOWN THE SLOPE" BAIT POSITIONING

Fig.16 PIKE SLIDER DEPTH MEASUREMENT SETUP

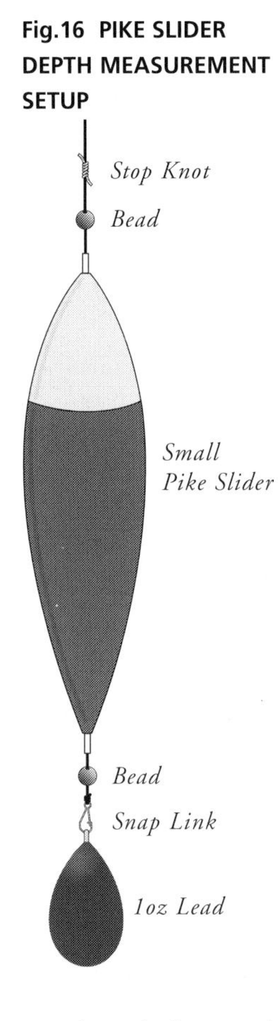

Slider

Accurate depth measurement, as in the example just described, is achieved by means of a sliding float (Fig 16). For close in, precision work I prefer a slider to the more usual through-the-lead feature finding setup.

An ordinary pike slider is my usual choice. In order to minimise disturbance I use a relatively small float - one which sinks with a 1oz lead.

Seasonal, Cyclical and Meteorological

In spring, when the sun starts to warm the margins, carp will move into very shallow water. I might have substituted the word "surprisingly" for "very" because - providing they are not spooked in any way - they will enter areas which, quite literally, are barely deep enough to cover them. They will feed in such places too - I know this to be so because I have caught carp from margins so shallow that it barely covered my vertical anti-tangle tube as I lowered the bait!

Late March, last year, I took several from the margins immediately adjacent to one of those naff table-top size wooden platforms which matchmen are so fond of. The water was about 15in deep, and crystal clear so I could see every pebble. One fish took me completely unawares and demonstrated just how confident - or daft - margin carp can sometimes be! I lowered my bait, then put the rod down in order to leave my hands free to toss in some feed. But the rod suddenly came alive and clattered across the top of the platform! Momentarily I was confused and looked down at my feet to see if the line had become entangled, when suddenly it dawned on me that I had a take! Fortunately the clutch was fairly loose set, so the carp was able to take line immediately. And how! It tore across the surface ahead of an impressive V-wake before deciding to dive and fight deep. At which point I managed to compose myself and take control of the situation. The fish itself was unremarkable - a mid-double common which I neither weighed nor photographed - but the circumstances of its capture make it unlikely that I shall ever forget it!

Throughout early summer, and possibly as late as mid July, I expect to catch carp from shallow margin spots. Not so shallow as during the late March to May period, but certainly 2-3ft.

From mid July there is a tendency to slip down the slope, and by the end of August I look for them in 9-12ft. Unlike carp which live in small, shallow pits, they will continue to feed close in, albeit steadily deeper, right through September.

This process continues very gradually until about mid October when I expect to find them in the 20ft region.

Why deep water carp should slip down the slope in this way is difficult to understand. It is not, as is popularly supposed, due to deeper water being warmer because most of the time the converse applies. All the while the water temperature remains above 4 Celsius (39 Fahrenheit) thermal stratification ensures that the surface layers - and consequently the shallower spots - are warmest. Only when the water temperature drops below 4 Celsius, and a phenomenon known as hydrogen bonding occurs, does the surface layer become cooler than deeper areas.

Deep water mirror - and still full of fight!

Mid to late February the migration reverses and the carp gradually move back to shallower water - which brings us back to where we started.

All of which seems nice and straightforward, and so it would be were it not for the fact that, as previously mentioned, matters are complicated by 24 hour cyclic movements. Also the weather. But we had better take them one at a time...

There is a tendency for summer carp to move up the slope in the daytime, and slip back down it during the evening. This is by no means an invariable rule - which is why I described such movement as a "tendency" - but it happens often enough to be a useful starting point when deciding tactics.

An intriguing observation I have made on the deep pits I fish is that few anglers catch much in the daytime; virtually all their captures come at night. This would make sense if the carp in those waters were primarily night feeders, but they are not - as is demonstrated by the fact that I catch mine in the daytime. I hate this to read like a brag piece, but let us put some flesh on the bones here. From a deep pit I fished for several weeks at the back end of last summer I took 26 carp - all between 9.00am and 8.00pm. The water was subjected to a lot of pressure - by some extremely capable anglers too - but I only saw two other carp caught in the daytime. The essential difference between the other anglers and myself was that they tended to fish the deeper water, while I concentrated on the margin slope. Which suggests - and I put it no stronger - that deep water feeding is more likely to occur at night than in the daytime.

The final factor influencing feeding depth is weather. As a generalisation I would say warm weather is a major inducement for carp to come into shallow water. Cool weather - especially if there is a chilly wind blowing - has the opposite effect.

Features

Thus far I have concentrated on the margins and just beyond because from spring through to late summer it is where I catch most of my carp. This is hardly surprising in view of the fact that the margins are, in most deep waters, their most significant feature. But sometimes they have other features such as islands, high rise areas and plateaux. Of them all, plateaux are the most common - although the nature of their formation (usually by a build up of sediment) means that a plateau, singular, is more likely than plateaux, plural. But whatever their number, they have an obvious attraction to carp.

High places in deep pits are like those in shallow pits, but on a grander scale. A deep water plateau, therefore, might rise from, say, 25ft to 10ft - and cover an area twice the size of a football field. Weed permitting, a large shallow(ish) expanse can be treated as though it was normal shallow water. Its edges, insofar as range permits, I treat as offshore margins, and apply the down the slope tactics described earlier. A word of warning, though; never assume that a plateau drops away in a gentle gradient - always plumb it carefully. The Pisces lake at Sundridge clearly demonstrates the importance of this advice because there is one spot where it drops steeply from 8ft to 20ft, another where it descends from 8ft to 32ft, and yet another where there is a cliff-like vertical plunge from 24ft to 44ft!

Through-the-lead Stop-knot Slider

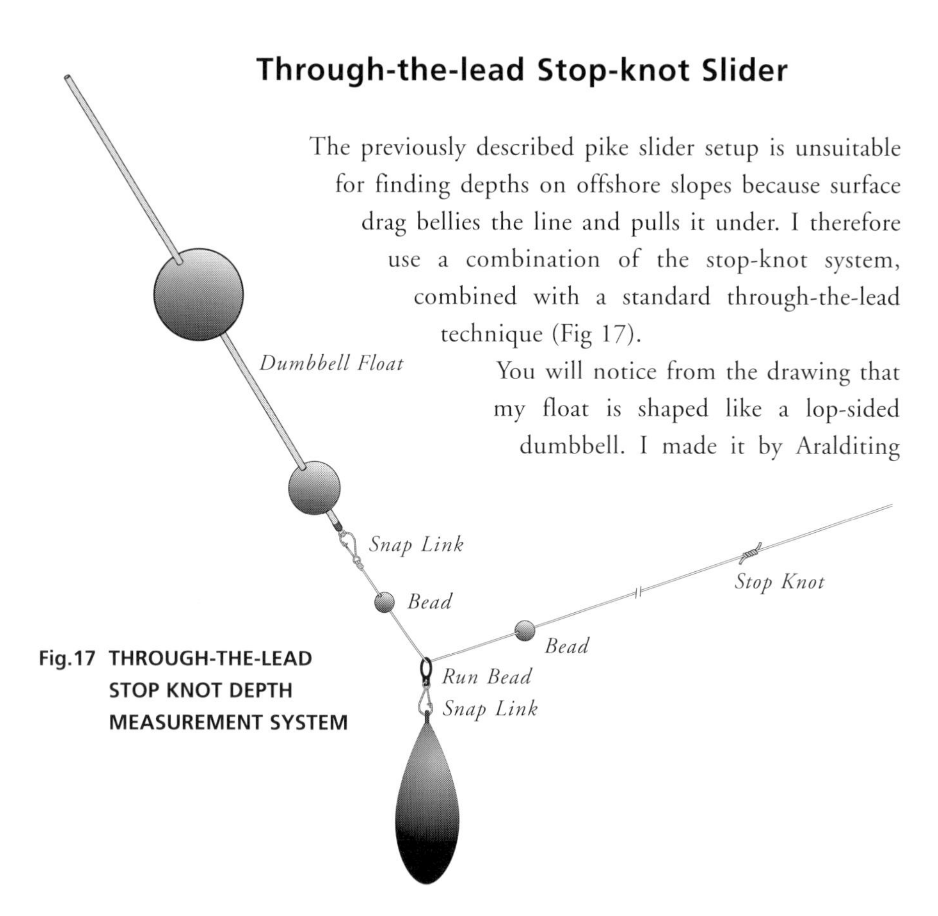

Fig.17 THROUGH-THE-LEAD STOP KNOT DEPTH MEASUREMENT SYSTEM

The previously described pike slider setup is unsuitable for finding depths on offshore slopes because surface drag bellies the line and pulls it under. I therefore use a combination of the stop-knot system, combined with a standard through-the-lead technique (Fig 17).

You will notice from the drawing that my float is shaped like a lop-sided dumbbell. I made it by Aralditing two different size pike pilot floats to a 1ft length of Drennan stiff anti-tangle tube. Based on the same principle, but an improved design, is an extra long antenna float made by Tight Lines Angling Products.

The procedure is similar to that employed with the slider but it operates upside down… if you see what I mean. The critical depth is estimated - just as described earlier - and the stop-knot set accordingly. The depth finder setup is cast out and, depending where on the slope it lands, the float will either lie flat or be submerged. It is then wound down, retrieved a short distance and released - and so on until it indicates the correct depth has been found.

The advantage of the long float over a more conventional design is that it gives the angler more information about the gradient (Fig 18).

Island margins, humps and bars are treated the same as plateaux - baits are placed at different depths down the slope.

Fig.18 LONG DEPTH TEST FLOAT GIVES MORE INFORMATION ABOUT THE GRADIENT

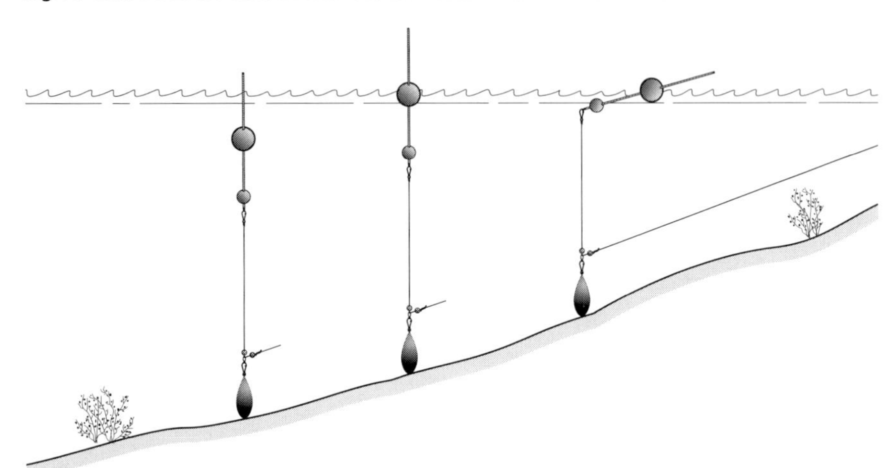

Wind of Change

You would not expect a gentle wind to exert much influence on a large body of water more than 20ft deep. But it does. I can recall a startling demonstration of this which occurred when I was floater fishing on the Blue Lake at Northfleet. For the benefit of those unfamiliar with the water, it is a chalk pit of about 30 acres. Vast tracts of it are more than 35ft deep, and by reputation it is 60-70ft deep in places. I was fishing the western end of the pit, towards which the gentlest easterly zephyr was blowing. It was a warm day and several fish were bow waving on the top. By late morning I had taken two fish, and was confident of a third, when the breeze dropped to nothing. Blue Lake was rarely flat calm, but on this occasion - albeit only for a few minutes - it was. Then the tiniest surface ripple became apparent, caused by a barely discernible breeze - but blowing in the opposite direction to the one it replaced. I rationalised the situation, and decided that the fish were unlikely to move on such an insignificant ripple. I looked over the water for an encouraging bow wave. Nothing. I rationalised further, and almost convinced myself that there was no point moving because no sooner would I be settled and the breeze would probably change again. But the maggot of doubt was gnawing away at my confidence, so I hastily dismantled my gear, loaded it in the car and drove to the far end of the pit. I walked to the top of the cliff face and looked down on three large groups of carp. Further out, others could be seen swimming purposefully towards me. Blue Lake is about one third of a mile long, yet a change of breeze had persuaded large numbers of carp to swim from one end of the pit to the other.

I accept that part of the reason those fish responded so quickly was because they were near the surface. Had they been deeper, perhaps they would have been slower to move. Or possibly they might not have moved at all in response to such a gentle breeze. But notwithstanding the somewhat exceptional circumstances, it was a dramatic example of how wind can affect carp.

From mid April through to late September, wind strength, direction and temperature are major factors which influence my choice of swim. But it is not a simple matter of following the wind because there are a number of important variables to consider. Features, for example. Big, deep waters tend not to be overly endowed with features, so the few which do exist can exert a strong attraction. How, then, do we weigh up the appeal of, say, a plateau at one end of the pit, against that of a warm wind which blows towards the opposite end? Or what about the island halfway down the pit - will carp which are moving on a wind remain in the island's vicinity when they reach it, or will they carry on past it? Other anglers come into the reckoning too. If it is a water where the carp have the reputation of following the wind, other anglers will respond by fishing the windward end. Will carp remain there despite the presence of lines, and the splashes caused by leads - in addition, that is, to the disturbance created by marker setups and freebie baiting?

None of the aforementioned elements are quantifiable in a purely objective way, so their evaluation is imprecise. If carp show by rolling or jumping, fine - they have done a large part of our job for us. But if they do not show - what then? Truth is, most of us rely as much on intuition as we do on logic. The "logical" part of the equation goes something like this:

- **If the wind is warmer than the water, and there are no anglers near the downwind bank, I follow it. If anglers are already in the prime area, I remain in the wind-affected half of the lake, but look for somewhere quiet, away from other anglers and their lines.**
- **If the wind is cooler than the water, a percentage of fish will still follow it, so if the downwind end of the pit is deserted I will fish there. If, however, other anglers are present I will probably ignore the wind and opt for a feature which I expect to attract fish.**
- **An en route feature (like the island mentioned earlier) will almost certainly delay fish which are following a warm wind, but rarely will it hold them for long. If, therefore, the wind is new, and not particularly strong, I will happily fish the feature - but if it has been blowing hard for more than 12 hours, or moderately for more than 24 hours, I would prefer the downwind bank.**

A classic demonstration of how a feature can delay carp, but only for a short time, occurred on RMC Angling's Larkfield One. Hereabouts it is not called Larkfield One, but The Ocean - a name inspired as much by its notorious difficulty as its size. The Ocean is 43 acres, and those of us who know the water estimate its population to comprise 30-50 carp. It is not its low population density which makes The Ocean such a hard water, however, but weed. Virtually everywhere under about 20ft deep is overgrown with pull-for-a-break dense weed. Deeper areas are clear of rooted weed, but covered in a thick bed of blanket weed. Only the deepest, darkest carpless holes are entirely weedfree. Successes on The Ocean are few and far between, and very hard won - just a handful are caught each year. Steve Edwards and I were therefore thrilled - and not a little surprised - to take two within 24 hours. Mine, a mirror, came during an after work Friday evening trip; Steve's, a common, came at lunchtime the following day. Both came from a high rise area which was being struck by a new wind. The forecasters promised the wind would last a couple more days, so we were confident the carp would remain in the area. We were wrong. Yes, the wind stayed constant, but the carp moved. What happened, I am sure, is the carp only paused near our high rise spot during which time we caught a couple - after which they carried on past us.

The Ocean is one of those waters where you cannot afford to miss opportunities because they occur so rarely - so I leave you to imagine my feelings following the incident I am about to describe. It happened last spring. I was fishing to a relatively large, uneven plateau cum bar, and had one of my baits in a semi clear area on top of the plateau in 15ft, with the second where it started to level out at 21ft. The morning passed uneventfully save for an eel to the "shallow" bait. Early afternoon I heard a gentle rumbling sound in the distance. I tried to convince myself it was an aircraft, but ominous looking clouds and periodic flashes over the North Downs soon dispelled that hope. Now, you have to understand that I am terrified of thunderstorms. It was not always so, and I well recall standing in a boat in the middle of Hickling Broad, with lightning flashing all around me and the water surface shimmering like Saint Elmo's fire, shaking my fist at the heavens and yelling, "You missed!" What brought about my current wimp mode I am not certain - but whatever the reason, my reaction to storms has metamorphosed from reckless bravado to undiluted terror! The ever darkening sky persuaded me that the wisest course of action was to pack up and return to my car. The first bait was retrieved, and the rod quickly dismantled. The second rod was lifted, whereupon it momentarily struck resistance which I presumed to be weed - and it too was retrieved. As I lifted my terminal rig from the water I could see something attached to the hook - it was a damn great mirror carp scale! There must have been a carp within a yard of my bait when I lifted the rod; it may even have been just about to suck it in at that very pico second! I had pulled a bait away from an Ocean carp! I did not know whether to sob, scream, shout, lay down and beat the ground with my fists, or impale myself Samurai style on the end of a bankstick! I considered recasting, but the proximity of the storm dissuaded me from doing so - and I had no wish to be zapped by ninety zillion volts and reduced to a pile of ash. On reflection, though, that might have been the most appropriate outcome... .

There is obviously something about The Ocean because bizarre incidents occur there more frequently than they ought. Like the time I was visited by The Nutter. There I was, quietly contemplating the water in front of me, when a rock came whizzing past me and landed just beyond my rods. Startled, I turned around and saw standing a few yards behind me a middle aged guy who was grinning dementedly and holding, somewhat incongruously I felt, a shopping bag. Normally I would remonstrate with rock throwers, but notwithstanding my lack of qualifications in clinical psychology, I immediately diagnosed this guy as being a fully paid up, card carrying crazy. I decided it would be best to ignore him. I turned back to the water, taking time to wonder what, in addition to rocks, he carried in his shopping bag. My curiosity was soon satisfied when a car's

40 acres plus, large tracts of deep water and heavily weeded - a corner of "The Ocean".

hub cap flew Frisbee-like over my head. "Oh God," I thought, "why me?" I scanned my tackle to see what I could use, should the need arise, as a weapon. My eyes fell upon one of Nashy's heavy duty stainless steel storm rods - that should ward him off. I waited to see what would happen next; desperately trying to resist the urge to turn and look. After a few minutes I could stand the uncertainty no longer. I looked, and to my relief saw that he had gone. I had heard neither his arrival, nor his departure. The Phantom of The Ocean! There was nothing spectral about the rock or the hub cab, though!

The Ocean has been the scene of at least one tragedy, too. And I witnessed it. It was shortly after sunrise, and I had been fishing for a couple of hours when I became aware of unusual goings on over the far side of the pit which, at that point, must be about a quarter of a mile across. A fleet of police cars arrived, and a number of divers entered the lake. Shortly afterwards the Kent Air Ambulance helicopter landed. I watched proceedings though my binoculars, and realised with a shudder that something awful must have occurred because I saw the divers pull from the water what, quite unmistakably, was a body. Seemingly a group of youths had been night fishing, and were swimming while waiting for their parents to pick them up. One had got into difficulties and failed to surface, whereupon the others raised the alarm but, sadly, too late.

The incident provides a sobering reminder that whereas we treat gravel pits - and lakes, canals and rivers for that matter - as recreation areas, they are potentially very dangerous.

Difficult

Some anglers find it difficult to come to terms with deep pits. First, there is the psychological barrier to overcome in that those whose experience is confined to shallow waters cannot quite get their head round the notion of carp living at depths of 20ft or more. They know from empirical evidence that it happens, but it nonetheless seems implausible. If they give a deep pit a try, they do so with complete lack of confidence. Early success might give them the spur to continue, but failing that they become discouraged and give up. All of which is understandable.

There are practical difficulties too. As already discussed, it is not enough to locate carp in the normal lateral sense - they have to be located vertically too. This means it is perfectly possible to choose the right area, but to have a twitchless blank because baits are fished at the wrong depth.

I have caught carp from fourteen different waters which had substantial areas deeper than 20ft. Twelve were pits, two were water supply reservoirs. And I can honestly say that none were intrinsically difficult, only insofar as some had such low carp stocks relative to their acreage, occasionally combined with problems such as heavy weed growth, they would have been difficult whatever their depth.

My advice to anyone who lacks the necessary confidence is to try to find a deep water which is heavily stocked. The size of carp does not matter - the important thing is to catch a few. If there are enough carp in the water, you should not have long to wait. Then tell yourself that while your carp may have been small, a carp is a carp is a carp... In other words, if small ones will feed in 20ft, 25ft or whatever, why should bigger carp be any different?

Acquire the necessary self belief, and deep waters will seem less intimidating - from which point on, the only way is up. Or down, if you want to be literal about it!

A long wait for a long linear! It came at dusk, just as I was about to pack up!

Chapter Four

Margins

An incident which occurred a couple of years ago at Aveley has stuck in my mind. I had just landed my fifth or sixth carp of the day when a neighbouring angler came along and said, "Well, now I've seen it for myself, I believe it. I've read your articles on margin fishing but didn't think it would work on the waters I fish." He went on to explain that he had always assumed I spent most of my time on exclusive, lightly fished waters, and my writing was not likely to be relevant to popular anyone-can-join fisheries.

Truth is, the bulk of my fishing is done in ordinary club waters, and far from being exclusive, some of those clubs actually advertise for members! A couple of my favourite pits are available to anyone who buys a season or day ticket. I fish commercial fisheries too, such as those run by RMC Angling. And yes, I have a syndicate ticket which, at £300, could be considered exclusive in a financial sense but it is not restricted in any sort of "closed shop" regard. I think, then, I can fairly claim that the waters I fish are similar to those fished by other carp anglers. But that said, I avoid the really busy waters because I hate being hemmed in on all sides by bivvies. Also I have no desire to catch fish which, in my opinion, have been caught too often already.

There is something else I would like to make clear; my penchant for margin fishing is not an idiosyncratic eccentricity like using cane rods or 19th century centrepins. The reason I do it is because I find it productive. But given circumstances when I think long range fishing will work better, I do not hesitate to kit-up with the big 13ft Eclipses and punch heavy leads at the horizon.

I think the pits I fish are fairly typical.

Swim Choice

It is important to realise that margin carp are rarely resident in the swim being fished; they are patrollers. That means they may have to pass other anglers before they get to you. If those anglers are sitting in full view of the water, chances are the fish will become somewhat nervous and as a consequence unwilling to feed. With that fact in mind, I try whenever possible to choose a swim immediately adjacent to a quiet, sanctuary area. Let me give an example: imagine a line of overhanging trees or bushes among which there are no swims, or a wide reed bed, or perhaps a stretch of marshy bank - any reasonable length (50yd plus) of bank which cannot be fished will suffice. At one end of the stretch is a swim; the first of several swims in fact. That is the one I would want to be in. At intervals during the day it is probable that individual carp, or even small groups of them, will leave the safety of the sanctuary and scout along adjoining stretches of bank. If nothing frightens them, and food is encountered, they may feed.

If there are no quiet places, and if the banks are continually busy, then frankly I think we need to be realistic and accept that margin fishing is best forgotten.

Undetected

My next requirement is cover. Ideally I like the swim to offer some sort of vegetation behind which I can sit - it does not matter what it is, just so long as it hides me from view or, at the very least, breaks my outline. If no cover exists, I will try to create it with my umbrella, or better still, a few cut willow fronds stuck in the bank. If neither course seems appropriate, but the nature of the swim permits, I will sit several yards back from the water's edge. Whatever the situation, I wear drab coloured clothing. It astonishes me the number of anglers I see sitting in full view of the water while wearing a white T-shirt and a red or yellow baseball cap - or an equally conspicuous ensemble.

In addition to remaining out of sight, I try to be as quiet as possible because only if carp are unaware of my presence can I expect them to feed.

At which juncture, and at the risk of causing offence, I will state that the main reason most anglers fail to catch fish close-in is because they are far too noisy. I am not just talking about obvious sources of noise like the use of a mallet to bash in bivvy pegs, but more subtle noises like a dropped tackle box or a tipped over flask. It is incredible just how noisy most anglers are - it starts when they dump their

Whenever possible I like to tuck myself behind cover.

Where no cover exists, I will create some.

tackle in their swim, and continues more or less unabated for the duration of their session.

Few carp anglers will think the foregoing applies to them, but observation tells me that those who take pains to remain quiet and out of sight are in a very small minority. Many anglers do not even realise that it matters - like the guy who stood adjacent to my rods as he inquired if I had caught anything. I replied that I had caught a couple, and then added that in view of the fact that I was fishing very close, I would be grateful if he would move back from the water's edge. His face acquired a look of genuine bafflement as in complete innocence he asked, "Why?"

He was not being awkward or obstructive, he just did not understand why it should matter - after all, carp fishing is all about rigs and baits is it not...?

In one of my Carpworld articles I cited the example of the angler who, like the previous one, stood right near the edge as he asked where I had my baits. "One of them," I replied, "is about a yard from your right foot."

I expected him to step back with an embarrassed apology. But not this guy! Instead he shielded his eyes with his hand, leant forward, peered down into the water and said, "Will they come that close, then?"

I closed my eyes, sighed in despair and quietly replied, "Sometimes they do."

What else could I say?

Occasionally, however, carp make nonsense of the rules. Like the time I was floater fishing at Handley Barnes. It had been a marvellous day and, if memory serves me correct, I had taken about ten carp.

The gorgeous colours on this deep water carp match those of the autumn leaves.

Gorgeous sparsely scaled mirror.

"Geordie" Mike plays a sunrise carp in a Seine Valley gravel pit.

High summer mirror.

"Will they come that close?" This one did!

But mid-afternoon a couple of jet-skiers arrived. They were of the mouth-breathing troglodyte variety whose idea of fun was to do aquatic "wheelies" just a few yards in front of me. There was no way I could continue fishing, so I retrieved my baits and left them dangling in the edge. The owner of the fishery, Chris Knowles, came across and said, "Sorry about those idiots, Jim - they'll be gone soon." As we stood there talking, making no attempt to remain concealed, with jet-skiers creating bedlam just a few rod lengths out, there was a splash at our feet. One of the mixer baited rigs had been taken!

Another example. On one of my early trips to Layer Pit my attention was attracted by ringing hammer blows. I looked across to the source of the disturbance and saw two anglers setting up - the hammer blows being caused by steel head mallets (no wimpy rubber jobs here!) being used to drive stainless steel banksticks into the rock hard banks. My lips probably set in the elongated "S" shape beloved by cartoonists when they want to signify disbelief! In mitigation, though, Layer was considered a "long chuck" water in those days, so bankside noise probably made little difference. But no, the new arrivals did not cast their baits to the middle - they lobbed them just over the edge! I turned away in disinterest. Within 30 minutes my attention was attracted again - this time by the sound of a bite alarm. One of them had got a run! The first of many as it transpired! The two anglers, who I did not know at the time but subsequently got to know very well, were Zenon Bojko and Mick Lindsell, whose astonishing catches at Layer became legendary.

Zenon and Mick are remarkable anglers, with an enviable track record of successes on a variety of waters. Where they deem it appropriate to adopt a softly, softly approach, they do so. But they considered it unnecessary at Layer - and on that occasion at least, they were obviously correct!

But exceptions, as they say, do not disprove the rule. And on 99% of occasions silence and discretion are not merely desirable, they are essential.

Thus far my swim requirements have been largely influenced by where I might find carp which feel safe, but other factors come into the reckoning too. If a warm breeze or wind is blowing I opt for a downwind bank.

If the weather is very warm, I am happy with margins as shallow as just 2-3ft; indeed, I have caught fish to 20lb plus from water little more than 1ft deep. If, however, it is cool, I prefer 9ft plus. Most times I look for something in the 4-6ft range.

Clear Spots

Many waters have weed growing all or part of the way down the margin slope - and well beyond, of course. If the base of the slope gives way to a weedfree bottom it is worth placing one rod there, but it is a mistake to ignore the weeded slope itself. The usual way of fishing in weed is to try to find clear spots, and this is invariably my first course of action. I especially like narrow channels between beds of vegetation, or cove-like recesses in the weed's outer edge.

Clear spots sometimes become overgrown as the season progresses, while others stay clear all summer - indeed, some remain weedfree year after year. How to find them? Diligent float-and-lead work is the only way I know; and having found them I do not rely on memory but record the details in a notebook. Often it is possible to relate these clear spots to naturally occurring markers: "2ft to the left of the single brown stem" - that sort of thing - thereby obviating the need to plumb around on subsequent trips.

In addition to looking for clear spots, I look for clean spots. These are places where, if I attach a short hooklink to my feature finding lead, it comes back free of dead weed stalks and other debris. I am convinced they are kept clean by regular browsing - so it seems reasonable to assume that baits placed in such spots have a very high chance of being taken.

When casting to mini clearings and weed edges it is important that rigs be allowed to rest where they settle because if they are moved it increases the likelihood of their becoming caught up. Great care, therefore, should be exercised when taking in slack or adjusting bite indicators; and on no account should the tackle be given "just a little tweak" to check that it is in the clear. Yes, we have all done it, and having found it was okay have then sat there in an agony of doubt wondering if our interference has messed it up!

Clear spots might also be found beneath overhanging trees where growth may be inhibited due to decreased light levels. Such places are most likely to be found on north facing banks which tend to receive less sun. If the lowest branches are a yard or two above the surface it should be possible to cast a bait beneath them, especially if the hooklink is folded back on itself Concertina Rig style - thereby shortening and stiffening it which prevents it flailing around in flight.

If the trailing branches are very close to the surface it is impossible to cast beneath them. Leastways, I find it so. Although I once read a recommendation to the effect that we should cast low and fast in such situations, and thereby skim our tackle in position...

I shall refrain from comment on that one!

On another occasion - and I think this appeared in an old B.C.S.G. (British Carp Study Group) journal - I read a description of how a terminal rig was floated beneath some branches by means of a Tom Thumb size raft, and pulled clear when it reached the desired spot. I tried it, and concluded it was one of those ideas which worked fine in the author's imagination, but never actually got used in practice! It was what Rick calls a "kitchen rig" - denoting that it has been cooked up at home...

Which, I suppose, brings us inevitably, albeit reluctantly, to the subject of bait boats. What can I say about bait boats? What do I even want to say about them? I think it best if I contain myself and merely describe them as an inappropriate accessory.

I shall say no more.

Were I unable to exercise such restraint I might be tempted to ridicule those who use the wretched things. Fortunately I am too mature to sink to that level, so nothing will induce me to suggest that if they want to play at being pond admirals they should go down to their local paddling pool and join other model boat enthusiasts. Nor will I allow the words "naff" or "anorak" to slip from my word processor keyboard - no matter how powerful the gremlin impelling my fingers...

Heavily overhung spots were beyond my reach until Mainline boss, Steve Morgan, offered the ingenious suggestion that I use a pole - not for fishing, just for

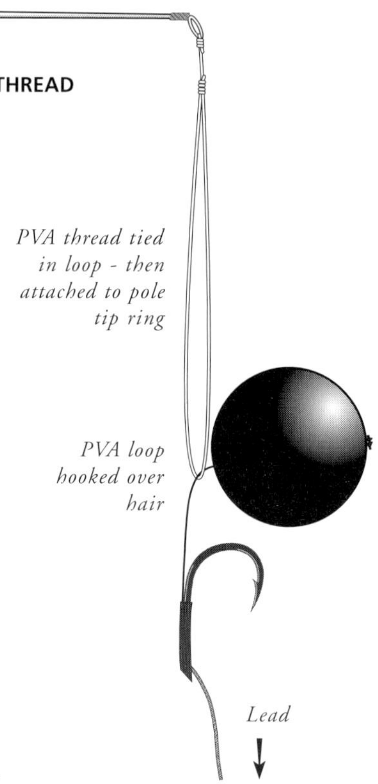

Pole Tip

Fig.19 HOOKBAIT TIED TO POLE TIP WITH PVA THREAD

PVA thread tied in loop - then attached to pole tip ring

PVA loop hooked over hair

Lead

bait placement. I thought it a brilliant idea, so I bought an inexpensive (about £20) seven metre telescopic glass pole. The tip section was excessively floppy so I replaced it with the top of a broken reservoir fly rod.

By tying the hookbait to the pole's tip ring with PVA thread (Fig 19) I was able to poke the end tackle beneath overhanging trees and bushes which had hitherto been impossible to access - my rod meanwhile being in the rests with the bale arm open. When the tackle was over the required spot, the pole tip was dipped beneath the water to allow the PVA to dissolve, whereupon the rig sank to the bottom. The pole was then withdrawn, and the rod's indicator system set up in the usual way.

It is somewhat awkward if there is a lot of vegetation or a high bank immediately behind the swim. And, seeing as how it utilises PVA, it is not very practical in the rain. So the system is not exactly user friendly, but it enables hookbaits to be placed in spots where carp have previously only encountered freebies. My friend Dennis Holding demonstrated the value of this when he used the tactic to extract one of the big fish from Sutton at Hone (bait placement by pole has since been banned there...).

After reading a description of this method in one of my Carpworld features, Brian Skoyles contacted me with the recommendation that I replace my tip ring with a "U" shaped holder. He sent me one to try - it looked like a mini two-pronged fork with its unequal length tines bent at right angles to its stem. It was intended, Brian explained, to replace the pole's tip ring.

If the bait is placed alongside the upright tines (Fig 20), with the hair passing between them, the boilie is held securely. When the terminal tackle is over the required spot, it is released by giving the pole a 180 degrees twist. Very neat! With

Fig.20 BOILIE HELD IN PLACE ALONGSIDE THE TINES OF BRIAN SKOYLES'S SPECIAL POLE 'FORK'

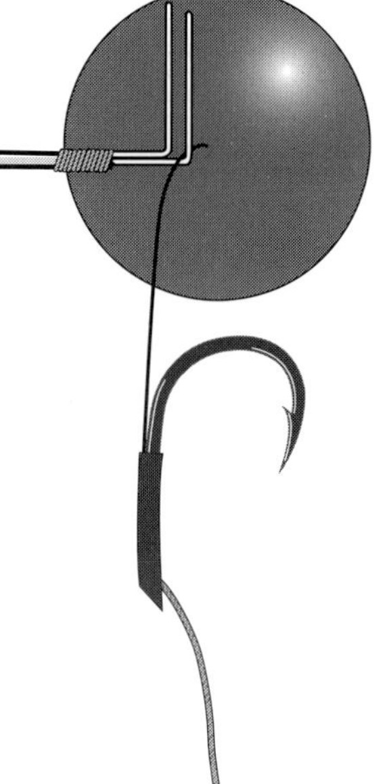

the added advantage, of course, that Brian's bait holder is unaffected by rain. I see no reason why it would not work efficiently with the pole tip completely submerged, thereby enabling a bait to be poked beneath branches which actually hang into the water.

In the Weed

If clear spots cannot be found, what then? We can, of course, play safe and cast to deeper, possibly weedfree areas beyond. Trouble is, such places might be carpfree too! So we need to psych ourselves up to fish right in the weed. Some anglers - Gary Bayes for one - have no qualms about fishing in weed. Indeed, Gary loves it! But then Gary is something of a specialist at this sort of thing. Others are happy to cast into weed with a cavalier, "If they want it, they'll find it."

For most of us, however, fishing in weed is a confidence eroding activity. The problem is one of presentation because a normal rig risks getting caught up as it plunges down through the fronds. There is no completely reliable means of avoiding hang-ups, but there are several approaches which give us at least a reasonable chance. These are discussed in Chapter Six.

Weed fishing is an uncertain business and requires a high level of determination and self belief on the part of the angler. I estimate that approximately 50% of baits fished in weed are poorly presented; trouble is - as the head of the giant Lever corporation said of the wasted element of his company's advertising budget - I do not know which 50%! After casting I therefore switch off - mentally that is - I clear my mind of doubts and have faith. Easier said than done, I acknowledge, but if carp will not take baits in clear spots, what choice is there?

Freshly made cubes cooling prior to being frozen.

Feeding

The presence or otherwise of weed affects how we feed. Fish in weedfree margins tend to be somewhat wary, they will stop to pick up a few items, but are unlikely to really get their heads down. Weedy margins, on the other hand, provide a degree of security with the result that carp will often be willing to stay and browse. I therefore feed very lightly when fishing weedfree margins, with just a small handful of boilies and maybe a couple of pouches of particles or pellets around each hookbait. On steep slopes I do not use spherical boilies, incidentally, but prefer cubes, discs or half-boilies to minimise the risk of their rolling down to deeper water. When fishing in or adjacent to weed I will double or treble those quantities, and am happy to use conventional boilies because there is little chance of their rolling very far.

Weed, or the lack of it, influences the sort of takes we can expect. Runs in weedfree water are usually extremely fast. This is primarily due to the fact that margin carp never completely overcome their apprehension at being so close to the bank, which results in them panicking as soon as they realise something is wrong. One of my Aveley fish took off with such violence that the Baitrunner was jerked into spin-mode and overran! Yes, I thought it was impossible, too! The culprit was only a low double which, after a failed but valiant attempt to cheese-wire the fingers from my hand as I endeavoured to unravel the tangle, was safely landed. Theories as to where it got its power from included the accusation that I incorporated steroids in my bait mix! One of the lake's regulars, on noticing that the carp had a lump on its tail root, suggested it had received a bionic implant!

The bionic, lumpy tail mirror which tried to sever my fingers!

Weedy water takes are often much more sedate affairs which just sort of trundle off in an unhurried, almost casual manner. This is presumably because they feel relatively safe in the weed and are thus in no hurry to leave it.

Tackle

Received wisdom decrees that stiff rods are unsuitable for margin fishing because they result in an unacceptably high number of hookpulls. For many years I accepted this dogma, and no doubt was as guilty as anyone for perpetuating the myth. Then I found myself catching a lot of big carp from an horrendously weedy Kent pit. These were very big fish, running almost to mid-thirties, and every one had to be hauled from dense Elodea and eel grass. The 2.25lb Eclipses I had been using hitherto coped admirably, but I felt I was making unreasonable demands on them, so I scaled up to the 2.75lb model. This is a relatively stiff rod - it is, after all, primarily intended for long range fishing - and I was concerned about hookpulls. My worries were unfounded. I continued to catch lots of big carp, and did not experience a single hookpull.

Until recently I used Shimano 8010 or 6010 Aero Baitrunners for margin fishing. They are faultless reels save for a somewhat "snatchy" clutch. It is not too bad once it gets going, but it has a tendency to stick after a period of non use. It is therefore advisable to give the spool a twist or two prior to every cast. Did you know, incidentally, that the 8010 and the 6010 are identical? Leastways, I cannot tell them apart. So why is the 8010 more expensive? Just one of life's imponderable mysteries, I guess...

I said "until recently" because dissatisfaction with the Aero's clutch prompted me to acquire some Shimano 3500 Baitrunners. They are lovely reels - far nicer than Aeros, in my opinion - and it is a revelation to experience a clutch which functions with silky smoothness.

The 3500, 4500 and 6500 models are the original Baitrunners, incidentally. They do not have the long stroke spool of the Aero, nor the lovely flat line lay, but as I use my 3500's for margin fishing this does not matter.

U.S.A. anglers evidently prefer the 3500, 4500, and 6500 models (sometimes referred to as "American Series") to the Aeros. They claim the gears are of better quality (Shimano describe them as "saltwater super gears", which I interpret to mean they are heavy duty and corrosion resistant).

Granite Juice significantly reduces line abrasion in weed.

Line

I have never understood why so many anglers use a main line of 10-12lb test when they can benefit from the increased strength of 15lb plus. I suspect it is a legacy of the notion that the use of heavy line is somehow brutal. Not so. The fact that an angler is using 15lb line does not compel him to adopt "heave and hold" tactics when he hooks a fish; he can be as gentle as he chooses but has the reserve of strength should it be needed.

Nor does the use of heavy line affect bait presentation because finesse can be applied beyond the lead.

There is no advantage to be gained from using fine diameter line when fishing close, so I use 15lb test in open water, and 18lb in weed. In addition to enabling me to play fish hard when necessary, relatively heavy line is better able to withstand wear and tear. Most anglers greatly underestimate the abrasion qualities of weed which due to its fibrous nature can damage line, as can the tiny particles of silt, sand and grit which become trapped in it.

Rick plays one of six or seven fish taken from just off the reed edge.

Even when using high breaking strain line, constant checking is necessary to ensure that no damage has been sustained. Obviously a tough, abrasion resistant brand is best. I use Power Plus - but Berkley Big Game, Sufix Supreme and GR60 are all good. If conditions are especially severe, I recommend you try Soft Steel, Pro Gold or Ultima Tournament.

Whatever brand is chosen, its slipperiness - and consequently its resistance to wear - can be enhanced by an application of Kryston's Granite Juice. Initially I was somewhat sceptical about the claims for this product, but having used it for almost three years I am completely converted. It lasts well - only requiring an application every two or three days fishing - and significantly increases the line's durability.

If the margin is strewn with large stones, or has a ledge over which the line might be dragged when fish are being played, I incorporate a 25lb Quicksilver rubbing leader.

Some clubs ban the use of Quicksilver - in which case I suggest a heavy mono leader, something in the order of 30lb test. It will not be as tough as Quicksilver - and certainly much less pleasant to use - but it should cope with all but the worst situations.

Rigs

Nine times out of ten I use a Concertina Rig. I shall not discuss it further at this stage because full details of how to construct it, and the rationale behind it, will be found in Chapter Nine.

Regular readers of my articles will know that I am a fan of inline leads, but even those who favour alternative setups generally acknowledge that inlines are the most suitable for use in weed.

Generally I opt for Korda's excellent, if misnamed, "Distance" model. The original Zipp inlines are good too, albeit not quite as well finished as are Kordas. Most times I use 1.5oz, but will scale up to 2oz or even 2.5oz if line bites are particularly prevalent or there is a lot of floating weed - either of which might pull the end tackle out of position.

Talking of floating weed... I have a real hang up about nodding anti-tangle tube. When floating weed catches on the line, it pulls tight and wave action causes the rod top to nod up and down. I can live with that. But what worries me is the probability that my anti-tangle tube is doing the same - even though it is backweighted. And whilst I have no evidence to support the fact, it seems likely that this will alarm carp. If, therefore, floating weed is a problem I use a 0.5oz backlead; or if there is a big chop on the water, 1oz. These are exceptionally heavy for me because most times when I use backleads I prefer the smallest size available - I even make ultralight versions from mini drilled bullets which are about the same weight as swan shot.

Slack Line

In a further attempt to mitigate the effects of line bites - and assuming my swim is free of floating weed - I allow my lines to hang slack. This provides leeway should a carp swim into them, and enables them to fall free before they pull tight. To provide even more leeway I use loose hanging long-arm lightweight indicators.

Another advantage of slack lines is that they lay along the bottom for the yard or two near the terminal rig - this decreases the likelihood of their being snagged by fish.

If lines lay across weed they will not lay flat, of course, and there is a high probability of carp swimming into them. Several times I have sat and watched big fish - in a pressured water too - swim into one of my slack lines and drag it almost tight without showing any signs of concern. I suspect it feels just like weed. Contrast this with what happens when fish swim into a tight line - they shoot off immediately.

When I refer to my lines being slack, incidentally, I mean really slack - with large loops hanging down between the rings. What surprises me is how much comment it evokes - I am frequently told that it "looks all wrong", and most say they could not bring themselves to fish in such a manner. Usually this is followed with doubts being expressed that a rig will work effectively without a tight line - plus worries that a fish could give me a gentle pick up without my knowing about it. Or it might eject.

I merely shrug my shoulders and reply that I am not on some sort of evangelical mission to convert others to my point of view. Which reply failed to satisfy one critic who, as he walked away, turned back to me and with undisguised indignation said, "Well, I think it's a fault in your fishing!"

As indeed it might be... I am only surprised that anyone cares!

Margin Weather

Margin fishing is at its most effective from spring through to midsummer. In all but very deep waters it is primarily a warm weather tactic. Most of my best margin catches have come when it has been hot and sunny - sometimes so hot that my choice of swim has been influenced almost as much by where I might find shade in which to sit as where I expect to find carp. And while I prefer a warm breeze, I am quite happy in a high pressure flat calm. I like muggy, sticky days too, when the humidity is high.

Low pressure, cloudy conditions are okay - even if it is drizzly - providing the weather remains warm.

If the day is chilly, or a cool breeze springs up, margins are unlikely to produce particularly well. I would, however, exempt from that generalisation the mid-April to late May period when even the shallowest margins can exert an almost irresistible attraction.

Earlier I made reference to margin fishing as a spring and summer approach, but it occasionally produces fish in winter - from surprisingly shallow water, too. Rick practically hand-fed and subsequently stalked out several early March fish from the margin shelf of an Essex pit. And I took carp just inches from the edge of a dyke where the water was so shallow that pick-ups were preceded by subtle vortexes and oily ripples.

Playing

Takes in weedfree margins, as already mentioned, tend to be fast. Often the fish runs parallel to the bank, with the rod stabbing violently as if to indicate, "That way! It's gone that way!" Meanwhile the Delkim's "diddley diddley" warble blends into one continuous note, drowning out the "buzz" of the Baitrunner. Exciting stuff!

I expect the rod to be wrenched down hard the moment I strike as the fish - which has already acquired a head of steam - accelerates rapidly. This is not the time to be fumbling with a tension knob or anti-reverse mechanism, so I ensure my clutch is preset to give line.

After 20yd or so in hyperdrive most fish slow down somewhat - although the run may continue at a more sedate pace for some considerable distance. At which stage I disengage my anti-reverse and may tighten the clutch a tad - this with the intention of playing the fish by backwinding which, I find, gives more direct control. It also significantly reduces the incidence of line twist. If, however, the fish is a particularly aggressive fighter, I continue to rely on the clutch.

When the carp comes within 20yd of the bank I loosen the clutch again - "beaten" carp often find a sudden burst of power which, on a short line, can lead to a hookpull or snap-off if it catches us unaware.

I almost always fish by myself, so I have to net my own carp. Other anglers sometimes come along when they see me playing a fish, and offer to net it. Some, with the best intentions I am sure, pick up the net without asking. Unless it is someone I know well, and in whose ability I have confidence, I decline assistance. I prefer to net my own fish.

Others tell me I look laid back and relaxed while netting a carp. Which, I can assure you, is a classic instance of appearance being deceptive! I have caught goodness knows how many carp but I still get dry mouthed and weak at the knees! The relief which swamps me when the fish is safely enmeshed defies words - especially if the carp is big and the fight has been a hard one.

At which point some anglers punch the air, others shout across the lake; I even saw one guy run round in circles! My reaction is somewhat more subdued. After lifting the fish ashore, I lower it on the mat and sink to my knees as I part the meshes, remove the hook and enjoy a quiet few seconds while I regain my composure. Then it is all businesslike efficiency while the fish is either returned, or placed in the sling/retainer in preparation for weighing and photographing.

Sometimes I recast immediately, but often I just sit and savour the moment.

Practising what I preach - staying well back, remaining behind cover and being as quiet as possible.

Chapter Five

Reaching Out

In autumn '97 I was contacted by an Essex friend, Carl Carlucci, who had obtained membership of a water which, by reputation, responded best to extreme range fishing. Carl had comparatively little experience of distance techniques, being primarily a stalking and floater specialist - so he had diligently searched through his stock of carp magazines in the hope of acquiring some helpful information. To his surprise - and, I confess, mine too - he found that little of real substance had been published. There were plenty of macho claims for prodigious distances, but very little hard information. After discussing a few of Carl's immediate concerns, I told him that, coincidentally, I had just completed a six-part series on long range fishing for "Crafty Carper" (subsequently published in issues 3 to 8). Simultaneously, and unbeknown to me at the time, John Carver was preparing a three-part series for "Carpworld". John's articles ("A Few Yards More", published in issues 89 to 91) were, and remain, the most lucid, authoritative and informative I have ever seen on the subject - essential reading for anyone wanting to extend their knowledge and refine their technique.

Notwithstanding the aforementioned "macho claims", what distances are we talking about when we refer to long or extreme range fishing? The furthest measured distance I have seen anyone cast a baited rig on sensible breaking strain line (0.27mm/10.5lb line, 30lb shock leader, 4oz lead and 15mm boilie) is 156.5 yards, which was achieved by Dave Kingsman, and was witnessed by Pete Overington (then of Summit Tackle), and also by my son, Peter. I suspect Dave's performance is very close to the attainable maximum; a conclusion drawn from having watched long casters on lots of different waters, both here and on the continent, and only having seen two other anglers - one of whom was John Carver - cast a comparable distance.

The furthest measured distance I have cast is 143 yards. But that was achieved with just a lead - no anti-tangle tube, hooklink or bait. I can pick up my 13ft/3.25lb Eclipse, equip it with an end-tackle and bait, and from "cold" (without prior practice) cast about 120 yards. If I practice, or am "tuned" after a period of distance casting, I can put another 10 yards or so on that figure. That is my limit. So what of the 180 yard casts we read about from time to time?

Pete Overington and my son, also called Peter, check out casting distances during a practice session.

What indeed...!

In summary; 100 yards is a long way. 120 yards is a very long way. 140 yards is prodigious. Anyone who can cast a baited rig that far is among the top few percent of long casters.

Rods

I apologise in advance if what follows reads like a Simpson's advertisement. But I had considerable input into the design and development of the Eclipse, Frontier and Advantage rods, so not surprisingly they are the rods I use for all my carp fishing.

First, some generalisations. A long range rod needs to have what is often termed a "fast taper" action - the description being a legacy from earlier times when the action of a rod was controlled solely by the taper of a blank and its wall thickness. If we think of a rod in thirds, "fast taper" translates as a rod which, when lightly loaded, only the top third bends to any degree. As the loading increases, so the middle third bends. Whatever the load, the butt should remain relatively rigid. Nowadays the action of the best quality rods owes as much to carbon composite blends as it does to taper and wall thickness. Such rods are described as being of "multi modulus" construction.

Rings should be few in number (my preference is for six, inclusive of the tip ring) to keep weight, and therefore inertia to a minimum; and also to reduce friction. The butt ring should be large (30mm for standard reels, 40mm for big-spool models), and situated near the top of the butt section. The remaining rings should graduate in size, thereby coning the line gradually to an apex at the 12mm tip.

I first proposed this "sparse ringing, long cone" system, as I then called it, in an article in the late '70's, and subsequently in my book "Modern Specimen Hunting" (Beekay, 1983). Surprisingly it caused quite a lot of controversy, and there was a great deal of resistance against its acceptance. I was told it would cause rings to groove; it was inefficient because it would result in distance retarding line-slap against the blank; and it would place undue stress on the rings when a fish was being played which would make them pop free of their whippings! Needless to say, none of those forecasts proved to be correct - which came as no surprise to me because my conclusions had not been reached theoretically, but as a consequence of taping rings to a blank and casting with it.

Now, of course, it is accepted as the norm, and old style ringing, with ten or more strung along the rod, has fallen into disuse. Talking of which, I am reminded of an incident which occurred a few years after I published my "sparse ringing" recommendations. I met an erstwhile rod consultant (who, in order to save his blushes, I will not name) at Johnson's Railway Lake. As he demonstrated his new rod's casting capabilities he said, "Daiwa" (there's a clue!) "are now using my ringing system on all their carp rods and..." Suddenly his mouth dropped open as the next half formed word froze on his lips. Somewhat red faced he spluttered, "I don't mean it was actually my system, I mean it was..." I saved him further embarrassment by interrupting with the suggestion that he quit while he was behind!

Earlier I made reference to lightness. John Carver has his rods made with single-leg rings - the top three of which have a titanium frame. John is a meticulous angler - the sort who wipes his rods before packing them in their individual sleeves... Most of us are less scrupulous - I simply lash mine to my landing net handle - so single-leg rings are impractical due to the ease with which they are damaged.

I divide my distance fishing into two distinct categories: long range, which I define as up to about 110 yards; and extreme range, which applies to anything beyond that.

A general purpose long range rod needs to be capable of full blooded, no-holds-barred casting with leads up to 3oz. I use the 2.25lb test curve Eclipse for this sort of fishing, and in all but very adverse wind conditions can cast comfortably in excess of 100 yards.

Sometimes, however, in order to contend with a fresh cross or facing wind, we need a lead of 3.5oz. In such circumstances a 2.75lb test curve rod is better.

For extreme range, or when having to cope with very strong winds, we may find it necessary to ratchet up the casting weight by another notch, and utilise a lead of 4oz. This is the stage at which we move up to the really powerful rods, those having a test curve of 3lb or more. The most popular designation is 13ft/3.25lb.

During the course of the last two or three years we have seen new materials such as Mitsubishi T900 carbon being incorporated in multi modulus rods - this enables them to cast heavier weights than their test curve would suggest. Simpson's 12ft/2.75lb Advantage and the 13ft/3.5lb Frontier are rods of this type. They will cast weights of 4oz and 6oz respectively.

Reels

Wide spool reels such as Shimano's 6010 and 8010 Aeros are perfect for standard long range fishing because line drops relatively slowly below their spool lip. This fact, coupled with excellent line-lay, ensures that line slips from the spool smoothly and with very little likelihood of tangles. I use Aeros whenever I deem line of 0.30mm or less to be suitable.

My big "bucket spool" reels I reserve for line in excess of 0.32mm. The reason for the switch is because thicker line drops rather too rapidly below the spool lip of the Aeros, which results in a retarding effect.

There are lots of excellent big reels from which to choose; I use Daiwa's PM4000 (now replaced by the Emblem), and Shimano's GT7000 Biomaster. Both are lovely reels, but a tad big for my taste; ideally I would like a model which is larger than the Aero, but smaller than the Emblem and Biomaster. Daiwa's SS3000 was probably about right - but I balked at a price tag of nearly £200 so did not acquire any. To the best of my knowledge they are no longer available.

Reel size is not simply a matter of aesthetics; big reels are heavy, a fact which exacerbates the effect of inertia. In an endeavour to mitigate the weight of my big reels I asked Jack Simpson to build me a "concept" 13ft/3.25lb Eclipse which had two winch fittings; one in the normal position, and the other just a few inches from the butt cap. By having the reel in the lower position - as is popular with South African beach anglers - its weight was close to the rod's pivot point. The rod felt wonderful - its improved balance was a revelation. And my upper (right) hand, freed from the need to straddle the reel-seat and hold the line, could grip the handle with reassuring firmness.

My intention was to cast with the reel in the low position, then move it to the conventional position before placing the rod in the rests. The basic principle was flawless, and had I been willing to practice, I have absolutely no doubts that it would have worked perfectly. Trouble was - and in truth this came as no great surprise - I found it extremely difficult to properly time the line release while using what, according to many years of mind/body programming, was the wrong hand. So, notwithstanding its theoretical advantages, the "concept" Eclipse rarely gets used.

Production model 13ft Eclipse alongside special 'concept' model.

If you want to use big reels Baitrunner-style you will need to have them converted with a free-spool unit, such as that developed by Gary Bruce and obtainable from specialist tackle shops. The alternative is to use a loose clutch - I call this "clutchrunner-style".

Another option which recently became available comprises the new range of big-spool Baitrunners. But of these I have no experience.

Line

I prefer fluorescent line for long range fishing. It offers two significant advantages. First, it shows up like a laser beam, even in poor light, which makes it possible to keep track of the whereabouts of hooked fish. This is a great help when they have to be kept clear of other lines, weedbeds, snags etc. But the main benefit is that it eliminates the risk of being wiped out by ducks, swans, geese, coots and other aberrant life forms which would otherwise blunder into it! Fluorescent line scares them, and they take pains to avoid it. Even most wind-surfers try to steer clear. Jet-skiers, of course, do not...

"But won't it scare carp?" is a question I am often asked.

It might if they got to see it, but I always use a shock leader of 7-8 yards; thereby separating the conspicuous main line from the end tackle.

Fluorescent lines are usually bought by sea anglers, so they are not readily available in diameters less than 0.40mm which is too thick for distance casting. I located some 0.35mm fluorescent yellow Sylcast, which is still thicker than I like, but it might have been pressed into emergency service had my bench tests not revealed its nominal 15lb breaking strain to have been overstated - it broke at just 13lb. Berkley do a peach coloured version of Big Game (Tournament Photochromic) which is suitable in every respect other than price - about three times the cost of standard Big Game. Nor is it generally available. Maxima produce a Fibre Glow mono which they describe as being "hi-vis and with aggressive luminosity". Which sounds about right! It is a reasonable price too - about £10 per 500 metres. Unfortunately I have been unable to find anywhere that sells it!

My French friends, who first persuaded me of the advantages of fluorescent line for distance fishing, use Water Queen. I brought some back from France, but having exhausted my stock have been unable to replace it. So fluorescent line, in suitable breaking strains and diameters, has been difficult to track down in the U.K.

Salvation, however, is at hand!

Recently, Ande line (which is made in Germany) has become available. I acquired some fluorescent yellow Tournament, put it through a battery of bench tests, and was sufficiently impressed to spool-up with it for actual fishing. While it is still early days, I have thus far been extremely pleased with its performance. It costs about £14 for a 4oz spool.

Just one word of caution - Ande Tournament is an IGFA (International Game Fishing Association) rated line, which means its designated breaking strain is spot on - so do not assume that it will be underrated, as is the case with many other brands. The 0.315mm version I am currently using has a breaking strain of 12lb, which compares very favourably with GR60, Big Game etc.

Where high breaking strain in conjunction with low diameter is the main requirement, the most suitable brands are Power Plus and Trilene XL. In their nominal 12lb versions, which have diameters of 0.30mm and 0.31mm respectively, they have an actual breaking strain of 14lb. Of the two, I prefer Power Plus because it has the higher abrasion resistance, so is better able to withstand the wear and tear of casting and being drawn through weed. Power Plus has lower than average stretch, too, which can be a benefit when striking at distance, particularly in response to drop backs. Its muted grey colour, however, is no deterrent to water birds - indeed I doubt that they can see it - with the consequence that they continually swim or fly into it. Its use is therefore best confined to waters where birds do not pose a problem.

In Chapter Fourteen I have summarised the findings of tests I undertook for a series of three Carpworld articles (Mono Multi Tests; issues 88, 89 and 90). The suitability of brands other than Ande, Power Plus and XL may be assessed from the information contained in that summary. An important point to consider - and something I have touched on already - is that nominal breaking strain often bears little resemblance to actual breaking strain. I therefore recommend that line for long or extreme range fishing be selected by diameter initially, then checked with a spring balance to establish its true breaking strain.

Shock Leaders

Shock leader options.

Occasionally I have read that, providing main line of at least 15lb is used, long casting with heavy leads is possible without a shock leader. I hope I never find myself directly opposite anyone fishing in this manner

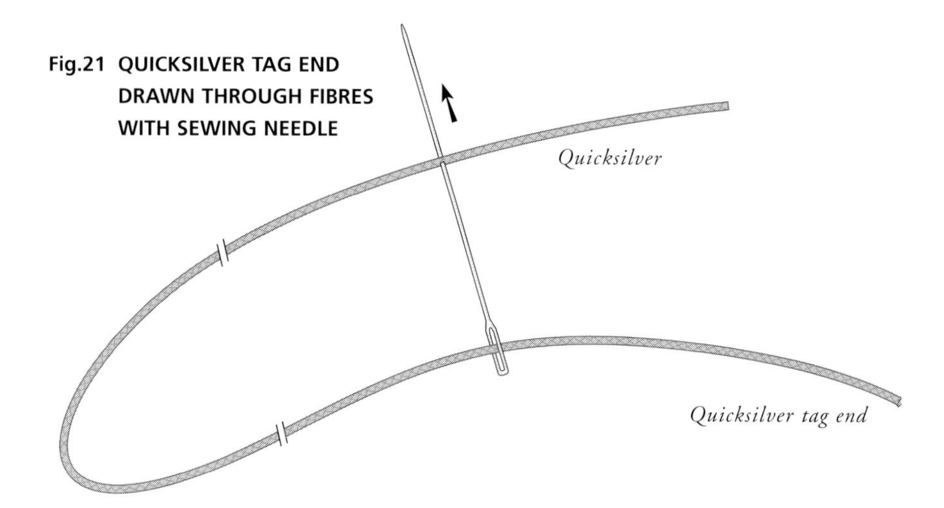

Fig.21 QUICKSILVER TAG END DRAWN THROUGH FIBRES WITH SEWING NEEDLE

because there is a high risk of a lead going into free flight after a snap-off. A shock leader is essential - to suggest otherwise is not merely stupid, it is irresponsible.

My preferred shock leader material is Quicksilver. It is obtainable in 25lb, 35lb and 45lb breaking strain, which is suitable for leads up to 3oz, 4oz and 5oz respectively.

The advantages of Quicksilver are threefold:

- **it is extremely supple, with no memory, so lays nice and flat on the reel**
- **it is very fine for its breaking strain, which enables the tying of a small junction knot which facilitates tangle-free casting, and allows the lead to slide free if necessary**
- **its high resistance to abrasion offers a significant level of safety when drawn across rocks or gravel bars.**

At which juncture I should mention that some clubs ban the use of Quicksilver due to their concern that a hooked carp might become tethered if the main line breaks. Whilst doubtless well intentioned, the ban is misguided because a carp will be just as firmly tethered on heavy mono as on Quicksilver. The problem lies not with the choice of shock leader material, but with anglers who cast across suicidal gravel bars, or use inadequate strength main line in order to achieve maximum distance.

My Quicksilver leaders incorporate a 50cm loop which reinforces the main load bearing part of the leader and enables quick and simple hooklink replacement.

I have devised a special Lock Knot for the purpose of creating the 50cm loop. First, the Quicksilver is pierced 115cm from its end with a sewing needle (Fig 21), which is used to draw a 15cm tag-end through the fibres. With this tag-end I tie a

Fig.22 QUICKSILVER LOCK KNOT

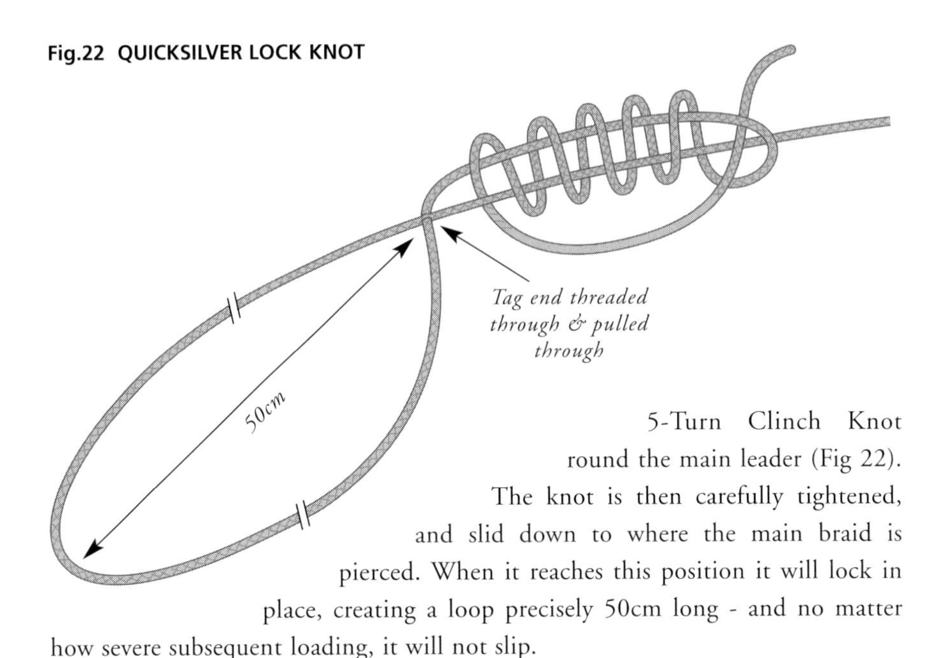

5-Turn Clinch Knot round the main leader (Fig 22). The knot is then carefully tightened, and slid down to where the main braid is pierced. When it reaches this position it will lock in place, creating a loop precisely 50cm long - and no matter how severe subsequent loading, it will not slip.

Next a 45cm length of 1mm No Spook anti-tangle tube - which will require pulling through with mono - is slid on the loop (Fig 23).

All the lead assemblies which I shall describe presently are based on my loop-end leader system.

To attach a hooklink, the loop is first passed through the swivel eye, after which the entire hooklink is pulled through the loop and drawn tight (Fig 24). This enables hooklinks to be changed without it being necessary to cut the shock leader and tie a new knot each time - a process which soon results in the shock leader becoming too short.

Fig.23 LOOP-END LEADER SYSTEM

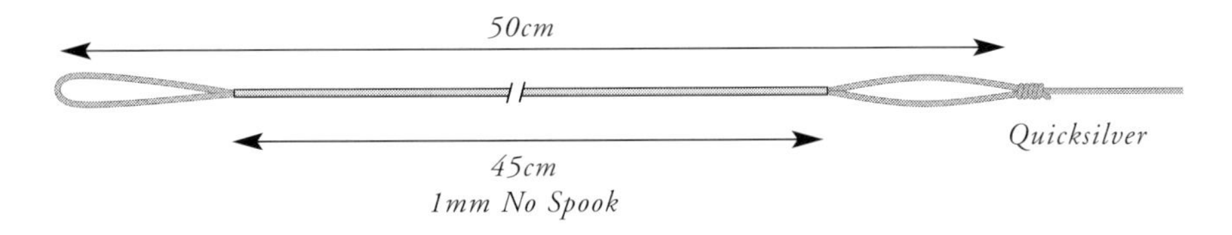

Fig.24 HOOKLINK ATTACHMENT TO LOOP-END LEADER

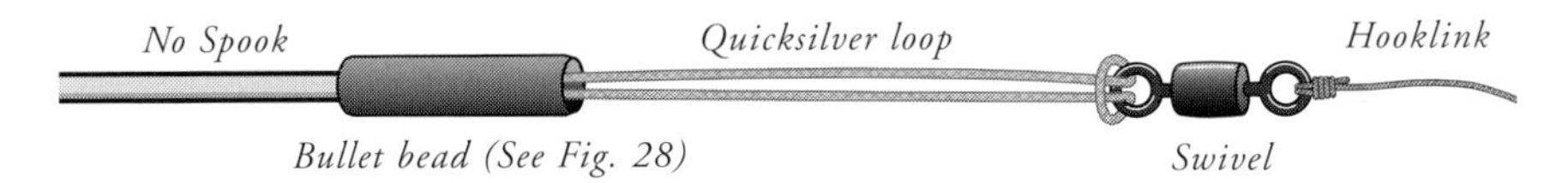

Secure Junction

A long range outfit is only as strong as the leader knot. It is essential, therefore, to use the strongest junction possible - and this is where Quicksilver poses a problem because it is incompatible with mono. I tried most of the commonly recommended leader knots and obtained disappointing results. With the 4-turn Water Knot, the main line withstood only 78% of its breaking strain. The Mahin Knot gave inconsistent returns: 85% at best, but only 70% at worst. The so-called Shock Leader Knot (a sort of wraparound Blood Knot) could barely top 60%. The best results by far were obtained by tying an Overhand Loop Knot in the end of the Quicksilver, then passing the main line twice through this loop and tying a 5-Turn Clinch Knot (or Uni/Grinner) just as you would when attaching a swivel (Fig 25). The resulting junction looks somewhat untidy, but its individual components are small and neat so it slips from the spool and through the rings smoothly. When tested to destruction it produced a minimum knot strength of 89%, and a maximum of 100% (by 100% I mean that the knot remained intact and the line broke).

This junction is based on Zenon Bojko's Leader Knot which he recommends in his Rig Book (published by Mainline). Zenon's version comprises a loop-ended heavy mono leader to which the main line is tied by means of a Tucked Half Blood.

In addition to being strong, the Modified Zenon Leader Knot is user friendly in that a shock leader can be attached in seconds. I carry several prepared Quicksilver shock leaders on an empty line spool (by "prepared" I mean that they are equipped with a 50cm loop, anti-tangle tube, and a small loop for main line attachment) so they are available for immediate use whenever required.

Fig.25 MODIFIED ZENON LEADER KNOT

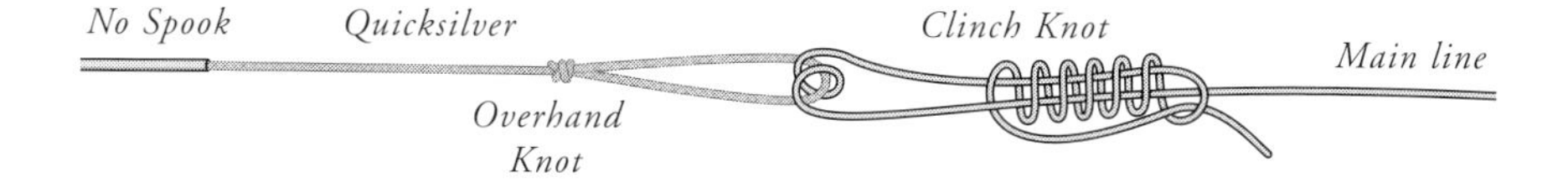

Mono Options

Some anglers recommend tapered leaders, such as those produced by Daiwa. Their primary virtue is that parity of diameter between leader and main line creates a very small knot which comes off the reel spool with minimal risk of snagging, and passes smoothly through the rod rings. Unfortunately they do not enable a sufficiently strong junction to be tied. When I attached a Daiwa 30-12lb tapered leader to 0.30mm main line with the 4-Turn Water Knot I got just 71% knot strength. To my surprise the Mahin Knot fared no better. I do not, therefore, use tapered leaders for long range fishing. They are, however, my preferred option on my spodding rod.

Heavy duty mono I do not particularly like - I only use it when, as previously mentioned, Quicksilver is banned. The best means of joining it to the main line is with the Mahin Knot (Fig 26).

One other option is the Bimini Twist. It was devised by saltwater big game anglers in the U.S.A. who fish to IGFA rules which ban the use of a separate leader. The Bimini Twist enables the end of the line to be doubled. It is a lovely neat knot, and has the additional virtue that it retains 100% of the line's strength. Its main disadvantage is that it is an absolute "pig" to tie! As a consequence few U.K. anglers use it. I considered giving detailed tying instructions, but then decided against doing so as I doubt that many readers would find it useful. Those who wish to try it, however, can find full information in my books "Modern Specimen Hunting" and "Big Water Carp" (Beekay).

In order to ascertain a safe breaking strain for a shock leader I recommend that the weight of the lead in ounces be multiplied by 8, and the resulting figure in pounds be taken as a guide. By that means we find that leads of 3oz, 4oz and 5oz require shock leaders of approximately 24lb, 32lb and 40lb respectively. For non stretch leader materials such as Quicksilver the multiple should be 9.

Fig.26 MAHIN LEADER KNOT

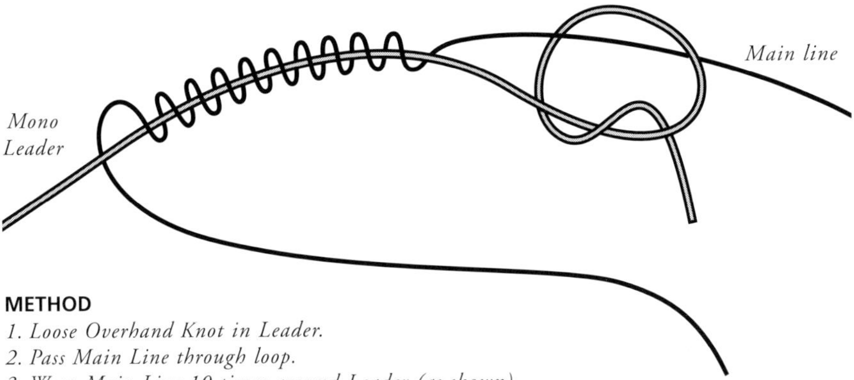

METHOD

1. Loose Overhand Knot in Leader.
2. Pass Main Line through loop.
3. Wrap Main Line 10 times around Leader (as shown).
4. Wrap tag end of Main Line 6 times round previous wraps - heading back towards loop.
5. Pass tag end back through loop so it points back up the line.
6. Moisten & carefully tighten ensuring all coils butt up neatly.

Lead Assemblies

The primary requirement of a lead assembly for long range fishing is that it be safe, both for other anglers and for carp. The first condition - as just described - is satisfied by the use of a shock leader of sufficient strength to prevent casting snap-offs. Unfortunately, the use of a shock leader has a downside in that the knot used to join it to the main line may prevent the lead being discharged if the line breaks; this can condemn a carp to having to tow the lead, or worse still, might result in it becoming tethered if the lead becomes snagged.

The next requirement of a long range lead assembly is that it should combine good aerodynamics with reliable non tangle characteristics.

Pendant Semi-fixed

Recently, following a discussion with Kevin Nash on the subject of long range rigs, I decided to take various end-tackle items and a selection of leads to a local pit, and have a "thrash". I did about 5-years worth of casting in one day! The conclusions were inescapable - swivels, links and run-rings are a liability. The most tangle-free setups by far are the simplest. This did not surprise me because I had already reached such conclusions by a sort of evolutionary process.

I confirmed a few other details too:

- **1mm anti-tangle tube resists tangles more effectively than 0.75mm (1.5mm or 2mm is even better, but increases air resistance and is more conspicuous)**
- **lead core resists tangles to a degree, but less effectively than anti-tangle tube**
- **pendant leads cast further and straighter than do inlines**
- **the shape of the lead makes little difference to range**
- **it does, however, make a significant difference to a rig's anti-tangle characteristics.**

Of the numerous pendant setups I tried, only two embodied all the required qualities of safety, good aerodynamics and freedom from tangles. To qualify as tangle-free, incidentally, they had to behave impeccably with the whole range of hooklink options: mono, combi-link materials like Snake-Skin and Snake-Bite, and braid.

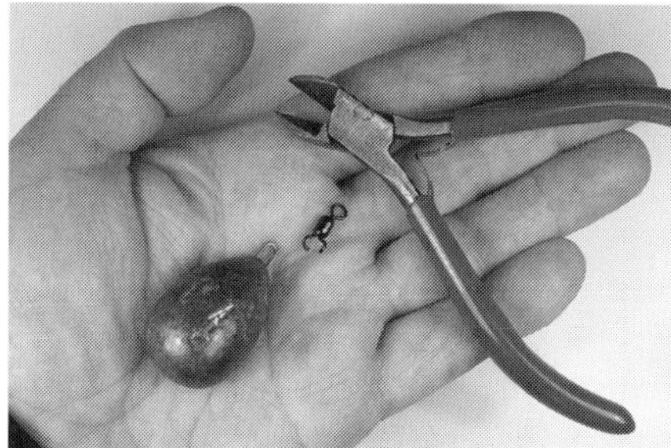

Removing the swivel enhances the tangle-free qualities of most rigs.

Fig.27 NASH SAFETY BOLT BEAD SEMI-FIXED LEAD ASSEMBLY

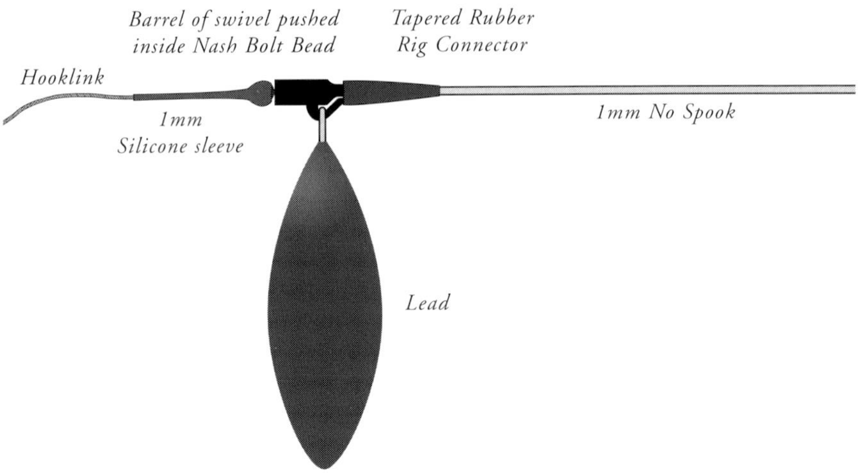

Barrel of swivel pushed inside Nash Bolt Bead
Tapered Rubber Rig Connector
Hooklink
1mm Silicone sleeve
1mm No Spook
Lead

Rig number one - which I use for leads up to 3oz - is Kevin Nash's Safety Bolt Bead (Fig 27). It is used in conjunction with a 45cm length of 1mm No Spook anti-tangle tube and a tapered rubber Rig Connector - the attachment of which will require a Tube Tool. Alternatively I use a parallel neoprene sleeve, which I Superglue in position, and round off the step created where it meets the No Spook with 2.6mm heat shrink tube.

The smooth contours of this setup make it virtually 100% tangle-free providing - and this is important - it is used with a lead from which the swivel has been removed. Korda's Distance and Pear leads are good. My favourite, though, is their original elongated Distance model.

Fig.28 "RUNNING" PENDANT ASSEMBLY

Barrel of swivel pushed inside Bullet Bead
Hooklink
1mm Silicone sleeve
1mm No Spook
Lead

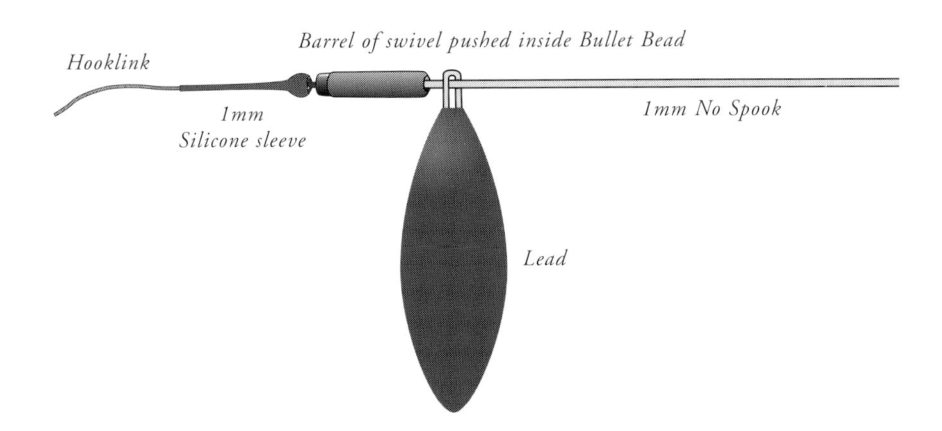

I am wary about using a lead heavier than 3oz with the standard version of the Safety Bolt Bead in case casting stresses result in the lead-clip opening prematurely. For leads in excess of 3oz, therefore, I choose the upgraded Continental version.

Alternatively I have the lead slide directly on the anti-tangle tube - which brings us to rig number two.

It again comprises one of the pendant leads mentioned earlier - swivel removed, of course - which rests against the hard rubber Bullet Bead (Fig 28) which Kevin Nash sells as part of his Long Range Running Rig. Solar, I believe, also produce a Bullet Bead, but I have not tried their version.

The end of a 45cm length of No Spook is poked inside the Bullet Bead (as with the tapered Rig Connector, a Tube Tool will be required).

Most anglers would class an assembly wherein the lead slides on the anti-tangle tube as a running rig. But is it? I carried out some experiments and discovered that running rigs do not function as such due to the combined effects of a tight line, line drag through the water, a loaded indicator and the resistance afforded by the Baitrunner or clutchrunner. There is some slippage - especially if the run is directly away from the angler - but not nearly as much as generally supposed. What actually happens is that the lead trundles along the bottom. So running rigs used at long range function, in effect, as unstable semi-fixed setups.

A problem associated with running rigs is that they do not like being cast with maximum force into a strong facing wind, especially if a stringer is incorporated. The combination of heavy lead and air resistance on the bait(s) results in line being drawn through the lead, which in addition to creating drag, increases the risk of a tangle. This tendency can be mitigated by feathering the cast just before splashdown, and preventing line spilling from the spool as the end-tackle sinks. The downside of feathering, however, is that it has a slight retarding effect on distance, which in some circumstances might not be acceptable.

Semi-fixed Inline

Few gravel pits have a serious silt problem - certainly nothing like that found in meres and estate lakes. But old pits sometimes have silty areas, notably in the north east corner where autumn leaves tend to accumulate. Depressions are occasionally silty too, again due to accumulations of dead leaves and weed. A pendant assembly can be a liability in silt, especially in shallow water, because it nosedives to the bottom where it can become quite firmly embedded. It can usually be freed with a steady pull, but the resulting cork-from-a-bottle jerk can cause the hooklink to

Fig.29 TIGHT FITTING SILICONE SLEEVE TO HOLD NO SPOOK IN PLACE WHEN INLINE LEAD IS USED

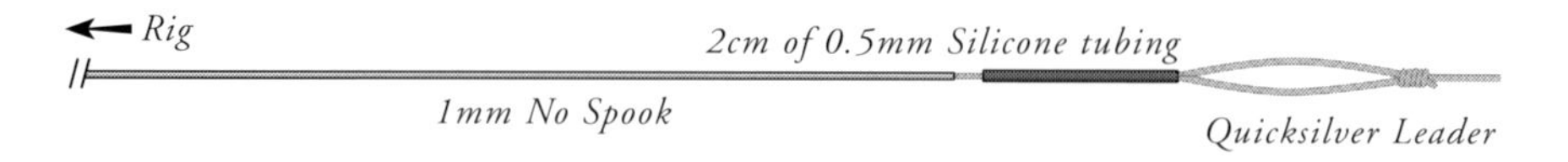

tangle. An elongated inline lead is better which, instead of nosediving, planes through the water at an angle. If a two or three bait stringer is incorporated, the extra front end water resistance causes the lead to sink in a horizontal posture. This results in a reduced tendency to bed in; and where the bottom is not too soft, it may not become embedded at all.

My inline assembly is described in Chapter Nine. The version I use for long range fishing differs only in that instead of a float stop to hold the anti-tangle tube in place, I substitute a 2cm length of tight fitting 0.5mm silicone sleeve (Fig 29). This enables the lead to slide off the shock leader in the event of line breakage. Leastways, it will if the knot used to secure the leader to the main line is small and neat. My preferred material, Quicksilver, lends itself to the tying of small knots - as does a tapered leader and the Bimini Twist - but a knot used to attach a heavy mono leader is likely to be bulkier, and may not readily pass through an inline lead's central tube. Mono leaders, therefore are better suited to one of the new generation of inlines which can detach from their central spigot. Nash Top-Liners and the Gardner Project 2000 range incorporate a tapered spigot as standard; while Korda produce what they call a Shock Leader Sleeve which is compatible with their Flatliner inlines. I have not used any of these for actual fishing, but my bench tests suggest that they work as claimed.

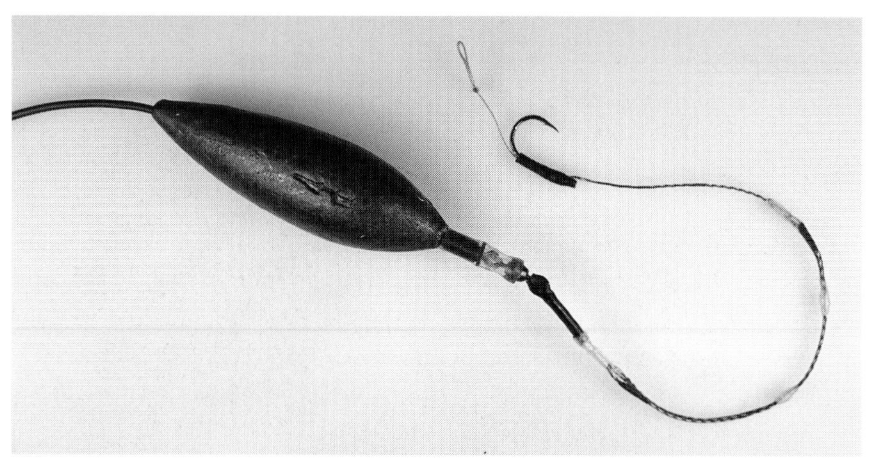

Inline silt setup (shown here with a Concertina Link).

How safe is Safe?

All this talk of safe rigs is somewhat misleading because most lead discharge systems only function effectively if the leader and main line remain free of tangles, algae and weed. But even when the mechanism works perfectly, there is the risk that the trailing line might become ensnared by vegetation or a snag. Only barbless hook rigs come close to being totally safe, but my experience has been that when used in conjunction with heavy leads they result in an unacceptable level of losses. So I opt for micro-barbed patterns. To reduce the likelihood of breakage, and its consequent danger to carp, I use sensible breaking strain main line - never less than 10lb, and more usually 12lb (I am referring here to actual breaking strain, not the nominal designations applied by manufacturers and distributors).

Casting

Casting is like knot tying - almost impossible to describe in words! Ideally, you need an instructor; someone who is able to demonstrate what to do, and who can correct faults as they occur. But not everyone has access to an expert, so notwithstanding its inevitable shortcomings I shall try to provide a written substitute.

Before embarking on "how it's done" details, I would like to stress the importance of finding the lead which ideally suits your rod. Adoption of the manufacturer's recommended optimum would seem to be the simplest way of achieving this, but it is not quite that straightforward because the ideal weight varies from one individual to another, depending on their casting style.

Greased Lightning reduces the risk of tangles.

One of the problems which afflicts long casters is the dreaded loose loop which wraps around the butt ring and causes a snap-off. There is no one hundred per cent sure way of avoiding this happening, but it is rendered less likely if the spool is filled to its lip, but not overfilled. The use of Greased Lightning lubricant also helps; it does so by reducing friction and thereby minimising the risk of wayward coils being lifted by the whirling line. It reduces friction in the rings too, so will add a few yards to the cast. Alternatively, the reel spool should be wetted with water immediately prior to the cast - water is not as effective a lubricant as is Greased Lightning, but it nonetheless makes a significant difference.

Something else which helps to avoid tangles is placing the leader knot at the back of the spool.

The risk of throwing a loose loop is further reduced if you extend your index finger so it is as close to the spool as is comfortable. If the line is held tight to the rod tangles are much more likely to occur; this, incidentally, is why mechanical release gadgets are unsatisfactory.

You will cast further with fine line than you will with heavier stuff, but do not take this to extremes and fish excessively light or you risk losing carp. 10-12lb test is a sensible choice for open water, while 15lb test might be necessary where weed poses problems.

Getting Technical

There are numerous different casting styles; the one I shall describe is relatively simple to learn, but provides considerable scope for improvement once the basics have been mastered.

First the stance. The angler should stand sideways to the water, his left side facing it (I am assuming a right handed angler; left handers will have to modify instructions accordingly), with the feet placed comfortably apart to provide stability. An imaginary line drawn across the toes should point in the direction of the cast; this will help accuracy.

The distance from tip ring to lead - known as "the drop" - should be about 4ft. You may modify it later, but 4ft is a good starting point. With the right hand grasping the reel seat (two fingers either side of the reel stem), the bale arm open, and the line hooked over the pad of the index finger, the rod is held as if it were a javelin. This puts it at about shoulder height, or maybe a tad above. The left hand takes hold of the lower end of the handle. Then, as smoothly as possible, push forward with the right hand, while simultaneously pulling down with the left. The upper body will automatically turn to face the water. The feet should be kept firmly planted until after the lead has been released.

Gradually the forward push of the right hand and the attendant pulling back of the left can be made progressively more forceful. But do not be in too much of a hurry to send a lead into the stratosphere; aim for smoothness rather than power.

Instinctive Release

Timing of the release is critical - too soon and the lead will fly high; too late and it will fall short. What we are trying to achieve is an elegant parabola with sufficient height to give distance, but not so high that the lead's energy is dissipated through gaining unnecessary altitude. Fortunately, judging the correct split second to release the line seems to be instinctive. Those who lack the instinct should try to aim for release at about forty-five degrees past the vertical; or if you prefer the clock face analogy, with the hour hand at half past ten.

Synchronisation is helped if the reel spool is always in the same position. Alan Partridge, writing on long casting in Korda's Advanced Rig Book, recommended that the spool be in its fully retracted position. John Doody, in an article in Catchmore Carp (October, 1997), took a different view and stressed the importance of having the spool in its fully extended position. Confusion would appear to reign! So who is correct? In my view, they both are, because I have not found the actual position of the spool makes a scrap of difference. Replication is what matters, so my advice is that you find the position which is most comfortable, and stick with it.

After the line has been released, the rod should be held at such an angle that friction is reduced to a minimum. This is achieved by pointing the rod along the line, not at the intended point of splashdown.

Hit it!

Boxers, I am told, are taught to punch from the shoulder, and not merely with the arms. Casting is the same. If the full weight of the right shoulder can be put behind the right arm as it pushes forward, considerably more power will be generated. Again, do not rush matters. Keep it smooth, and build up the power gradually.

Bend the Knees

When taking up the stance in preparation for the cast, the knees should be bent. Initially it will feel uncomfortable, but a cast which starts with legs bent (they will straighten automatically as the cast gets underway) will benefit from significantly increased power. The final ingredient is practice - lots of it. The aim should be to get the disparate elements I have described flowing together in a smooth, perfectly synchronised movement. The more you practice, the better you will get.

Developing further

You might, as mind-body coordination develops, discover ways of modifying the basic "javelin" style in order to achieve improved performance. My preference, for example, is to extend my right arm until it is almost straight, resulting in the rod being held further back than hitherto described. Also, I like to lean back so most of my weight is on my rear (right) leg.

Sometimes I swing the lead gently back immediately prior to sweeping the rod through its arc; this serves the dual purpose of increasing compression and helping to keep the terminal tackle clear of vegetation. An alternative means by which these objectives can be achieved, and one which combines well with the basic "javelin" cast, is John Carver's guttering technique. This involves the placement of a length of rainwater guttering (minimum length about 4ft) at a right-angle to the bank, between the angler and the rod's tip ring. The end of the guttering nearest the angler is pegged to the ground; and a bank-stick used to lift the furthest end so it looks like a take-off ramp (Fig 30). The terminal tackle is placed near the bottom of the ramp, whereupon the cast then proceeds as normal. If you try this, do not expect to see an immediate increase in distance; but perseverance will bring its rewards - and before long you should see an improvement of at least 5%, and possibly as much as 15%. But even without the distance benefits, it is a technique worth mastering because it mitigates the effects of a steeply sloping bank or vegetation which can otherwise interfere with the drop and thereby restrict the casting arc.

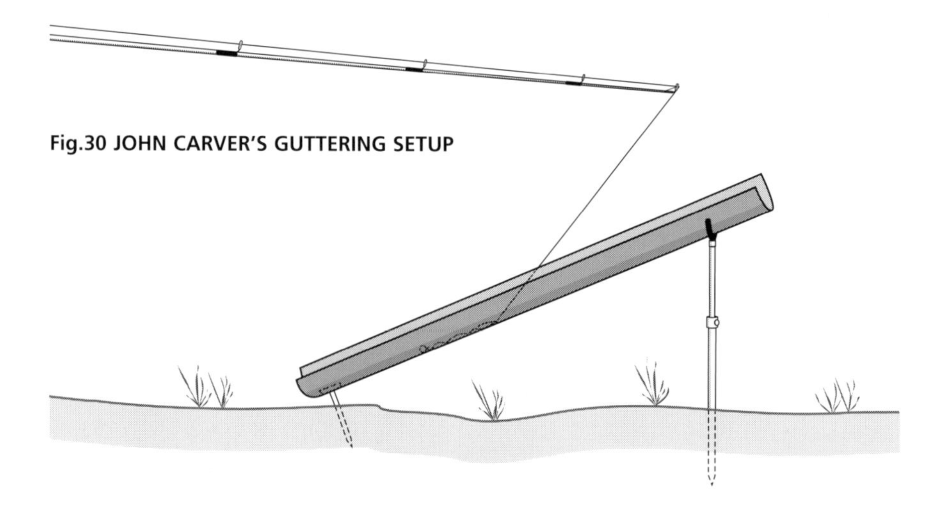

Fig.30 JOHN CARVER'S GUTTERING SETUP

Fall Short

Apart from the obvious benefit of being able to cast a long way - that of being able to reach distant fish - it has the added advantage that it improves shorter range accuracy. If you push your technique to the point where you can top 120 yards, you will find that 100 yard casts become easy. And distances which can be achieved without effort gain from greatly enhanced accuracy. So even if you never have the need to fish at 120 yards, it is worth acquiring the ability to do so.

The wind was so strong I sheltered behind these waterside straw bales - this pretty common took a bait cast as far as the conditions allowed.

Learn from the experts

Carp anglers are relatively new to long casting, but sea anglers and tournament casters have been refining their techniques for many years. I therefore endorse the advice given by John Carver in his aforementioned "A Few Yards More" series - read what top flight casters like John Holden, Nigel Forrest, Neil Mackellow and Paul Kerry say about casting. There is at least one video on the subject, too ("Mastercast" with Neil Mackellow; produced by Sea Angler magazine).

Range finder tactics

The standard long range tactic of casting both (or all three... four?) rods as far as possible exploits the swim laterally, but not longitudinally. If, for example, the terminal tackles land 100 yards away, carp which cross the area, parallel to the bank, at distances shorter than about 95 yards, or beyond 105 yards, are unlikely to encounter the hookbaits. To reduce the likelihood of this happening, I use the air resistance created by a stringer to vary the length of my casts. Where I am allowed to use three rods, I cast one as far as possible using just a hookbait. The second will be rigged with a one or two-bait stringer, and the third will carry a three or four-bait stringer. This will cause each of them to drop at a different distance from the bank. The extent of the difference will depend on bait size, and on the wind strength and direction.

Duplicate the range

I doubt that I would change tactics on the strength of just one take, but if a second take came to the same rod I would be tempted to conclude that carp were travelling along a relatively narrow "pathway", so I would retrieve the other rod(s) and incorporate the appropriate number of stringer-baits to enable me to duplicate the required range.

Many anglers will think it improbable that five or ten yards nearer or further will make much difference. And sometimes they would be correct. But my experience convinces me that there are many occasions when it matters a great deal. Some of my best long range catches have come after I have used range-finding tactics to identify the critical distance, then cast both, or all three rods, so they lay in a precise line.

Spot-on

The aforementioned range finding technique works perfectly when we have a certain amount of leeway, but may not be sufficiently accurate in situations where the casting has to be very precise - when baits have to be dropped as tight as possible to a far bank tree line, for example. We can still apply the basic principle, but need to refine it somewhat and consider not only the number of stringer-baits, but also the line diameter and the weight of the lead. To enable us to find the range safely and accurately we "creep up" on the target by gradually increasing our casting distance. We start with a combination which guarantees we fall short - it might comprise a 3oz lead, 12lb main line (plus shock leader, of course) and a five-bait stringer. We then reduce the number of stringer-baits, one at a time, to enable us to get closer. If, after dispensing with all the stringer-baits, the target remains out of reach, we increase the weight of the lead. We might, if it is safe to do so, change to a lower breaking strain line. Eventually we will find the combination which enables us to drop our baited terminal tackle perfectly every time. The big advantage of this technique is that it does not rely on muscle memory, we simply hit the cast as hard as

October afternoon and an immaculate long range common.

possible (resisting the nervous temptation to "wimp out" - a tendency in darkness, I find!) and the laws of aerodynamics do the rest.

An alternative method is clipping-up. The procedure I use, utilising a Power Gum harness, is described in Chapter Two.

Versatility

When I introduced the subject of accurate range finding I used the example of a far bank tree line. Other situations which require similar precision include casting to the nearside of a gravel bar, the edge of a plateau, an island, a channel between weedbeds, a baited area... to name but a few. All of which demonstrate that whilst the ability to cast a very long way can be an asset in itself, effective long range fishing does not begin and end with the "big chuck"!

Baiting

One of the difficulties associated with extreme range fishing is that of getting free baits and hookbaits in close proximity. Many of us, myself included, can cast further than we can free bait, so whether we intend to or not, we often find ourselves fishing single hookbaits. Normal long range fishing - which you will recall I defined as up to about 110 yards - is a different matter, and getting freebies that far is not a problem.

Most long range free baiting will be undertaken with baits of 20mm or larger. The best means of getting them out to the fishing area is with a throwing stick. Only very hard baits will withstand being given a really good "whack" because the ultra fast spin generated by a throwing stick, and its consequent centrifugal force, causes all but the hardest baits to disintegrate in flight. Wetting the inside of the stick reduces the amount of spin imparted to baits; but whilst this mitigates the disintegration problem, it results in significant loss of distance.

If baits are air dried it makes them harder, but it also makes them lighter - and light baits do not go as far as do heavier ones! It would appear, if I may allow myself the cliché, to be a classic "Catch 22" situation. But if the right balance between hardness and mass is achieved, it produces boilies which withstand throwing stick use, and go the distance, too. I cannot give a definitive guide as to how long baits should be dried because it depends on the ingredients contained in your boilies, the density of the baits before drying, and the ambient temperature of the

Long range Cobra baiting - and not a gull in sight!

environment in which they are dried. My best suggestion, therefore, is that you work in 24 hour increments. Dry them for a day and see how they turn out - if they are not hard enough, give them another day... and so on.

Those who make their own boilies might care to try incorporating some sort of heavy additive in the mix. I have heard of powdered limestone being used for this purpose (obtainable from animal feed suppliers where, I understand, it is sold as a calcium additive for horse diets). I have not tried it myself, so I cannot comment on how it might affect the acceptability of a bait.

Of Nina Sansome's Cobra range I like the lightweight Ace best - the Jumbo is a ruthlessly efficient tool but I find it a tad heavy. John Carver obtained a titanium model for me; it is lovely, but would doubtless prove too expensive to be commercially viable.

My French friend, Alain Besnier, made an impressive looking double-handed throwing stick. It must have been at least 5ft, maybe 6ft in length! With his droopy moustache, long "hippy" hair and this enormous throwing stick, which immediately put me in mind of a shepherd's crook, Alain looked distinctly biblical! Unfortunately the stick's performance proved less miraculous than its appearance suggested!

Spodding

A major league problem associated with long range freebie baiting is that of gulls. I once read advice to the effect that if baits are thrown high, they will achieve sufficient velocity on their descent to avoid being intercepted. Additionally, the author assured us, on striking the water the baits plummet to a safe, gull-proof depth almost instantaneously.

Excuse me while I snigger!

Immediately anyone picks up a throwing stick on some of the waters I fish, the gulls gauge the range with microchip precision, and then wheel over the spot with reflexes so finely tuned that it takes them just three baits - absolute top whack max - to sort out trajectory and speed. From that point on, it is game over - you are lucky to get one bait in a hundred past them! So, if gulls are troublesome, I put the throwing stick aside and reach for my spod rod. There are several good spods available commercially, including the Boilie Rocket from Trev's of Wilmslow, and the Gardner Bait Bullet. They fly a long way, and fly straight too. And both have a reliable release system which enables them to be retrieved nose first after they have emptied.

The Boilie Rocket has an open end, so it tends to lose between one and three baits per cast. The Gardner version does not suffer this problem because it has a trapdoor which retains its contents in flight.

Trev's Boilie Rocket is topped up with water before it is cast; this makes it heavy in air, but very light after splashdown; it therefore sinks extremely slowly, which enables it to be skimmed back along the surface immediately it has discharged its contents. The Gardner Bait Bullet has a sliding metal collar which causes it to sink quickly, which in turn delays its ascent to the surface on the retrieve. The significance of this only becomes apparent if baiting is done over end-tackles which are already in position, when there is a risk of a line being picked up.

As can be seen, each model has its own particular merits. I use both and, frankly, would find it extremely difficult to state a preference.

There are a number of alternative spods available - some of the best being limited production models made in garden sheds and garages. Obviously there is little point my giving details of these because they are not widely available.

Fully loaded, the Boilie Rocket and the Bait Bullet each weigh about 3.5oz, so they require a powerful rod. I have seen inexpensive, poker-stiff beachcasters recommended for the purpose; but they do not perform at all well and I prefer a proper distance rod such as the 12ft/2.75lb Advantage. If there is no danger of snagging in weed I use 0.25mm (about 6lb test) mono in conjunction with a 30lb Diawa tapered shock leader. I like a tapered leader in this instance because it enables the use of a very small junction knot, the strength of which is fairly irrelevant.

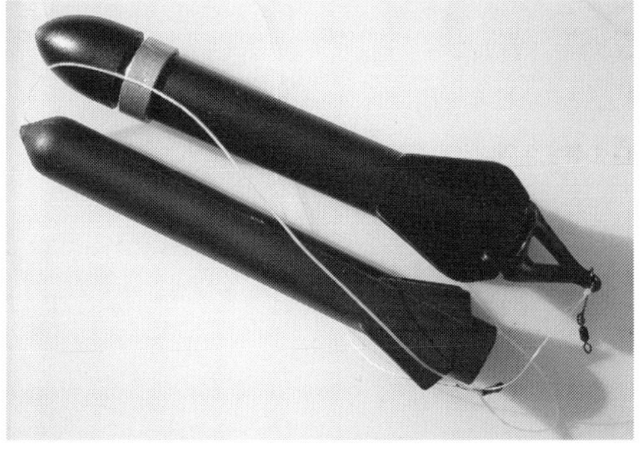

Gardner Bait Bullet (with metal collar) and Trev's Boilie Rocket.

I find it beneficial to modify my usual casting style when using a spod. I use a shorter drop (about

3ft), and aim somewhat higher. In reasonable wind conditions a spod will go a very long way - certainly in excess of 100 yards. During a Gardner demonstration I understand spods loaded with lead were cast more than 150 yards, but I doubt that anything like such distances are possible with boilies or particles.

Stringers

Another gull-proof means of getting baits out the required distance is to use a PVA stringer on a separate baiting rod. Baits go further too - I can get boilies 15-20 yards beyond my maximum spodding distance by this means, but each cast takes longer to set up, and is not really tenable in heavy rain.

Free baits (the actual number depending on the distance I am trying to achieve) are threaded on a short length of PVA string. This is tied to a link-swivel, to which is attached a 4oz lead. The rod, leader and main line combination remain the same as that described for spodding.

Spook fears

The disadvantage of both spod and stringer-baiting systems is that they create a lot of disturbance, especially if cast repeatedly. I think this is mitigated if there is a strong wind blowing, or if fishing in deep water, but I worry that carp will be spooked if the surface is quiet and the water relatively shallow. If possible, therefore, I try to bait my swim at least two hours before the anticipated feeding time. If I think carp are already in the area, and circumstances suggest free baiting might scare them, I confine free baits to one, two or possibly three attached to the hookbait by means of a conventional stringer.

Boats

There is one final possibility - a boat. Whereas I feel strongly that hookbaits should be cast into position (the practise of boating out hookbaits strikes me as more akin to saltwater set-lining than angling), I have no hang-ups about free baiting being done by means of a dinghy providing it does not disturb other anglers.

I repeat, however, what I said before - no one should go out in a boat without wearing a lifejacket.

Remote control bait boats I cannot abide. Were it within my power, I would ban them. I shall not justify the comment beyond saying that in my opinion they have no legitimate role in angling.

Setting-up

High position Wasps ready to show drop-backs or runs.

In open water I try to cover the area laterally by fanning my end-tackles in a sort of fleurs-de-li configuration. If I am not casting to features, I explore the swim longitudinally, as previously described, by varying my range. If I am using three rods, the middle bait will be cast furthest, so carp can approach it from either side without having to cross either of the other lines.

After casting, and taking in windblown slack, I place the rod in the rests and engage the reel's anti-reverse mechanism. Subsurface drag will pull the line harp-string tight, whereupon I switch the reel to Baitrunner mode if using an Aero, or slacken the clutch if using one of my "bucket-spool" models. The spool should just resist revolving in response to wind and water drag.

Now the indicator is clipped on. I use the spring loaded Nash Wasp for most of my distance fishing (the original version with the gate-latch release system - now, unfortunately, no longer available). It is placed in the high position, and tensioned so it will respond immediately should a drop back occur. Weighted indicators will require at least an intermediate loading, which may have to be upgraded to maximum if a strong crosswind is blowing.

Striking

How we respond to a take depends whether it is a run or a drop-back. If, as is most likely when long range fishing, the take is a lovely one-note flier, it is merely necessary to pick up the rod, engage the Baitrunner (or give the adjustor knob a quick turn or two if fishing clutchrunner style), then wind down. As soon as the fish is felt, the spool should be cupped with the reel hand to lock it, and the strike be made as hard as possible. If the rod stops solid in mid strike, all well and good - if it does not, strike again.

In the event of a drop-back occurring, the procedure is similar, except that the winding down phase is likely to take considerably longer.

Playing safe

Carp hooked at long range rarely do much at first; generally they just sort of wallow about - but it is necessary to be prepared for the occasional maverick which rips off on a rapid run. It is therefore sensible to disengage the anti-reverse as soon as a carp is hooked.

Whenever possible - as stated in a previous chapter - I play fish by backwinding, which affords better control and reduces the incidence of line twist. But when the fish comes within 20 yards or so of the bank, I ensure that the clutch is able to yield line in case a sudden, unexpected run occurs.

Hooked carp sometimes swim in a wide arc (known as "kiting"), which can cause them to cross other lines. In the daytime it is usually possible to steer a safe course, but not so in darkness when there is a high risk of a snarl-up. If the water is relatively even bottomed and weedfree it might be beneficial to use backleads. But if there are intervening bars, troughs or weedbeds, backleads are best avoided because they can exacerbate the problem. The safest course is to ask a nearby angler to retrieve your other rod(s). If you are alone, I think it best to confine yourself to using just two rods. Three, or even four rods may increase the likelihood of takes, but at the cost of a greatly increased risk of fish being lost amidst a tangle of mono.

Choice

My first articles on long range fishing attracted quite a lot of criticism - from some unexpected quarters, too. One erstwhile carp fishing luminary wrote, "If Jim learnt to fish the margins he would catch more carp than by fishing at distance." Truth is, I catch about two thirds of my carp within a few rod lengths of the bank - a high proportion from right in the edge - but being able to fish at distance does not make me a worse margin angler, nor blind to its opportunities. The fact that I can fish at distance does not compel me to do so, but it enables me to do so when the need arises. The angler who fails to acquire the necessary long range skills does not have that choice.

Chapter Six

Weedy Waters

Near my home are several well known gravel pits, the most notable of which are the Johnson's group of lakes and RMC Angling's Larkfield complex. When I first fished them, more than twenty years ago, they were virtually weedfree. Now they are heavily weeded.

The story is not unique to Johnson's and Larkfield. All over the country, pits which were once weedfree, almost barren even, now have lush jungles of Elodea, milfoil and hornwort. The most common explanation is that it is something to do with global warming which, with its attendant hot summers and mild winters, provides an ideal environment for plant growth.

It is a neat hypothesis.

It is also incorrect.

Global warming has little or nothing to do with it. The reason our pits are very much weedier now than they used to be is primarily the consequence of eutrophication. This is the name given to the enrichment of our waters via nitrogen and phosphorous compounds - the main sources of which are agricultural fertilisers, sewage effluent and detergents. Occasionally these chemicals reach our waters directly via run-off or feeder streams, but more usually through contaminated groundwater. Gravel pits, which obtain most of their water from underground sources, are particularly susceptible to the last named.

For detailed and authoritative information on the subject I recommend "A land awash with nutrients - the problem of eutrophication" by Professor Brian Moss (pages 407-411, "Chemistry and Industry", 3 June, 1996). You should be able to obtain a copy from a university technical library.

Another factor which plays a part is low water level, such as occurs during periods of drought, which not only concentrates the nutrients but allows sunlight to penetrate to the bottom in areas which previously were too deep. This encourages plants to grow where they might previously have been sparse or completely absent. Once established they tend to retain their hold even when water levels return to normal.

Big Fish

In many waters carp grow faster and larger than they used to. By undisputed general consensus this phenomenon is due to boilies.

I very much doubt it.

In addition to making pits weedier, eutrophication results in increased algal growth and an attendant proliferation of zooplankton. Carp (also tench and bream) thrive particularly well in these food-rich eutrophic environments. It is this, and not boilies, which has led to improved growth rates.

I am not disputing that bait can be a contributory factor, but other than in grossly overstocked waters where carp become bait dependent, it comes a long way behind natural food. Look at it logically; if boilies were the primary reason for carp growing big, vast quantities would need to be consumed which, in turn, would result in far more anglers catching many more carp than is currently the case.

In support of my contention let us put carp to one side for a moment and look at tench. It seems incredible, but prior to 1950 only two tench over 7lb had been recorded. Yes, two! Ever! By the mid-'80's the situation had changed dramatically, and 7lb tench were relatively commonplace. Target fish for tench specialists became previously unimaginable fish of 8lb plus. Now, every year, genuine double figure tench are caught.

Likewise bream. If you read accounts published at the beginning of the century it is evident that 6lb bream were considered big! Nowadays, 7-8lb fish are caught routinely, and double figure specimens are by no means rare.

Some big tench and bream live in carp waters, which invites the argument that they benefit from carp baits. Which would be a difficult proposition to refute were it not for the fact that many are found in pits which either do not contain carp, or are so rarely carp fished that they hardly see a boilie from year's beginning to year's end.

So, I do not think the "carp grow big on boilies" hypothesis withstands scrutiny. If we slung vast amounts of bait into carp ponds and never fished for them, it would be different, and no doubt our boilies would soon become a prominent food source. But we try to entrap them, which results in a caution-induced reduction in the amount of bait they consume.

Another point. If bait is the main reason carp grow large, why do those which have hitherto grown rapidly suddenly stop doing so and start to "freewheel" when a water comes under heavy angling pressure? Where pressure intensifies further, carp weights can actually drop - and this despite prodigious quantities of bait going in.

Before I leave the subject of carp growth, there is one more factor we need to consider. Cormorants. I loathe and despise cormorants, and were I a roach specialist or a matchman I would be tearing my hair out at the failure of MAFF to recognise the extent of the problem. And as for the RSPB's astonishing obtuseness on the subject - words fail me. But as a hardcore spessy-type I acknowledge the likelihood that cormorants are one of the reasons carp, tench and bream are bigger than ever before. Untold thousands of roach and skimmers have disappeared down the throats of cormorants, resulting in increased food supplies for the big fish which remain.

Cormorants are part of the reason why carp are bigger than previously.

Difficult Fishing

While the presence of weed indicates a fertile water, which in turn enables carp to grow large, it is a mixed blessing in that it makes the fishing much more difficult. Odd patches of weed are no problem - what I am talking about are extensive, almost impenetrable beds of the stuff. I fish a couple of waters where weed is so thick that retrieving a terminal tackle has sometimes been touch-and-go, and even with heavy line I have come close to pulling for a break.

I have tried dragging. This works reasonably well in shallow water, but where the depth is greater than about 12ft and the fronds reach almost to the surface it is difficult to make much of an impression. What happens, I suspect, is that adjacent weed closes in to create a sort of canopy. One of my more recent failures in this regard occurred in a 15ft deep swim on a big pit where I spent two mud-spattered hours trying to create a clear spot. To judge from the mountain of weed I accumulated in the margins, the bottom ought to have been bald - but the drag continued to come in fully laden every time!

A better bet is to look for clear spots. Dave Lane has described how he goes out in a boat and actually looks for such places with the aid of goggles or a glass-bottomed bucket. Willingness to make the effort and subject his waters to detailed scrutiny is doubtless one of the reasons Dave Lane is so successful. In most of the waters I fish, however, boats are not permitted; I therefore have to rely on tree-climbing and direct observation - which is okay in clear, shallow, close-in swims adjacent to a suitable tree(!) - or a feature finding rod.

I have discussed feature finding elsewhere, so will not expand on it here other than to say that whenever possible it should be avoided immediately prior to, or during a fishing session because repeated casting will scare carp. Where it is unavoidable, I recommend that a small float and light lead be used, and it be cast as infrequently as possible. I further suggest that where weed is thick, clear spots be sought close in; this makes them easier to target with baited terminal rigs. Close fishing also increases the chances of carp being safely landed. I know it is accepted practice to go out in a boat in order to land weeded fish, but it sits uncomfortably with me. I am not talking here of the occasional emergency, but of fishing in situations where it is accepted and expected that any fish hooked will have to be landed from a boat. It raises the issue of whether we should be fishing such spots in the first place... I shall leave the subject of playing fish in weed for the moment, and return to it later.

If a clear spot is fished and baited regularly, feeding activity may keep it weedfree. I get the impression that hempseed is particularly effective in this regard - probably due to the way it encourages carp to scour the bottom for every last grain. A couple of seasons ago I fished one particular pit twice, sometimes three times a week throughout the summer, and by baiting with about half a kilo of hemp each time I packed up, I was able to keep a handful of spots more or less clear. They were not large spots - about as big as a tea tray - but sufficiently large to be easy targets at the close range at which I was fishing.

Rob Maylin, among others, has described how heavy baiting can result in clear spots becoming enlarged. I do not recall having experienced this myself, but I have no doubt it can happen. One of my local pits occasionally has its water level radically lowered, exposing wide areas of "beach". When this occurs, large basin-like depressions are revealed which, I am convinced, have been dug by carp. Fish capable of scooping out a hollow in a relatively hard bottom are undoubtedly capable of dislodging and uprooting weed.

Some clear spots appear in the same places year after year; others come and go. There is an extensive shallow area in one of my favourite pits which, since the mid-'80's, has been heavily weeded. Last summer it was almost weedfree. What happened in that instance, and in similar situations, is that where weed is particularly prolific it eventually renders the bottom devoid of nutrients, with the result that a "fallow" year occurs. During the rest period, nutrients become re-established, whereupon weed colonises the area again.

Weed Types

Many writers - and I have probably been as guilty of this as anyone - use the term "weed" without making it sufficiently clear what sort they are talking about. I am not referring to the actual species when I say this, so much as its physical characteristics. In an endeavour to rectify this omission, and make my advice more readily translatable to readers' own fishing situations, I shall describe approaches which can prove successful with regard to particular weed types.

Thin Bottom Weed

Usually this will take the form of what is usually called silkweed. It is grassy in appearance, but much more delicate and with a slippery, sometimes almost gelatinous texture. If we want to be pedantic about it, we should not refer to it as weed at all, because it is actually an algae - a species of cladophora.

Silkweed can be somewhat disconcerting in that the end-tackle invariably comes back clogged up, but this only happens when it is moved. If the tackle is allowed to stay where it lands, silkweed presents few problems.

Silkweed rarely grows more than a few inches long, so the easiest way of dealing with it is to use a popup. This achieves the dual effect of ensuring the bait remains readily visible, and holds the hook in a bend uppermost configuration which significantly reduces the likelihood of a hang-up.

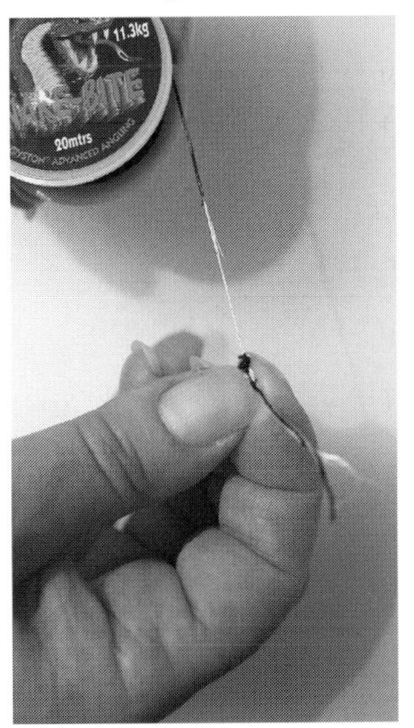

Snakebite is my choice for popup links.

Popups do not seek to mimic free offerings, so there is no need for a long hair - the ideal length being that which will enable the bend of the hook to just clear the bait. In presentation terms there is no need for suppleness, either - but I prefer to use a soft, flexible hair in order to aid hook rotation.

My hooklinks are shorter than those I use for bottom baits; 25cm from swivel to counterweight. The remaining portion - from counterweight to hook - is sufficiently long to clear the weed which, in the case of silkweed, will usually be 5-10cm. I like Snake-Bite for popup links - the portion from bait to counterweight being stripped, the rest with the coating intact (Fig 31).

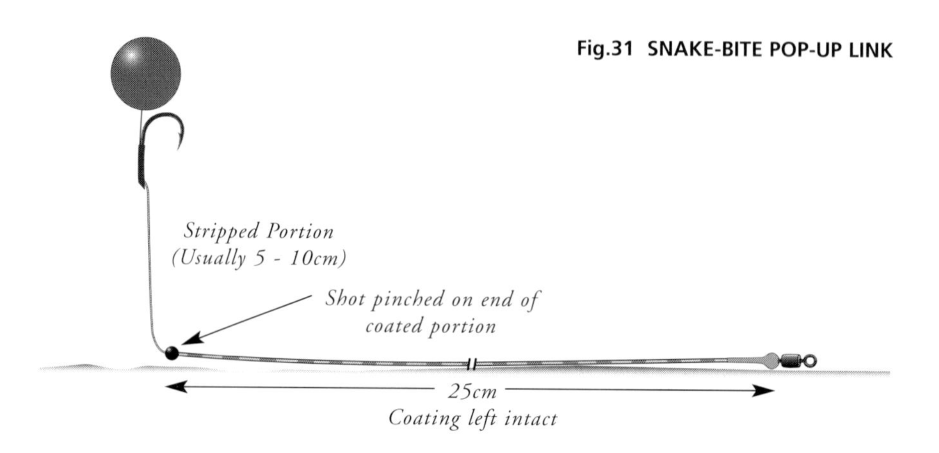

Fig.31 SNAKE-BITE POP-UP LINK

My usual counterweight comprises a split-shot, pinched on the end of the coated portion. Where I require the bait to be critically balanced I use tungsten putty which, as an insurance against slippage, is moulded around a stop-knot tied with pole elastic.

Related to silkweed, but much less benign, is blanket weed. There are many varieties - some carpet the bottom, others grow in great billowing heaps like underwater cumulus clouds, some form dense floating masses. All are extremely difficult to deal with, and at worst can render every method other than the use of floating baits untenable.

It is evil stuff.

The only truly effective response is to shift attention to another water. And that is not the flippant comment which, at first sight, it might seem.

Thick Bottom Weed

Branched weed like Canadian pondweed (Elodea canadensis) sometimes grows in a thick, mattress-like bottom layer. It may be only a few inches in depth - especially in autumn when it starts to break up - but more usually will be a foot or two.

I used to struggle with this sort of weed, but a couple of seasons ago I made substantial progress - and I have Rick to thank for giving me the confidence to do it.

All the shallow areas of the water I was fishing at the time were heavily weeded. I tried casting beyond the thickest of the weed to a depth of about 12ft; but whilst I caught a few I never felt it was the answer. Rick suggested I use a long mono link, a slow-sink bait, and the lightest lead possible. At which juncture I ought to explain that Rick's "slow-sink" baits are only one nano notch away from being floaters. He ascribes the power of reason to them, and reckons they think, "Shall I sink? Shall I? Oh, all right then...!"

Fig.32 SLOW-SINK BAIT FOR FISHING ON WEED

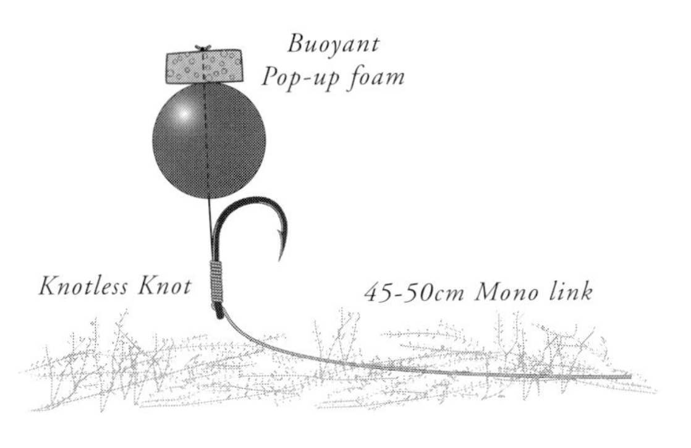

To achieve this just-sink effect, Rick uses baits buoyed with foam so they become "hook sinkers" - popups which sink with thistledown lightness when weighted by a hook. As with a conventional popup, it comes to rest hookbend uppermost, which reduces the risk of the hookpoint snagging on a weed stem when a carp takes the bait (Fig 32).

The first time I tried Rick's technique I had three carp - they fell to foam-buoyed tigernuts. Subsequent trips produced more fish on tigernuts, and others on pulses and boilies.

In those instances I used a 45-50cm mono hooklink in conjunction with a 1.1oz or 1.5oz (depending on the density of the weed) inline lead.

Next time I encounter this situation I intend replacing the lead with a 50cm length of lead core - a Nash Limpet, perhaps - which "dummy runs" suggest will lay across the weed rather than sink into it.

Hook sinker buoyed with foam.

A difficulty with Rick's on-the-weed approach is that it does not work where there is any degree of turbulence. It will tolerate a ripple, even a reasonable chop, but if the wind is sufficient to generate a significant amount of subsurface drag, the bait becomes "balled" in weed. I presume this is because underwater currents cause the bait to waft about and the fronds to undulate - whereupon they become entwined. Disturbance created by water skiers and jet-skiers has the same effect.

Fig.33 ZIG RIG

45 - 50cm Anti-tangle tube

Various Length Strands

Elodea does not always grow in mattress fashion - often its strands vary in length. Other weeds which are relatively common in gravel pits are milfoil (Myriophyllum spicatum), hornwort (Ceratophylum demersum) and starwort (Callitriche); these never grow in mattress-like beds, but always have multi-length strands. They are branched too. This makes them very difficult to deal with. The most practical method, I feel, is to use an extra long popup - what is often described as a Zig Rig (I think Zenon Bojko christened it thus). It requires that a hooklink of sufficient length be used to put the bait above the worst of the weed (Fig 33).

To minimise the risk of the hook fouling weed as it sinks - and this applies to all my weed fishing setups - I sheath it in PVA tape (Fig 34).

I think the Zig Rig was developed at Layer Pit - not to overcome weed, because Layer is virtually weedfree, but simply to present a bait at "midwater". I put midwater in inverted commas because it does not necessarily signify mid-depth, but anywhere from, say, a foot off the bottom to a foot below the surface. Layer is a prolific high-doubles, low-twenties water these days, but it used to hold a large population of single figure carp which were targeted by matchmen. They devised a special technique which involved the use of a heavily weighted missile float in conjunction with a long, unweighted tail which allowed buoyant maggots (created by placing them in water just a millimetre or two deep, whereupon they took in air to become floaters) to sink ever so slowly when weighted with a size 18 hook. Groundbait balls laced with casters

Fig.34 HOOK SHEATHED IN PVA TAPE

encouraged carp to feed in the upper layers, where the matchmen's slow-sink maggots were intercepted. A few carp anglers decided to try anchored "midwater" baits in an endeavour to capitalise on this behaviour - and the Zig Rig was born.

It has since been used widely - notably to fish over the weed in the Carp Society's Horseshoe Lake. I saw the same tactics used successfully at Handley Barnes - that was in the winter when 4ft hooklinks took fish from over the top of dying weedbeds. Rick rates it as a hot weather tactic, and has used it to catch a number of carp from a small Essex pit. So, bizarre though the method seems, it has a good track record. But that said, I never feel wholly at ease with it, and tend to reserve it for those occasions when I am unable to find clear spots.

As a somewhat uncommitted Zig Rig user I am not really qualified to advise on the best setups, but as a starting point for those who want to try the method I will say that I use Super-Silk (which is buoyant) for low-level presentations - by which I mean those up to 2ft from the bottom - and a combination of mono and Multi-Strand when fishing higher in the water (as per my long tail floater paternoster - see Chapter Twelve). Leads are inline - and used in conjunction with my standard 45-50cm anti-tangle tube. The fact that the anti-tangle tube will likely be shorter than the hooklink is not ideal, but it still helps resist tangles. A stringer made from floating dog biscuits also helps in this regard.

Long, Stringy Weed

Several of the deep pits in the Medway Valley contain what we hereabouts call eel grass. I have tried to find eel grass in books on freshwater plants, but as yet have been unsuccessful. So what its Latin name might be I have no idea - nor, for that matter, do I know if "eel grass" is the correct nomenclature. But it is a long, ribbon-like weed - almost like a soft rush - which in clear water can be found down to about 16ft. Where the depth is less than 13-14ft, it reaches the surface and collapses to form a floating raft.

As you might expect, the deeper you get, the less dense is the eel grass, and I have caught a fair number of carp by casting right into it with an inline lead and Concertina Link setup. In this, as in all weed fishing, presentation is an act of faith - you hope it is okay, and try hard to believe it is okay, but you can never be certain... It is therefore necessary to cast and forget it. I used to find this very difficult and went through all the agonies of doubt which culminated in my giving it "just a little tweak" to check if it was hung up. If, as was often the case, my "tweak" moved the rig - indicating it had been all right - I was then tortured by the

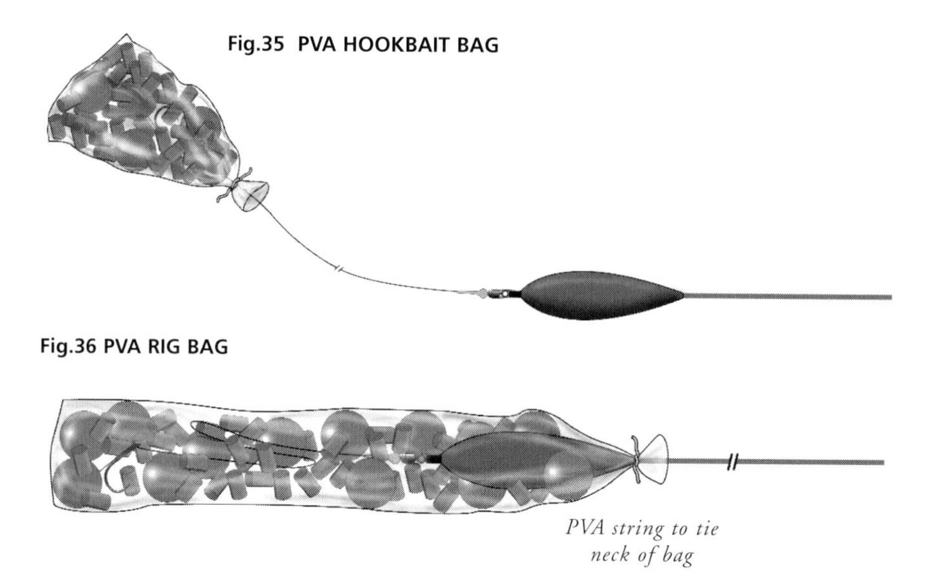

thought that I might have pulled it into weed! So I retrieved it - tied on a new Concertina Link, and recast... But did the doubts disappear? Did they hell! Eventually I acknowledged that the only way to prevent a negative dynamic setting in was to cast, and then forget the damn thing! I had to disassociate myself from what my end-rig might be doing and read a book, listen to Talk Radio, compile swim notes, draw, doze - anything except succumb to the burning desire to give it "just a little tweak"!

Now, I am pleased to say, I have cracked it! After doing a lot of fishing in eel grass, and having taken numerous carp from it, I find the process of disassociation relatively easy. Yes, I have the occasional bad day when the doubts take hold - but in truth, they are rare.

As an alternative to the Concertina Link and PVA cocooned hook, PVA bags are worth a try. I have used both hookbait bags, and rig bags (Figs 35 and 36). They work well, with the additional advantage that the great "glops" of bubbles which appear on the surface when the bag starts to dissolve provide an accurate marker for free baiting. "Why not include free baits in the PVA bag?" you might be wondering. Dry items like boilies, boilie bits and pellets are included; but wet baits like hempseed, sweetcorn, maize etc. have to be loose fed.

As an alternative to casting among the eel grass - and this is an approach which can be effective with any sort of weed when it grows down a deep water margin slope - is to fish its outer fringe. I have read occasional references to anglers casting beyond the weed fringe, then gently pulling back until the lead locks against its

Fig.37 "DEPTH - 0 - MAGIC"

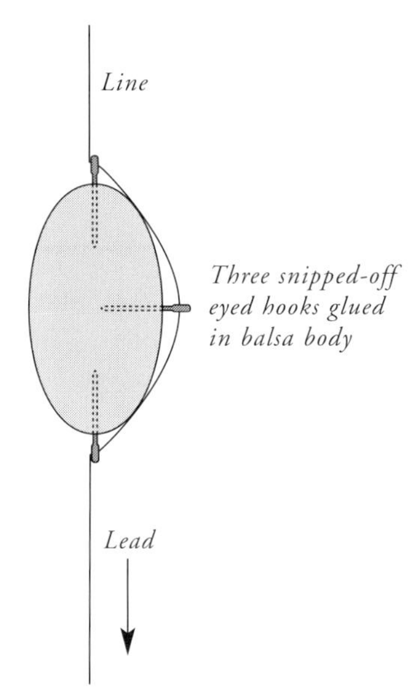

furthest edge. I know this is one of Gary Bayes's favourite tactics, and one he has used with considerable success, but I lack the "bottle". I never, ever pull back, being paranoid about the hookpoint fouling bottom debris or wayward weed strands. I therefore have to locate the weed's outer edge by means of a marker float. My preferred float in this instance is a homemade self-locking pattern to which I long ago appended the seemingly naff but actually joke name, "Depth-o-Magic"! (Fig 37). The principle behind this design is that it slides on a slack line, but locks in place when placed under tension. Leeda produce what they call a Depth Finder Float which, to judge from the catalogue description, works on the same principle. Dave Thomas's Long Tom Locslide floats have a very neat base-mounted locking system, which again works on the same principle. I have not tried either the Leeda or Locslide versions, but see no reason why they should not prove effective.

Fig.38 LOCATING OUTER FRINGE OF WEED

The float - which should be used in conjunction with a lead sufficiently heavy to sink it - is set at approximately half depth. It is overcast by a few yards, taking care to maintain tension as the setup sinks or the float will run up the line. When the lead hits bottom, it is carefully pulled back until it catches on weed. At which point the line is released, which allows the float to rise to the surface vertically above the weed's outer fringe (Fig 38). The baited terminal rig is then cast alongside.

I always retrieve my marker rod, incidentally - not just in this situation, but whenever I use one.

Alternatively I use a modified version of the feature-finding method described in Chapter Two - but in this instance I dispense with the float. First I establish my casting direction by lining up with a far bank marker, then as before, overcast and pull back until the lead snags against the weed fringe. A heavy duty elastic band is placed on the spool, and the lead retrieved. I then pay out line along a clear area of nearby bank until the elastic band restrainer is encountered. The distance from lead to tip ring, plus an extra foot as a safety margin, is marked with a couple of banksticks or, if suitable bankside features such as fence posts, shrubs, swim number pegs(!) exist, I use them. If this distance is measured off prior to casting, and the line restrained with a heavy duty elastic band, I will drop "on the button" every time. Clipping-up (or "harnessing-up") works fine too - but for gentle close-range casts a heavy duty elastic band is adequate.

The precise distance - either via bankside markers or an actual measurement made with a surveyor's tape - is recorded in my swim-plan notebook. This enables me to duplicate the range on subsequent trips without having to disturb the swim.

In the foregoing account I have referred to the weed's outer edge - and while this can be productive, I prefer bay-like recesses. They are not easy to find, but are worth the effort because they are extremely reliable hotspots.

Surface Weed

Lilies (Nymphaea alba and Nuphar lutea) and floating leaved pondweed (Potamogeton natans) are the surface plants most likely to be encountered in gravel pits. Their surface coverage is far greater than the underwater rooted area because they spread. Due to reduced light penetration, bottom weed is often non-existent beneath both lilies and Potamogeton. Chances are, then, a bait which descends without hang-up through the various stems will land on a nice, clear bottom. It is necessary to take care, though, because the swollen stems, or rhizomes, from which lilies and Potamogeton grow can have the texture and thickness of small tree branches.

In the margin chapter I described how I sometimes use a telescopic pole to place baits beneath overhanging trees and bushes. Steve Morgan - who recommended the tactic to me - developed it for poking baits beneath lily pads. I have not tried this for myself, but I can see its merits. I usually rely on my PVA hook cocoon system and cast or lower my end-rigs in position.

Immature lilies, or those which are in water too deep to enable them to reach the surface, grow in underwater clumps which look exactly like cabbages. When I lived in Northampton I heard them referred to as candocks - but I suspect it was a local name because I have not encountered it elsewhere.

Candock leaves (I like the name, so notwithstanding its lack of universal acceptance, I shall use it!) will support a light lead, but it tends to roll out of sight, pulling the bait with it. A long hooklink provides a reasonably effective solution, especially in conjunction with a neutral density, slow-sink bait which completely masks the hook. I have caught a number of candock carp on breadflake, also dampened, compressed crust - but these were from the Upper Nene, not a gravel pit. I suspect luncheon meat would be equally good - possibly better - but I have not tried it in this context.

An alternative - and one which enables hook-out presentation - is the long popup Zig Rig. I used this system last spring to fish over extensive candock beds in one of my local pits. It produced carp - and bream too, as a matter of fact - but I never really had the chance to refine my approach because the water was sufficiently shallow for the candocks to quickly develop into full blown lilies.

A floating plant which, thankfully, is absent from most gravel pits is duckweed (Lemna minor is the most common, but other localised varieties are encountered). I say "thankfully" because when duckweed becomes established it can cover the surface completely. A couple of the rivers I fish, also a canal, are so choked with it that in high summer they resemble long, thin fields rather than waterways! The main reason it is absent from most gravel pits is, I suspect, because organic nutrients are fully exploited by rooted weed - Elodea, milfoil etc - thereby leaving insufficient to encourage colonisation by duckweed.

A further factor which ensures big pits remain clear is their exposure to wind, which results in duckweed being dumped on the bank - thereby keeping it in check. Small pits, however, are vulnerable - especially if they are tree girt and thereby sheltered.

Duckweed does not create presentation difficulties because an end-rig can be encased in a PVA bag and "bombed" through it; the problem is its tendency to drift in large clumps which accumulate on the line and can drag the end-tackle out of position. This annoying characteristic is exacerbated by the fact that the eutrophic conditions in which duckweed proliferates also encourage floating blanket weed - which not only drags end-tackles along the bottom, but manages to

Pegged branch weed barrier.

spot-weld itself to the line so immovably that it jams in the tip ring and makes retrieving impossible.

Elodea also causes drift accumulation problems. It has a tendency to break up all through the summer, but gathers pace in early September. Any attempt to fish across the wind when Elodea fragmentation is well underway results in the lines becoming strung with pennants. If the floating strands are confined to the surface, it is sometimes possible to create a barrier where lines enter the water - I often cut a leafy branch which I trap upwind of my lines, and at right angles to the bank, with a couple of banksticks. But if, as tends to be increasingly the case as September progresses, the weed strands are found midwater too, the problem becomes more difficult to deal with. Backleads help. As does a heavier lead. But it can get to the stage when accumulations of weed are so great that, in combination with a big wind, even a 4oz lead will drag. When that point is reached, I quit, because I am not prepared to scale up to leads of 5-6oz.

Fishing directly into the wind usually mitigates the situation. If the rod tips are submerged, weed runs up the line and thence up the rod, where it can be removed. Fishing the upwind end of the pit solves the problem completely, of course; but such a solution is of little benefit if the carp are elsewhere!

Playing

Whether we fish in, on or near weed, sooner or later we have to extract carp from it. The process is helped, of course, if fish are struck soon after they take the bait. Being a day trip angler, this rarely presents difficulties because I can be off my chair and beside my rods in seconds. It is somewhat different if the angler is in a bivvy, possibly cocooned in a sleeping bag, and perhaps asleep. In such circumstances there will be a significant delay between the onset of the run and the fish being struck. Whilst not a desirable situation, it is unavoidable. What is avoidable, however, is the practice of wandering away from the rods. There is a tendency on some waters for carp anglers to gather together in little social groups - at best they might be about 50 yards from their rods, but in the worst examples they can be round the other side of the pit. A carp which takes the bait under these circumstances will likely have become inextricably weeded before the angler (sic) reaches his rods. There then ensues a lot of unceremonious brute-force heaving and hauling to try to release the unfortunate carp. Inevitably this proves unsuccessful, after which a raucous, "Get the boat!" will be heard.

Being away from the rods is unacceptable at any time. If the water is weedy, it is worse than unacceptable, and should result in expulsion from the controlling club or syndicate. It is bad for carp, which are subjected to excessive hook pressure. It is also extremely selfish, and the resulting disturbance handicaps those who are fishing responsibly. And frankly, I am sick to the back teeth of having my close-in fishing ruined by the thumping feet of clod-hopping cretins pounding past me as they run to their rods.

So, the first requirement is that the fish be struck as soon as possible.

No matter how diligent the angler, a percentage of fish will manage to get right in the thick of weed from the outset. If they are big and powerful they will probably plough even deeper immediately after being struck. It is somewhat disconcerting to see the line entering the water 10 yards from the bank, while the surface heaves and rocks some 30 yards beyond! I never try to hold big carp - they are unstoppable anyway - but I make them fight for every foot of line they take.

When a hooked carp comes to a stop, I maintain steady pressure until I feel it kicking on the end - at which point I pull hard. The fish's struggles are relatively ineffective in propelling it forward because it is trying to accelerate from stationary - but those struggles tear the weed, thereby releasing the fish from its hold. Usually, after a few feet of progress, everything grinds to a halt once more. Steady pressure is again maintained until the carp gets its second wind, whereupon it will struggle and, all being well, a few more feet can be regained. And so on. The process is not a continuous haul, but rather one of synchronising heavy pressure with the carp's struggles.

Occasionally - and this is relatively rare in my experience - the fish stops and refuses to budge. This, I suspect, is a consequence of thick weed covering the carp's eyes, which acts not unlike a falcon's hood and encourages it to lay quiet. This is not a good situation because we rely on the carp's struggles to help it free itself. In these circumstances I slacken off and wait. This achieves two things: first, it enables the carp to "think" it is no longer tethered; and second, it allows the weed to return to its original configuration whereupon the carp's vision might be restored. After five to ten minutes, the fish will usually start moving of its own volition. I allow it to take a yard or so of slack, then apply heavy strain again.

If that does not work? Well, I guess we are compelled to resort to a boat if one is available. But of the innumerable carp I have hooked in weed, I have only twice had to take to a boat.

Playing carp in weed is inevitably a somewhat heavy-handed procedure, but it need not be the brutal heave and haul we are sometimes led to believe. The five golden rules are:

- **if possible, fish close in**
- **strike the fish as early as possible**
- **utilise the fish's struggles to enable it to fight its own way free**
- **be patient**
- **use adequate tackle.**

Landing

Occasionally a carp will be enveloped in weed when it comes within netting range, which is one of the few circumstances in which I welcome the assistance of a netsman. I have landed weed-balled carp by myself, but there is no disputing the fact that a second pair of hands makes the task a whole lot easier.

Another difficult circumstance arises when the margin weed is so thick that it becomes difficult, if not impossible to submerge the net. The drawstring of a conventional net is not sufficiently rigid to push through weed - actually it sort of collapses which exacerbates the situation. Three years ago I lost a very big carp as a consequence of this - three times I drew the carp to the drawstring, and three times it powered off while I endeavoured to manipulate the net beneath it. The third time the hookhold gave. It was not the first time I had encountered difficulties in this regard, but it was the first time I had lost a fish as a consequence.

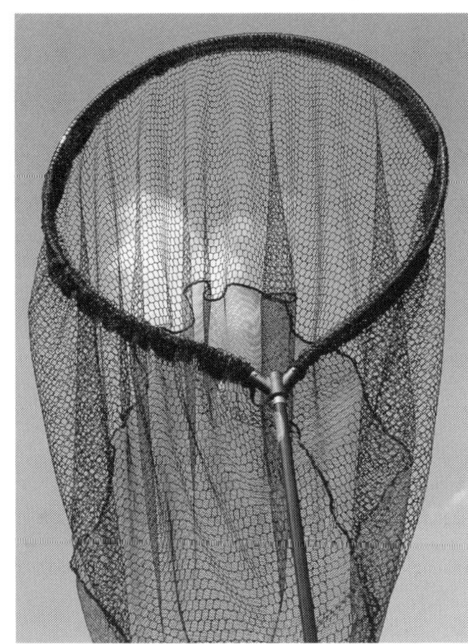

Leeda Predator Net; ideal for landing fish in thick weed.

I decided I needed a rigid frame, preferably a circular one with which I could push the weed aside, so I bought a Leeda Predator net - designed, as the name suggests, for pike. It is inconvenient in that it does not fold down, but performs exactly as required in thick weed.

Kevin Nash encountered similar problems - in the Essex Manor, I believe - and as an interim measure also acquired a Predator net. Meanwhile he worked on the development of a custom carp version which folded down - and came up with the Springbow. I had a small amount of input into the design, but my main claim to fame lies in the fact that I tested the prototype and have the distinction of landing the first ever U.K. carp in a Springbow net!

A powerful, heavy bodied mirror which was extracted from thick weed.

Tackle

I discussed tackle for weed fishing in Chapter Four, so my comments here need only be brief.

First, a cautionary comment. The butt of a heavily loaded rod should never be pulled past the 11 o'clock position. A modern rod is incredibly strong, but its tubular cross-section will not withstand overloading because it is designed to resist ovality - if the integrity of the tube is compromised, the blank will shatter. When I see someone leaning into a snag, or occasionally a hooked fish, with his rod bent over his shoulder, I flinch in horror. The fact that rods usually survive this treatment owes more to the amazing qualities of modern carbon composites than to the common sense of the anglers concerned.

Weed is abrasive, so a hard wearing line is essential. It should be strong, too - 15lb minimum for medium weed; heavier if it is thick. My normal choice is 18lb Power Plus, which has an actual breaking strain of about 21lb. Why so many carp anglers are reluctant to use high breaking strain line, I do not understand. A typical response was that of a friend who had just completed a week-long session on one of my club pits and was packing up as I arrived. I stopped to exchange pleasantries and ask how he had got on. “It’s driving me mad, Jim; I’ve hooked three fish and lost them all.”

“What happened, did they shed the hook?”

“No. Snap-offs; all three.”

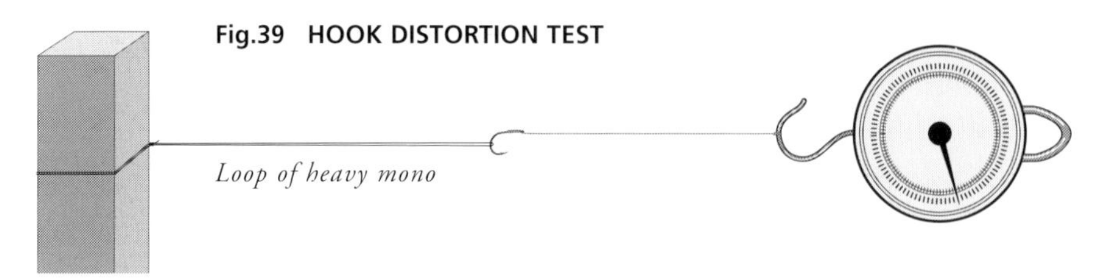

Fig.39 HOOK DISTORTION TEST

I inquired what strength line he was using. "12lb Big Game," he replied. Now, 12lb Big Game is tough line - it is underrated and has an actual wet breaking strain of about 15lb. But 15lb is not strong enough for big fish in thick weed. Tactfully I suggested to my friend that perhaps he ought to use something heavier. "I've caught loads of fish on 12lb," he said, "I'm sure it's okay."

Clearly it was not okay - as my friend reluctantly concluded when he deliberated on events subsequently. Next trip he was armed with 15lb Big Game, which has an actual breaking strain in the order of 18lb. It solved the problem; as was demonstrated by the fact that he hooked two fish and landed both of them.

Hooks must be strong, too. Nash Fang are excellent; as are Owner spade-end, Fox Series Three and Gardner Talon Tip. All are relatively heavy-wire hooks.

There is a school of thought which holds that fine-wire hooks are satisfactory providing they go in all the way to the bend. Only when a hook fails to penetrate - so the theory goes - and leverage is applied to the point will hooks open out. Not so. Leastways, not in my experience. Anyone in doubt should try this simple test. Tie a hook to a link in the normal way; then tie the link to a spring balance. A loop of heavy mono - which should be tied to a fence post or somewhere secure, is then placed in the bend of the hook (Fig 39). The balance is pulled, and readings noted as the hook distorts. You will find that most carp patterns show significant distortion - sufficient to result in a lost fish - with a loading of 6-9lb. Continue pulling and they either snap, or acquire an "L" shape. Such hooks are adequate for open water fishing, but what is the logic of using them in conjunction with 18lb test line? Or even 15lb, for that matter? Heavy wire hooks - such as my aforementioned foursome - achieve higher readings. They are sufficiently strong to be safely used in size 6; even size 8 is satisfactory in all but the most severe conditions. Size 4 I do not like because it is much too heavy and ungainly for my taste. I exempt Fox Series Two from that comment. While an excellent open water hook, I do not consider Series Two in sizes 6 or 8 to be strong enough for weed fishing; size 4, however, is almost indistinguishable from a 6 - so is not too large - but is made from heavier wire, which gives it the necessary strength.

If you undertake the hook test I have described, please wear spectacles or eye protectors. When a hook snaps, the point flies off at tremendous speed - certainly fast enough to become deeply embedded in an eyeball.

I do not like barbless hooks for weed fishing. If club or syndicate rules demand their use, I use them - but I do so reluctantly and in the certain knowledge that lots of hookpulls will occur.

A weedy swim on one of my local pits - eel grass is one of the varieties present.

Eel Grass Enigma

Mid-October, much of the weed will start to die back. With the first frosts - which here in the south-east usually occur early November - the process accelerates. Areas that were previously unfishable - or could only be fished with considerable difficulty - become accessible. On some waters this leads to a brief "honeymoon" period when carp are caught from places where they hitherto felt safe. This is not, however, the case with regard to eel grass. At the first signs of autumn browning - and I mean at the very first signs, but when it is still predominantly green - carp vacate it. I can only assume the process of decay releases a noxious chemical into the water.

Despite its tiny tail, this torpedo shaped linear fought hard and ploughed through several weedbeds.

I cannot recall having tried to catch winter carp from eel grass, but I know they are happy to feed among the dead strands in spring - so I suspect it is only the onset of decay which makes it unacceptable.

Strange stuff, eel grass. Where it grows, it is rampant; but to date I have only encountered it in four waters - all of which, coincidentally or otherwise, are deep, steep sided gravel pits. But strangely, it is absent from adjacent, apparently similar waters.

If anyone reading this thinks they can identify it, and can tell me more about it, I would be both interested and grateful to hear from them.

Chapter Seven

Carp Weather

Recently, while enduring a blank in a bitterly cold north-easterly wind, I endeavoured to lift my confidence by foraging through my memory-banks in the hope of recalling an occasion when I had done well under such conditions. No such recollection came to mind.

Dispiritedly I hung on until about an hour after dark, and then decided that as there was not a hope in hell of my catching anything, there was no point my sitting there any longer. So I packed up and went home.

I had not long been indoors when the telephone rang - it was Rick; "Been out today?" he asked.

"Yes," I replied, then added, "I knew my chances were virtually nil, but I'm working the rest of the week so today was my only opportunity to get out. How about you?"

"I had three," said Rick, "a twenty and a couple of upper doubles." Which demonstrates that even the most unpromising conditions can produce a good

Fishing into a big, mild winter wind on a day which produced half a dozen carp.

catch. The converse also applies, and we have all experienced twitchless blanks in conditions which looked perfect.

So where does that leave us? If we cannot dismiss any day as being entirely hopeless, and find that an apparently ideal day can throw up a blank, is there any point in trying to "read" the conditions? If not, then this chapter is redundant even before it has begun! But I believe we can make a reasonable assessment of our chances, and notwithstanding the occasional surprises which occur, I have found carp in most waters to be fairly predictable.

The first important fact to establish is that individual waters respond in different ways, and to an extent those responses depend on how we approach our fishing. There are, for example, pits which I classify as being "big wind waters", by which I mean they generally fish best when the wind is strong enough to produce whitecaps. But is my preference for a big wind due to the fact that I am primarily a daytime angler? Certainly those who fish the same pits after dark would disagree with my assessment because they are often successful in a flat calm. Then again, my "big wind" designation only applies when I am using bottom baits, because completely different preferences apply if I am fishing floaters.

By contrast, there are several deep gravel pits where I favour hot, sunny weather - especially when fishing the margins. Indeed, on those waters I have caught well on days which were so sweltering that even in the shade of my umbrella the heat was almost unbearable.

So "best weather" depends on the water, the angler and the method.

Wind

Albert Buckley was one of the first carp anglers to recognise the importance of wind. He realised that a cool wind which chilled Mapperley Reservoir's weeded shallows persuaded carp to move to deeper, weedfree water. Having identified this response he used the knowledge to take his one time British record (26lb, circa 1930).

An even earlier reference was brought to my attention by my Belgian friend, Peter Goossens (who, sadly, died in an industrial accident three years ago). It was a leaflet - published in Belgium about 1920 - which contained a chapter entitled "Influence of the Wind on River Carp". That the writer was well ahead of his time was further demonstrated by his description and drawing of a version of the hair rig which he recommended for the attachment of pieces of cattle cake to the hook!

I became aware of the wind's significance very early in my carp fishing career as a consequence of being attracted to larger than average waters which, by their nature, were exposed to the elements. The first and most obvious observation was that surface activity, such as rolling and jumping, was far more evident at the downwind end. So, not surprisingly, that is where I fished. It did not take me long to realise that as well as being an aid to location, wind often seemed to induce feeding. So my fishing became very wind oriented. But then anomalies occurred - well, they were not anomalies really, but they seemed so at the time. I noticed, for example, that not all wind was beneficial.

As a broad generalisation I would say that carp will follow a warm wind, but will only occasionally follow a cold one. My definition of "warm" and "cold" in this context being relative to the temperature of the water. Up to a point, the stronger the wind, and the greater its temperature difference to that of the water, the more noticeable will be the carp's response - favourable or otherwise.

The tendency to follow a warm wind is not, however, an all-year reaction because it becomes progressively less evident after late September. A cold wind, on the other hand, exerts an influence all through the year, and often prompts carp to seek shelter in the lee of a high or tree lined bank.

The direction of the wind matters too, partly for its inherent characteristics, and partly as a result of the meteorological conditions which cause it. But that said, there is no wind direction which is always good or always bad. As an example, consider the summer south-easterly which is usually warm when it precedes a low-pressure system, but it can also occur as part of a high-pressure anti-cyclone which drags cold air down from the north. The direction may be the same, but its characteristics are completely different.

The U.K.'s most predictable weather system is the Atlantic depression (a "low") which comprises winds which rotate in an anti-clockwise direction. The circulating air mass usually tracks north-east, eventually moving across the North Sea towards Scandinavia. The typical depression will be preceded by a south-easterly wind. It will probably be fine at first, but will become increasingly cloudy and possibly wet as the pressure falls. It is generally warm, or at the very least mild, and in all its manifestations - anything from a gentle breeze to a raging "hoolie" - it can provide good fishing. It is my favourite summer wind.

As the depression locates itself over the British Isles so the wind will veer to the south-west, often accompanied by a mixture of sunshine and showers. In summer, if the wind is warm, carp will probably follow it; while if it is cool, they may move to its tail and seek the shelter of an upwind bank. But whether they follow it, or move against it, carp will probably feed because the south-westerly is a reliable "catching" wind.

As the depression slips away, so a north-westerly is likely to develop. It tends to be cold and squally, and may become strong and very wet. Occasionally it will be accompanied by thunderstorms and hail. It does not, needless to say, feature high on my "all time favourites" list - but I have sometimes done well in north-westerlies, especially the quieter versions. If it is classed as fresh or stronger, I will normally choose a swim which offers a degree of shelter because although I have often seen carp rolling and jumping in areas receiving the full force of a big north-westerly, I have rarely caught much by fishing such spots.

With the departure of the depression, winds will probably moderate - which provides an opportunity for non depression-related winds to take effect. Southerlies are the most welcome of these; they can be extremely warm, sometimes coming laden with fine Sahara sand which leaves everything coated with a thin layer of ochre dust. I like southerlies whether they be hot, oven blast jobs, or cloudy and wet. Occasionally they can be extremely strong. But whatever form they take, I am confident of doing well.

Although I dislike cold north-easterlies, the gentle summer version which sometimes occurs when a warm, high pressure system takes hold, can be very good. Especially on its first day - but that is something I shall come to presently.

Westerlies are usually cloudy and often wet, having come direct from the Atlantic where they pick up a lot of moisture. I have mixed feelings about westerlies, and have found that they often look better than they prove to be - for which observation I can offer no explanation.

Perfect, distortion-free reflections on a rubbish fishing day!

I mentioned earlier that there is a change in a carp's response to wind which usually occurs late September, but may sometimes be delayed until mid-October. It is a distinct summer/autumn divide, and marks a clear change in carp behaviour. Before this time, carp tend to follow a warm wind; after it, they cease to do so. Why does this happen? Is it simply cyclic, or is there a critical temperature cut-off?

Before attempting to answer that question, I would like to ask another - why do carp follow the wind at all? The usual explanation is that it is in order to take advantage of drifting food supplies which accumulate at the downwind end of a water. If we examine this proposal objectively we have to conclude that it does not withstand scrutiny. Admittedly there is in any body of water a certain amount of drifting food - nymphs, pupae and possibly daphnia - what biologists call the "invertebrate drift". For surface feeding fish like rudd and rainbow trout this is undoubtedly a primary food source - but is it sufficiently abundant to persuade large bottom feeding fish like carp to go from one end of a lake to the other? Only in exceptional circumstances, such as a daphnia bloom, will the invertebrate drift be able to compete with semi-static food supplies such as snails, mussels, crustaceans, larvae, and in some waters, crayfish - all of which are to be found on and in the bottom, and in weedbeds.

Another suggestion is that the water at the downwind end will be better oxygenated. This is more credible than the drifting food idea, especially as a carp's tendency to follow the wind is most pronounced in summer when, due to high temperatures, water is least capable of holding dissolved oxygen. But notwithstanding the apparent logic of this notion, I doubt that it is correct. Why, for example, will carp vacate weeded shallows where, as a result of photosynthesis, the water may be supersaturated with dissolved oxygen (and thereby incapable of holding any more), in order to follow a wind which blows towards deeper, weedfree water where dissolved oxygen levels may be lower?

So, if they are not following food, and not moving to an area which is better oxygenated, why do carp follow the wind? I think the essential appeal of wind is the water flow it creates. Carp were originally river fish; its native waters were the large rivers flowing into the Mediterranean, Black, Caspian and Aral Seas (Freshwater Fishes, J. Vostradovský, Hamlyn, 1973). This fact, combined with their known capacity to be great "wanderers", provides a compelling argument for their having a well developed instinct to move against a flow of water. If they did not do so, their peregrinations would have eventually resulted in their ending up in the estuaries and evolving into sea fish!

So, let us consider what happens when wind blows across a big pit. In response to the flow of surface water moving with the wind, a subsurface layer moves in the opposite direction. This undertow can be quite powerful - ask any float angler and he will tell you how it is sometimes possible to trot float tackle back against the wind. It is this undertow, I believe, against which carp swim - they are, in effect, responding to their instinct to move upriver.

Which brings us back to my earlier questions - why do carp not follow a cold wind; and why is there an autumn switch-off as regards response to the wind?

I think a cold wind which chills the water creates an uncomfortable environment, and the need for temperature stability takes precedence over the instinct to swim against the flow - so they seek sheltered areas.

In autumn and winter, as temperatures drop, their instinctive responses become dulled - a not improbable reaction when you consider that we compel carp to live at a latitude beyond their normal distribution limits. But this is not the whole story. I suspect thay are also strongly influenced by day length. And that, I believe, is why carp will rarely follow a late autumn "Indian summer" wind, even when it appears to fulfil the required temperature criterion. Late October '96, for example, was marked by several days of unseasonably high temperatures - news broadcasts showed people sunbathing on Brighton beach - but on the waters I fished during that period I saw nothing to indicate that carp were following the warm southerlies and south-westerlies which accompanied the sunshine.

New or Old?

Here is a short extract from Big Water Carp:

"It is widely believed that it (the wind) needs to have been blowing for some time before it has a major effect on carp location. Often I have read such things as, "The wind had been piling into the willows for four days, so I knew the carp had to be there."

My experience is completely at variance with that belief. I have found that the wind that has the greatest effect is the new one. The day to be on the water is the first day of a new wind. The second day can still be good, but with every subsequent day its influence becomes progressively diminished."

I wrote that in 1988. At the time it was a radical notion and was initially received with some scepticism, but it quickly gained acceptance.

But whilst most carp anglers now agree that the new wind is the one which matters most, I doubt that they fully appreciate the immediacy and determination with which carp respond. Frequently I have read something along the lines of, *"The wind changed direction and blew away from me, towards the far end of the pit, so I put a big bed of bait out in an attempt to hold them."* Most such accounts end with the writer's hopes having been dashed! When the wind changes, carp move. Even on big waters - 30 acres or more - I would expect a significant proportion of the population to be at the downwind end within an hour or two of a new wind's commencement.

How Strong?

Although carp will move on any warm, new wind, they do so most purposefully if it blows fairly briskly. My "designer wind" falls in the moderate to fresh category. If it increases to strong or gale force, I am less enthusiastic. There comes a stage when it ceases to offer extra benefits, and merely increases the physical difficulties. I have caught carp in ludicrously strong winds, like the big, late summer catch I took from Bysingwood when the forecasters categorised the south-westerly as "severe gale, gusting to storm force." My journey to the water was most disconcerting as I had to negotiate several overturned lorries along the M2, and minor roads were strewn with broken branches! Fishing, not to say survival, was only possible because I found a swim in the lee of an island. I was able to sit in relative shelter, but beyond the island huge waves raced down the pit!

That incident occurred many years ago. What lunacy prompted me to do anything so daft as go fishing on a day like that I cannot imagine. I would not willingly set foot outside the door in such conditions now!

Bars, Weed and Hotspots

Often, on my first visit to a water, I have been given the well meant advice, "They don't follow the wind here." I always disregard the information because while I hesitate to say that no such waters exist, I have yet to find one. In fairness, though, the tendency is much less marked in some waters than others. I doubt that the carp themselves are any less responsive, but the physical characteristics of the water can minimise the wind's influence.

Take very weedy waters, for example. If the weed is extensive and dense it will inhibit subsurface flow and may prevent the creation of an undertow. This - if my "against the flow" hypothesis is correct - explains why carp in very weedy pits are less responsive to wind.

Carp in pits which have their main body of water divided up by long parallel bars or islands appear to show inconsistent and unpredictable responses to wind.

But if we examine wind induced movements closely, a pattern can be discerned. If the wind blows lengthwise, along the channels, carp are likely to follow it in the standard manner. If, however, the wind blows crosswise, the bars and islands act as barriers which limit the generation of subsurface currents. The situation is further complicated by the fact that each bar or island acts like a sort of false downwind bank which delays the carp's progress. They move round and beyond such features eventually, but this may take anything from several hours to a couple of days.

So, while I maintain that all carp follow the wind, I qualify the statement with the acknowledgement that in some pits responses are affected, and sometimes seemingly negated, by weed, bars and islands. Before leaving the subject of wind anomalies, I need to mention long, narrow pits. I have fished several such waters over the years, the most recent being one known somewhat evocatively, if inappropriately, as "Heartbreak Lake". It is about half a mile long, but nowhere more than 100 yards wide. When a warm wind blows lengthwise along the pit there is a marked tendency for carp to follow it, but when it blows crosswise it has little effect, and carp are found in the vicinity of favoured holding areas such as reed beds and low rise plateaux.

So, when fishing long, narrow pits - ignore crosswinds, and opt for hotspots.

Coastal Pits

Thus far I have been concerned with what we might call "proper" winds which result from weather systems; but what of local winds such as are produced near the coast in response to temperature differences between land and sea? Everyone is familiar with the sea breeze phenomenon whereby reduced pressure created by warm air rising from the land during a hot, summer day causes cool air to be drawn in from the sea. The consequent sea breeze is very deceptive; by mid afternoon it can be sufficiently strong to convince us that it is a proper isobar induced wind, so we conclude that it will blow for the duration of our session. But at dusk, or shortly after, the breeze will die away to nothing, while an hour or two later a land breeze may spring up - this occurs when the water is warmer than the adjacent land - which blows the opposite way. We therefore find ourselves in the irritating circumstance whereby after setting up with the wind in our face, it swings through 180 degrees and proceeds to blow at our back! When the water concerned is a 50 acre pit requiring a gut-busting yomp in order to change ends, this is not an ideal situation in which to find oneself!

Only those winds classed as moderate or stronger will retain their integrity against the influence of sea and land breezes. So before setting off for a day on a coastal water, I obtain the inshore waters wind forecast from television text channels (BBC Ceefax 409, ITV Teletext 158).

This is probably a suitable juncture at which to give details of the abbreviated Beaufort Wind Scale used by television and radio forecasters:

Description	Speed (mph)
Calm	less than 1
Light	1-12
Moderate	13-18
Fresh	19-24
Strong	25-38
Gale	39-46
Severe gale	47-54
Storm	55-63

While in "facts and figures" mode, I will add that regional general weather forecasts are obtainable from television text channels (BBC Ceefax 402, ITV Teletext 154).

Continuous exposure to the pruning effect of wind ensures coastal pits remain relatively treeless and open to the sky - which I like. Many swims comprise shingle - which I also like because in addition to being clean and dry, shingle is comfortable and easily contoured to accommodate my chair and rucksack. And those stones are not "just stones" - I often amuse myself searching for fossils among them, and have collected numerous examples, mainly ammonites. But it is not only the environment I find so appealing; I enjoy the challenge of trying to "read" these fascinating waters. Often I will start the day at the end towards which a land breeze is blowing, then switch to the other end late morning or early afternoon in anticipation of the sea breeze springing up - taking into account, of course, the influence of whatever "proper" wind exists. If I get it right, I can have baits and feed in position before the carp arrive.

We all have waters where we feel deep, inner contentment; "big sky" coastal pits are mine.

Rain

Persistent rain depresses me. I sit beneath my umbrella feeling trapped, and my mood gets as leaden as the sky. When I fished at night it was even worse, with the additional problem of trying to keep bedding dry; sometimes I have actually lay there hoping I would not get a run!

But what about carp? How does it affect them?

Only on a few occasions have I been successful in continuous heavy rain, or when it has been cold and squally. Showery rain, however, is a different matter entirely, especially when borne on a mild wind or interspersed with spells of warm sunshine. During late summer '98 I fished through some torrential downpours - one of which prompted Maria to ring me on my mobile 'phone to tell me that our rainwater guttering was overflowing in a passable imitation of Niagara Falls! But dramatic though some of the showers were, none lasted longer than an hour or so; then the sun would come out. I caught well on such days. Interestingly, though, I cannot recall a run occurring while the rain was actually falling.

Rain is particularly welcome in a heatwave because protracted periods of calm, hot weather can result in waters becoming seriously depleted of dissolved oxygen. In extreme cases carp might die; but long before this stage is reached, appetite will be suppressed. Rain is supersaturated with oxygen, so can have an immediate beneficial effect. Additionally, heavy rain agitates the water surface and can encourage oxygen to be dissolved from the atmosphere. The consequent increase in dissolved oxygen might stimulate feeding.

On a related subject. Thunderstorms can sometimes induce feeding, but they can also produce the converse effect when, due to atmospheric, chemical and biological interactions, lakes suffer sudden and severe oxygen depletion. This phenomenon, known as an oxygen crash, is most likely to occur at night. At best it will inhibit feeding; at worst it might result in fish dying.

Rain is often acidic, so may have a radical - albeit temporary - effect on the pH of a water. Whether this is likely to trigger or suppress feeding I cannot say, but I offer the thought for consideration.

Fog and Mist

How large does a wood have to be to qualify as a forest? When does a stream become a river? At what stage does a pond become a lake? And with the previous subject in mind - for how long does a shower have to last to be classed as rain? Which reminds me... when Terry Eustace, the late Ian Gillespie and I were on an Irish pike trip, we paused in our conversation to listen to the weather forecast on the car radio. We heard - and I swear this is true - a dulcet voiced colleen say, "It will be a day of showers. Between the showers will be periods of prolonged rain." We had to think about that one..!

To continue. Is there a precise transition point at which mist becomes fog? I ask this because weather forecasters often refer to "mist or fog" - the inclusion of the word "or" suggests that they are not the same thing. But my research to date has failed to reveal what the difference might be.

Hot summer sunshine, and one from the margins.

Notwithstanding the lack of definitive demarcation, both mist and fog develop as a consequence of the air temperature falling to a level at which the relative humidity becomes 100% and water vapour condenses into minute airborne water droplets. This is known as the dew-point.

But no matter whether it is classed as mist or fog, few carp anglers like it. Kevin Maddocks, writing in Carp Fever (Beekay, 1981) said that he had never caught a carp in thick fog. I can recall catching only one. Brother Martin, on the other hand, has no hangups about fog, and demonstrated why when one winter morning he took four big carp in quick succession. The fog was so thick that the angler in the next swim - only about fifteen yards away - did not realise Martin was there until he heard his Delkim!

Why should fog make a difference anyway? It descends, as previously mentioned, when the air is cold and still. Its presence creates an all-pervading dullness. How many anglers would put cold, still and dull conditions near the top of their "favourite weather" list? Very few, I suspect.

So, if fog has an adverse effect - and I emphasise the word "if" - perhaps it is not the fog itself which matters, but the conditions which accompany it?

In my case its negative attributes tend to be self-fulfilling in that I do not go fishing if fog seems likely. If it catches me unawares, and I am already by the water, I pack up and head for home. I have, therefore, put in very few "fog hours", so my lack of success is hardly surprising!

Sunshine

Bright sun in isolation is neither a benefit nor a debit. It depends on other factors, notably temperature and wind direction. Bright sun combined with a warm southerly can provide excellent conditions; but if the wind is a cold north-easterly fishing is likely to be difficult.

It also depends on the sort of fishing - several times in preceding chapters I have made reference to hot sun being beneficial when fishing the margins. In many waters it is conducive to surface feeding too.

Type of water and time of year also come into the equation. A sunny flat calm after an overnight frost is one of my favourite conditions - but only on deep pits, and only in November!

Atmospheric Pressure

In summer, high pressure generally results in hot, sunny weather. In winter it leads to night frosts and cold, bright days. Lack of wind is a factor frequently associated with high pressure whatever the time of year.

Low pressure usually brings wind, cloud and rain.

So when carp anglers say something like, "Fishing won't improve until low pressure moves in," are they actually wanting a drop in pressure, or the change in the weather which is likely to accompany it?

As to the importance of a rising as against a falling barometer - again, I find it difficult to come to meaningful conclusions. How, for example, does high but falling pressure compare with when it is low but rising? Or high and rising further? And so on...

Truth is, I can make very little sense of atmospheric pressure as an isolated entity. I have preferences and dislikes, but they are always in connection with other aspects. As already stated, I like high pressure warm winds, but do not like high pressure cold winds. In common with most carp anglers, I much prefer low pressure warm winds to low pressure cold ones. But if asked to state a preference for high pressure warm or low pressure warm, I could not do so because I doubt that either "high" or "low" pressure is intrinsically superior.

Low Oxygen

I referred earlier to the serious consequences of an oxygen crash such as occasionally occurs during a thunderstorm. It can also be a problem in autumn when, as a result of a sudden algal bloom die off, a water may suffer radical oxygen depletion. When the demand for dissolved oxygen (known by the acronym BOD, which stands for Biological Oxygen Demand) exceeds supply, carp can become distressed and lose condition. In extreme cases their immune system shuts off and they become vulnerable to infection. At best the fishing will slow right down, and may grind to a complete stop - at worst, particularly if the water has correspondingly high levels of dissolved ammonia, fish will die.

If autumn oxygen depletion occurs, the best course is for the water to be closed until circumstances improve. On no account should free-baiting be permitted or, as it rots on the bottom, it will exacerbate matters by placing increased demands on already critically low levels of dissolved oxygen.

Mechanical intervention (spraying etc) can reduce the risk of fish deaths occurring, and I understand that granular hydrogen peroxide has been used to boost oxygen levels. But such measures are best left to qualified people such as fisheries experts from the Environment Agency. Generally the situation improves of its own accord when the temperature falls in November and, typically at that time of year, the water is reoxygenated by wind and rain.

Full Moon

The phase of the moon, while not "weather" in any literal sense, seems to fit comfortably into this chapter so I decided to include it.

In summer, the appearance of a big white moon has usually condemned my Delkims to silence. In autumn, however, the situation changes - and I have sometimes wondered if a bright moon is actually beneficial. But it is difficult to draw meaningful conclusions because accompanying weather conditions have to be included in the reckoning.

Many anglers believe that it is not merely the presence of the moon in the night sky which matters, but its cyclical phase. They are convinced that it influences carp behaviour, and our chances of catching them, quite independently of weather conditions. In daylight too. ABU's "Tight Lines" catalogue used to contain a "Solunar Table" in which days were designated as being excellent, good or fair. A similar lunar calendar currently published in the USA goes further and has certain days marked with a little lawn mower symbol - which indicates that fishing is likely to be so poor you may as well stay home and cut the grass!

Why should the moon matter anyway? It is easy to see how it can influence the behaviour of sea fish due to its effect on tides - but "tidal" rises and falls on a lake or pit are likely to be insignificant, and certainly far less than would be produced by wind and rain. So it seems illogical that the moon's gravity should influence carp. But what about the light it emits? All creatures have an inborn metabolic clock which is synchronised to daylight, and there is abundant evidence to demonstrate that animals can have their body clocks reprogrammed by exposure to light at the wrong times - indeed, this procedure is widely used in animal husbandry. Is it not possible, therefore, that the appearance of a bright moon is sufficient to disorientate a carp's body clock, with the consequence that its feeding patterns go awry?

Fascinating

Low lying mist over a Belgian pit.

Meteorology has always fascinated me - even as a child I would watch through the window as mini-spires produced by heavy rain "marched" down the road. I still do! Had I not gone into teaching, I suspect meteorology would have been my chosen profession. As an angler - and more particularly as one with a preference for big pits - it is an interest which has practical application because it helps me to visualise how the weather will affect the waters at my disposal. This enables me to choose which water will probably be the best option on any given day. It influences my choice of swim, too.

Sometimes the weather behaves in a manner completely contrary to expectations and confounds my attempts to mentally compute the variables. Often enough, though, things go according to plan. And I have no doubts whatsoever that, taken overall, the use of weather-study as an angling tool has enabled me to catch many more carp than I would otherwise have done.

Chapter Eight

Let Us Talk Again

The title for this chapter is derived from my erstwhile monthly Carpworld column. So too is its style which comprises a mixture of the serious and the satirical. I hope the difference is obvious!

Overseas Trips

A question I am frequently asked is, *"Why don't you fish overseas any more?"*

Mainly, I suppose, because with all-year fishing now available in England I feel no need to take a close season break on the Continent.

Also - and this may sound strange - I do not want to catch the carp of my dreams. Anglers tell me they can separate overseas fishing from that back home. An audit of the cast list of those who have caught foreign monsters suggests otherwise because many no longer fish for carp, either here or abroad. This, I suspect, is because after catching a 50 or 60 pounder it is difficult to keep one's perspectives intact.

Excessively prolific fishing can have the same effect. My son, Peter, has twice fished the St. Lawrence in Canada. Both trips he caught a stack of big carp and had

Late May on a French gravel pit. The abandonment of the UK close season has reduced the incentive for such trips.

a wonderful time, but it left him with little wish to catch any more. With his appetite for carp sated, he now concentrates on tench and bream.

I have had personal experience of the same phenomenon. Some years ago I was heavily into pike and travelled all over the U.K. and Southern Ireland. By a combination of hard work and fortuitous timing I enjoyed excellent fishing on lots of lakes and gravel pits, also some well known big pike waters such as Abberton Reservoir, Loch Lomond and Horsey Mere. Then I met Ken Crow. Through Ken's contacts and generosity I gained access to some superb pike fishing in a group of virtually untapped Kent pits. I caught a lot of big pike. But it spoiled me. I became "all piked out". Now, I no longer fish for pike.

To say I was pleased would be an understatement!

I am determined that the same thing will not happen with carp. In the last twelve months I have been invited to fish for carp in Romania, Poland, Italy and Canada. Whilst being extremely grateful to those who extended the invitations, I have declined them all.

I live for carp fishing. Even after all these years and after catching countless carp I still retain the level of excitement which can keep me awake at night prior to an early morning start. I do not want to lose that.

Imports

Not that I need necessarily go abroad in order to catch foreign fish! Some fishery owners are honest about it and readily acknowledge that all or some of their carp are imported. Others seem reluctant to admit to the fact, and claim that the big fish which unexpectedly appear are unknown specimens which have suddenly "come through". Some of the anglers who fish such places try to convince themselves that such is the case, the rest of us know that "come through" is carpspeak for *"recently introduced"*!

And from where do such fish come? Most are imported legitimately, but a few show a remarkable similarity to the typical pointy-headed, high backed Chantecoq fish. This may, of course, be pure coincidence. Or not, as the case may be...

Carpspeak

Talking of carpspeak. Carp fishing has developed its own linguistic conventions, idiomatic phraseology and esoteric vocabulary. Nowhere are these characteristics more pronounced than in anecdotal writing. Take the word *"well"*. To most of us it either signifies freedom from illness, or a water-filled hole down which pussy is apt to fall. In angling writers' carpspeak it is neither. It is an ancillary which when combined with a verb's transitive form signifies magnitude. As an example; extreme disappointment - such as might be experienced after suffering a hookpull - is expressed by the term *"well gutted"*. Used in isolation, *"gutted"* still signifies disappointment, but to a less intense degree. Occasionally, *"gutted"* is prefaced by the indefinite article and expressed in its noun form, *"a gutter"* - a ploy used by our more erudite writers to reduce the incidence of repetition within a narrative.

By contrast, the phrase *"to say I was pleased would be an understatement"* applies to the converse circumstance, namely when the intention is to convey jubilation.

"Mega", *"magic"*, *"over the moon"* and *"what a result"* are alternative means by which pleasure consequent on a particular triumph might be denoted; but long term success is more usually conveyed by the phrase *"doing the business"* - or *"done the business"* if expressed in its past or passive form.

In the event of success being unexpected - and this applies whether it be short or long term - it is described as leaving the captor *"gobsmacked"*. This being the colloquial alternative to the now redundant *"astounded"* or *"astonished"*.

The phrase *"a bellyful of grease"* refers to a particular form of dietary abuse which, while potentially applicable to any meal, generally applies to breakfast eaten in an establishment known as *"the caff"* (abbreviated form of "cafeteria", not as commonly supposed a corruption of the French "café").

Accounts of long periods of time spent at the waterside risk an author being perceived as someone who has difficulty relating to women. To eliminate this possibility, writers endeavour to make it clear that they are far from being emotionally dysfunctional and actually have abnormally high levels of hetero-testosterone coursing through their veins. Session fishing narratives are therefore punctuated with sexual innuendo and amusing references to "mucky mags".

On a related theme, photos showing anglers in various states of partial undress are not uncommon. Such pictures usually illustrate the practise known as *"mooning"*, which involves the baring and subsequent display of the buttocks. Although the purpose of this activity among carp anglers (and, incidentally, football fans) remains unclear, biologists have long been aware of its importance among groups of chimpanzees and baboons. References to bodily functions are frequently encountered. Some writers specialise in virtuoso descriptions of defecation. Others, with admirable decorum, stop short of this and concentrate on humourous allusions to excessive flatulence.

The reader might occasionally feel confused and excluded by the use of nicknames. This, of course, is the writer's intention, and is the means by which status as a core member of an exclusive big carp hierarchy is established.

Here I am getting it all wrong - I should be wearing a bait-logo T-shirt!

In trophy pictures, authors invariably wear a T-shirt which bears a bait-dealer's logo. In addition to indicating their corporate worth, it ensures free or heavily discounted supplies of bait. It should not be assumed, however, that the T-shirt bait was actually used to catch the fish in the photo. Indeed, it is well known that some writers endorse one bait, yet use something entirely different. This is known as ambiguous allegiance, and reached its zenith with the celebrity angler who allowed the capture of a particularly impressive common to be attributed to not one, but two different baits; from different manufacturers too! Initially he caused some bewilderment by appearing in both their advertisements, but he subsequently clarified the apparent anomaly by explaining that his hookbait was made from one manufacturer's mix, which he fished among free offerings made from the other manufacturer's mix! Such ingenuity deserved, and indeed received enormous respect from every bait-logo T-shirt wearer in the country.

At which juncture it is worth mentioning that the noun *"bait"* is often replaced by the idiomatic nomenclature *"gear"* - as in, *"We decided to go in with Nash/Mainline/Nutrabaits gear."* Bait dealers support the validity of their sponsored writers' preferred terminology by making reference in promotional literature to someone *"having it away with our gear."* The term *"having it away"*, along with its variant *"having it off"* are not, incidentally, in any way connected with its more familiar usage in the context of copulatory activity, but are alternatives to *"doing the business"* as a means of signifying consistent success.

Syntactic subtlety, or what!

Orwellian Hell

My more astute readers may have detected that I am not exactly wild about jet-skiers. Indeed, I have been known to express the wish that they return to the

Bless!

primeval slime from which they prematurely emerged and, following another six or seven million years of evolutionary development, have another try to see if they are ready to walk upright and develop an opposable thumb.

Close behind jet-skiers in my list of angling-related hates come dugouts. As well as being ugly, they can be rock hard dust-bowls in summer and filthy quagmires in the winter. They can be dangerous, too, with bank reinforcements shored up with lengths of scaffolding pole which always, but always protrude a foot or two above ground level. What is it about nice, sloping, grassy embankments that compels carp anglers to vandalise them in this appalling manner? Part of the reason, I suspect, is because many anglers live in an urban environment and, quite simply, feel ill at ease when surrounded by nature. They therefore feel the need to urbanise their angling surroundings. Also, presumably they want a flat bank on which to pitch their domes. It does not occur to them to use a shelter which is compatible with the contours of the bank. No way! Make the bank fit the shelter, instead!

Mallets. These have no place on, near or within earshot of a carp lake. They may serve a useful purpose if you are setting up a bungalow-tent in a New Forest campsite, or for securing an awning to a caravan so you can qualify for one of those amusing rear window stickers saying something like, *"Caravanners would do it if they only knew what it was"* - but mallets are no more an appropriate accessory to carp fishing than are Laura Ashley curtains.

Darenth - once a lovely water, now spoilt by ugly dugouts.

Talking of caravans. Can you think of anything more naff? And have you noticed what inappropriate names they have? *"Pioneer"*, *"Adventurer"* - that sort of thing. But best of all, *"Marauder"*! Can you believe it! You can just imagine Genghis Khan leading his plundering hoards while towing his Wendy house!

Marauder... I ask you!

Dogs. I cannot abide dogs. My profound dislike of the wretched things is primarily due to their utter and complete gormlessness. Their only function in life would appear to be the consumption of perfectly good protein which they convert to excrement and dump on lakeside paths (a characteristic they share, unfortunately, with some carp anglers). In addition to which they leap into the water, run through your lines, shake themselves dry over your clothing and kit, try to make off with your bait or sandwiches, and generally qualify as a confounded nuisance. They give being dim a bad name. And as for those who subscribe to the sobriquet that dogs are *"man's best friend"*, I can only conclude that there are some pretty sad people out there.

All things bright and beautiful...

Close behind dogs come tufties, cormorants, coots, geese, swans, ducks, gulls, wasps, mosquitoes and slugs - and anything else which bites, stings, crawls, slithers or interferes with the efficient deployment of floaters. According to the book of Genesis, God frittered away his time during a very tight-schedule creation week making *"the birds of the air and the beasts of the field"*, when he would have been far better employed relaxing with a nice single malt and flooding Kent in preparation for stocking it with carp.

On a gentler level, I dislike careless misuse of language. Like the occasion when I was compelled to prematurely guillotine a fantastic day's fishing because I ran out of bait; an event which prompted a nearby angler to comment, "There's nothing worse than running out of bait when you've really got the fish feeding, is there?"

"Bubonic plague," I said.

"Pardon?"

"Bubonic plague - you know, the black death - that's worse," I suggested. "Or a hurricane. Or your run-of-the-mill earthquake." I warmed to my theme, "At a rough guess, and without really trying, I reckon I could think of about ten thousand things far, far, far worse than running out of bait."

The poor guy had innocently and inadvertently touched on one of my pet hates, namely the blatantly obvious inappropriateness of the crass, *"there's nothing*

Literally taking a Kent pit apart!

worse" phrase.

"At the end of the day" makes me cringe, too. The only occasion when it can be justified is when talking of a sunset. *"That's what it's all about"* is another - and usually uttered by people who have precious little clue of what anything is about.

And the word *"literally"*. There is nothing wrong with it in its correct sense, but people use it when they mean *"metaphorically"*. Bait companies are prime offenders with phrases like, *"The water was literally destroyed by those using our predigested pH adjusted neutral density wondermix."* What they are actually saying, albeit unintentionally, is that the water was, well, destroyed - as in H-bomb annihilation. Or else they claim the water was *"literally taken apart"*. Which is impossible, of course, unless your name happens to be Moses!

An Apology

I apologise if anything contained within this chapter has caused anyone embarrassment. My intention has not been to induce discomfiture, but to amuse - after all, there is nothing worse than upsetting people when, at the end of the day, having a laugh is quite literally what it is all about.

Know what I mean?

At the end of the day...

Chapter Nine

Rigs

Carp anglers are obsessed with rigs. Read almost any issue of any magazine devoted to carp fishing and there will be an article - or more likely, articles, plural - on the subject. On occasions there will even be special rig editions!

Part of the reason, I suspect, is because the concept of "the revolutionary rig" is deeply ingrained in carp anglers' folk memory. It stems from when Lenny Middleton and Kevin Maddocks developed the Hair Rig. The importance of this development can hardly be overstated. It was, and remains, the most outstanding rig-related innovation which has ever been made.

Since then we have tinkered with the basic concept, and all manner of variants have been spawned - hence the plethora of "I gotta rig" articles which range from the informative, through the misleading to the downright daft!

Simplicity

My credo is simple; if carp can be persuaded to feed on free baits, they can be caught. I realise this conflicts with the enormous volume of anecdotal evidence which suggests otherwise - you know the sort of thing, *"The only baits which remained in my swim at the end of the session were my hookbaits."* I do not doubt that it happens, but whether it need happen is another matter entirely. In my opinion, hookbait rejection - in situations where freebies are being eaten - is a consequence of defective presentation.

If I am correct, the remedy is obvious - it merely requires that a different rig be used. And providing the substitute is one which allows for greater subtlety, the problem will most likely be solved. What is unlikely to work, however, is a gimmicky "advanced" rig which makes the hookbait behave even less like a freebie than it did originally. What is worse is that some "advanced" setups are mechanically inefficient, and are cluttered with unstable elements which, notwithstanding drawings which show how the rig should sit on the bottom, are wholly unpredictable and are just as likely to settle in an ungainly heap.

I try to make my hookbait indistinguishable from free offerings.

Anti-Eject

We hear and read a lot about anti-eject rigs. These are based on the premise that the only way a carp can ascertain whether a bait is safe, is to pick it up; so if a rig can be rendered anti-eject it will not matter if it is "sussed". While I have no doubt that some rigs may be more difficult to eject than others, I do not believe there is any such animal as a truly effective anti-eject rig. Indeed, I go further and say that some of those which purport to embody anti-eject qualities are so crude that they will result in fewer pickups and a lower percentage of successful hookings. If you believe otherwise, there are plenty of published versions for which potent anti-eject qualities are claimed.

Rather than attempt to render my rigs anti-eject, I concentrate on trying to increase the likelihood of a pickup in the first place. If a carp takes my bait confidently, and nothing happens to alarm it, I have no need to worry about ejection.

The aforementioned objective is achieved with a comparatively limited repertoire of rigs. If I needed more, I would use them - but I have yet to be persuaded that such is the case.

Efficiency

An effective rig should embody the following qualities:

- **Most important of all, it must be safe. It should cause minimal damage to a carp's mouth, and in the event of a fish escaping due to line breakage, the lead should be readily capable of being discharged. It is also important to ensure that there is no risk of a casting snap-off or premature lead-release which might pose a risk to other anglers.**
- **The rig must provide for tangle-free casting - not some of the time, nor even most of the time, but virtually 100 per cent of the time.**

- **The bait should be presented in a manner that is compatible with the nature of the swim (silt, stones, debris, silkweed, rooted weed etc.).**
- **The rig must provide unimpeded access to the bait.**
- **A high proportion of pickups should result in a hooked fish.**
- **Hookholds must be secure.**
- **The rig's components must be sufficiently strong to ensure that, barring unforeseen disasters, every hooked carp is landed.**

It is a common sense list, and I doubt that many anglers would find fault with it - why, then, do they persist in using rigs which fail on one or more counts? Take tangling, for example. Often I have seen someone retrieve a snarled-up rig and comment, "That probably happened on the way in." Possible, of course - but unlikely. When a rig comes in looking like a pot-scourer, chances are it lay that way on the bottom, too. But why take the risk? Why use tangle-prone rigs when there are alternatives which behave impeccably?

Then there are hookpulls. We all have occasional fish come adrift, but if it occurs on a regular basis (exceptional circumstances apart) it suggests that there is something fundamentally wrong with our rig. To persist with it would be foolish. But anglers do, and they rationalise their difficulties with such comments as, "They're not taking the bait properly," or, "They've got really riggy and are only being lightly hooked."

There are two categories of rigs - those which are efficient, and those which are inefficient. Most cases of refusal, rejection, ejection and hookpulls are a consequence of using something from the second category.

Enough of generalities; now to details.

The Delicate Touch

Whenever possible, I use a lead of 1.5oz or less. Only casting distance, adverse wind conditions, drifting weed or rig-dislodging line bites will persuade me to go heavier. A light lead lands with less disturbance, allows greater subtlety of bait presentation, places less stress on a hookhold, and can result in better bite indication.

I shall repeat that last bit, "and can result in better bite indication."

This runs contrary to received wisdom which holds that a heavy lead is necessary in order to produce an effective prick-and-run shock effect. Observation on the waters I fish suggests that the majority of anglers favour 3oz or more. Do not misunderstand me; I am not suggesting that they are wrong because there are many

My choice of leads: Gardner Stealth Bomb, Korda 'Distance' inline, Nash Wisp inline, de-swivelled pears.

occasions when the use of a heavy lead in conjunction with a harp-string tight line, and with an indicator loaded to maximum, will produce a lot of carp. I have caught plenty by such means myself. But not all fish which pull the hooklink tight to the lead will run. Some - and what proportion this represents we can only guess - will pull tight, have their suspicions aroused, and will eject. And this, I believe, is where the use of a light lead can be an advantage, because it can result in hittable registrations which would otherwise pass undetected.

Let me give an example.

One of my favourite pits has a stretch of almost unfishable bank which can only be accessed from an awkward, swampy swim. On the day in question I adopted my usual policy when fishing this particular spot of angling my rods steeply upwards to keep my lines clear of the wide reed margin. Late afternoon, while I was engrossed in watching a dragonfly nymph crawl up an emerging stem, one of the Delkims gave a brief "bleep". I glanced at my indicators, but neither had moved. An investigative twitch from a skimmer, perhaps? I then looked at the rod tips and noticed that they were not quite in alignment, one had been pulled ever so slightly downwards; so in one movement I picked up the rod, cupped the spool with my reel-hand, and struck. The "skimmer" proved to be a big, two-toned leather!

A question which arises from the capture is, why did the fish not run? I cannot answer that. Nor have I any way of knowing if it would have run had I been using a heavier lead than the 1.5 ounces with which my rig was equipped. It might have done; but then again, it might not, and perhaps I would not have seen the take at all?

Then there are those takes where the indicator lifts, perhaps almost to its full extent, but no line is taken from even a loose set Baitrunner. When this happens I pause for a moment to give the indicator a chance to fall back in case a line bite is responsible; if it does not do so, I use the previously described spool-cupping, quick strike technique. I have caught a lot of carp this way. But as before, unanswerable questions arise; do these lift-and-stop takes occur as a consequence of my using light leads? Were I to use heavy leads would they manifest as full blooded runs, or would they fail to register at all? In the absence of definitive answers to such questions I am compelled to rely on belief - and I believe that my use of light leads has resulted in my detecting takes, and consequently catching carp, which would otherwise have ejected the bait and left me none the wiser.

My reason for making that assumption is that a lead of 1.5oz or less is more readily dislodged than is, say, a 3oz version. And if the lead becomes dislodged, even if only slightly, a sufficiently sensitive indicator/alarm system should respond.

"But," you might be thinking, "if the carp is pricked, it won't be able to eject the bait." At this initial stage, with a cautious carp moving slowly, I doubt that the hookpoint does more than nick ever so lightly. If the fish fails to move off, and manipulates the bait and hook in its mouth, I am convinced that it is readily capable of ejection.

All this talk of tiny bites may give the impression that I am forever hovering over my rods in anticipation of the slightest movement. Not so. Winter apart, mini pulls are not a frequently encountered feature of my fishing, and most of the takes I get on my "delicate touch" tactics are lovely one-note fliers!

Which demonstrates that the prick-and-run sequence does not depend on the use of a heavy lead. Once the carp starts towing the rig - no matter how light the lead - it becomes scared, causing it to accelerate. At which point ejection becomes difficult if not impossible - a situation which is compounded when the Baitrunner comes into play. In any event, I am convinced that I get no fewer runs as a result of using light leads. Which, combined with a higher incidence of recorded mini takes, persuades me that taken overall, light leads are the best choice.

Semi-Fixed Pendant

I once wrote something to the effect that if Kevin Nash ever decided to withdraw his Safety Bolt Bead, I would buy all his remaining stock. I rated them that highly. I still do.

The Safety Bolt Bead was designed, as the name suggests, with carp safety in mind. If used correctly it will allow a snagged lead to discharge, thus reducing the risk of a fish becoming tethered. But its virtues do not end there. When used in conjunction with anti-tangle tube it creates one of the most tangle-free rigs yet devised. No matter whether it is equipped with 3oz (its maximum safe loading) and cast to the far distance, or just 1oz and flicked out with a gentle underarm lob, it behaves impeccably.

In common with other pendant assemblies, it is not particularly well suited to weed, nor when used in conjunction with a heavy(ish) lead in soft silt. But those

Fig.40 FLAME USED TO CHAMFER ENDS OF TUBE

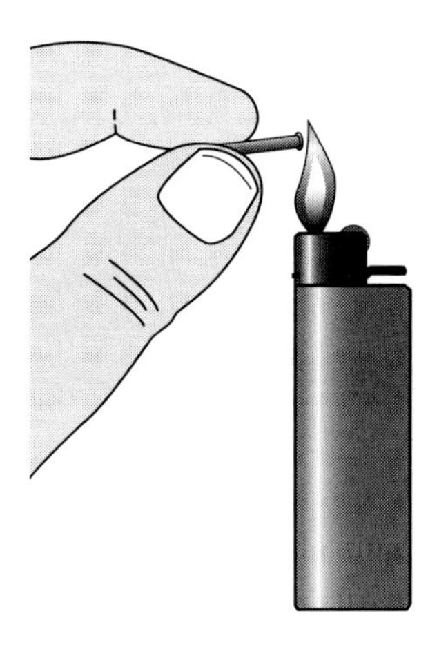

circumstances apart, it is an excellent go anywhere, general purpose rig.

It is my favourite setup for hard bottomed pits because no matter how high and long the cast, or how shallow the water, the lead always hits bottom first, thereby eliminating the risk of the hooklink or main line sustaining impact damage on stones, flints or mussels.

My margin to medium range version of this rig is the same as recommended for long range fishing, except that I incorporate a small backweight. This comprises a 2cm length of 0.5mm hard tubing, around which I roll a small piece of tungsten putty. To ensure the plastic tube is line friendly, I chamfer its edges with a flame (Fig 40). The backweight is kept in place by means of a large rubber float stop (Fig 41). In conjunction with a slack or droopy line, it ensures the anti-tangle tube is held flat to the bottom.

My hooklinks are equipped with a size 10 Berkley Swivel, the upper eye of which is pulled into the barrel of the Safety Bolt Bead. This grips the swivel sufficiently tight to provide a fixed lead when a carp picks up the bait, but it will release readily should the need arise - indeed, nine times out of ten I find that the whole assembly is free sliding when I land a fish.

Fig.41 MINI BACKWEIGHT

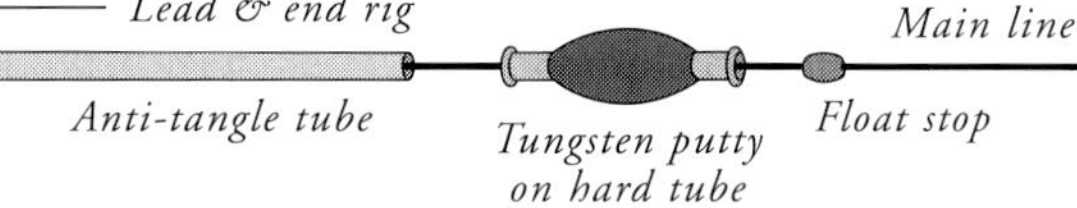

Inline

Some years ago Zipp produced an elongated, slightly front-heavy inline lead. It was an excellent shape, but fell short of perfection due to variable quality finish. Korda addressed the issue, and developed a more refined, but otherwise almost identical model, which they call their "Distance Inline". This is a rather unfortunate designation because its tendency to wobble in flight has an adverse effect on both range and accuracy! Nor is it suitable for use in hard, stony bottomed gravel pits - especially if the water is shallow - due to the risk of the hooklink or main line sustaining impact damage. But for mature pits, where the bottom is usually covered in a thin layer of detritus, or where the water is over about 10ft deep, it is ideal.

Its slender shape and smoothly tapered ends make it perfect for fishing in weed. I have caught a great many carp from really dense jungles of the stuff, and cannot

Fig.42 INLINE LEAD ASSEMBLY SHOWING THICK WALLED SILICONE SWIVEL GRIPPER

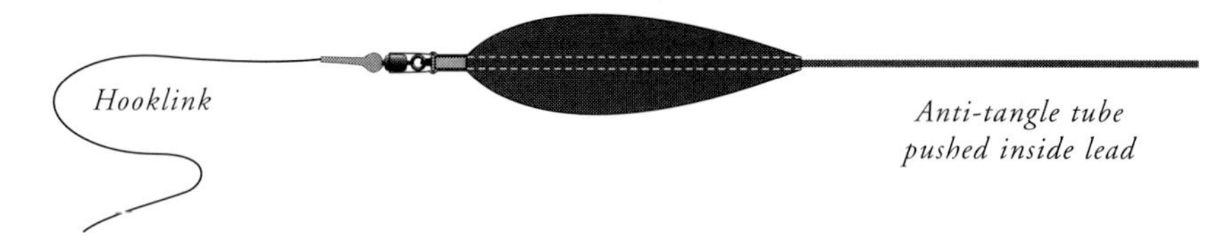

recall a single occasion when the lead has been responsible for a hang-up.

As explained in the section on long range rigs, it is ideal for fishing over silt due to its reduced tendency to become embedded.

It is my usual choice for margin fishing, too.

My inlines are prepared by first Supergluing the hard plastic through-tube in place. A centimetre is left protruding from the lead's thicker end, and this is given a chamfered lip by lightly touching it with a flame. A 2cm length of thick-walled silicone tube is slid over the protrusion - this will grip the upper eye and barrel of the size 10 hooklink swivel (Fig 42). On no account should neoprene or thin-walled silicone be used because they stretch under load and clasp the swivel too tightly, which adversely affects the lead's ability to discharge. The tube protruding from the lead's thinner end is cut off; after which the upper shoulder is examined for any roughness or moulding irregularities. Korda leads, and indeed those from most other manufacturers, are of very high quality, but the odd one needs a light touch-up with fine Carborundum paper (I am talking here of uncoated leads). A smooth shoulder is essential to minimise the risk of tangles.

The end of a 50cm length of 1mm Nash No Spook is poked inside the lead. It is held in place by means of a large rubber float stop (or two if I am casting more than 30 yards or so). A mini backweight is sandwiched between the float stop(s) and the end of the anti-tangle tube. In addition to using this setup in its standard form, it is the rig I favour for Method fishing. A hard stony bottom - even where the water is shallow - presents no hazards in this circumstance because the groundbait ball slows the rate of descent.

Before moving on, I must make the point that the inline assembly I have just described is not suitable for use in conjunction with a leader because the float stop(s) and backweight will jam against the junction knot and prevent the lead discharging.

I have been unable to obtain elongated inlines lighter than 1.5oz, although both Korda and Kevin Nash produce a slightly stubbier 1.1oz version. Neither, in my opinion, are quite as good as the "Distance" shape, but both are satisfactory.

Anti-Tangle Tube

Some anglers worry that anti-tangle tube will scare carp. I think it might do so if it rises steeply from the bottom, or nods up and down due to waves plucking the line, or is a conspicuous colour, or has a shiny, reflective surface. But providing it lays flat on the bottom, and is an unobtrusive, natural colour, I am convinced it has no detrimental effect. In any event, this is a situation where we need to balance disadvantages against advantages; and I believe the theoretical debits of anti-tangle tube are far outweighed by its proven benefits.

With one exception - when using a running rig.

Running

Occasionally, as previously mentioned, I get lift-and-stop takes instead of full-blooded runs. When it happens, I cup the spool with my free hand and strike. Most are successfully hooked, so I do not regard them as a problem. But, summer before last, on one particular coastal pit, most of the takes I received were of this sort. I do not recall missing any, but I thought it would make life simpler if the carp could be persuaded to run, so I adopted the tactic I normally reserve for winter, and replaced my semi-fixed setups with running rigs. This change led to an immediate cessation of lift-and-stop takes; and conventional runs ensued. They were not fliers, indeed most were slow trundlers, but they were all nice, easy to hit runs.

Why a running rig should amplify indications I do not know; especially when, most of the time, I doubt that it functions as a proper running setup anyway. In the instance just mentioned I was casting about 60 yards with a 2.5oz lead; and I am convinced the lead shifted when a carp tightened the hooklink. The pit had a hard gravel bottom, which made it even more likely that the lead was dislodged. My droopy line and ultralight indicator may have allowed the rig to perform as semi-running initially, but as soon as the Baitrunner came into play the lead would simply have been pulled along the bottom.

If the mechanical efficiency of a running setup is questionable at the best of times, I believe it to be compromised to the point of nonfunctionality if anti-tangle tube is incorporated. There is no way a running rig can operate if the line has to run through tubing, or if the lead slides on tubing. There is too much friction, especially if the take is in any direction other than directly away from the angler. I tried all sorts of combinations of wide bore beads, run-rings and swivels, and finally concluded that the only means by which the lead could be persuaded to slide - albeit partially, and only until the Baitrunner came into play - was to dispense with anti-tangle tube. Fortunately this was made tenable by Kryston's introduction of their coated multistrand product, Snake-Skin, and the braided version, Snake-Bite. More of which later.

Fig.43 STEALTH BOMB RUNNING RIG

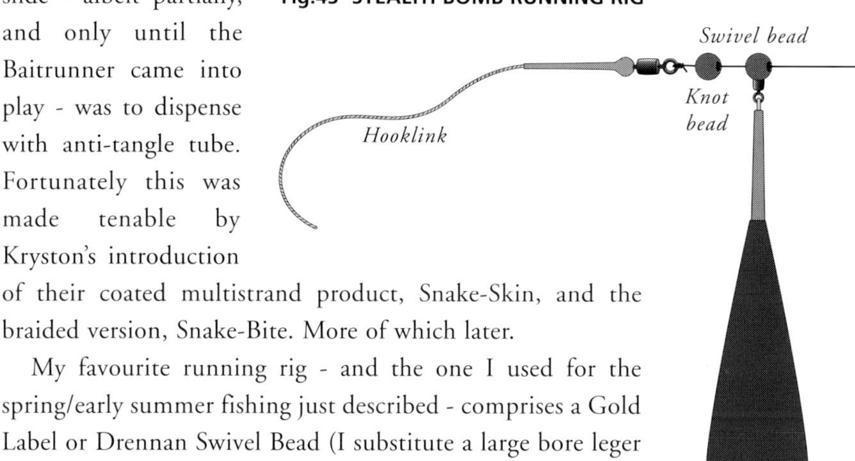

My favourite running rig - and the one I used for the spring/early summer fishing just described - comprises a Gold Label or Drennan Swivel Bead (I substitute a large bore leger bead if using a leader) to which is attached a Gardner quick-release Stealth Bomb or Long Tailed Carp Bomb (Fig 43). Not many anglers are aware of the existence of these excellent leads because few tackle shops stock them, and Richard Gardner does not even give them a mention in his catalogue! Which might explain why lack of demand has led to production of the Carp Bomb being discontinued, and the future of the Stealth Bomb put in doubt. I remain unfazed by this impending disaster because I took the precaution of acquiring a lifetime's supply while they were readily available!

A tip here; when casting with this or any other running rig, the line should be feathered just before the lead hits the water, and as it sinks. Alternatively the rod tip can be dipped beneath the surface to increase drag. This prevents the hooklink and lead separating which can, occasionally, result in the main line becoming wrapped around itself.

Snag Rig

Fig.44 LUG OF JOHN ROBERTS BEAD SLIT WITH KNIFE

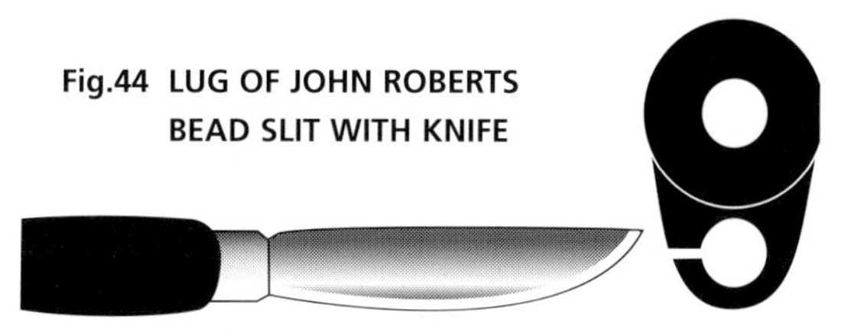

I use one other running assembly; but in this instance its running characteristic serves no real function, it is merely a by-product of the way the rig is assembled.

It employs a John Roberts Leger Bead, the lug of which I slit with a knife (Fig 44), thereby enabling a de-swivelled pendant lead to pull off easily if it becomes trapped.

Fig.45 SNAG RIG - BULLET BEAD VERSION

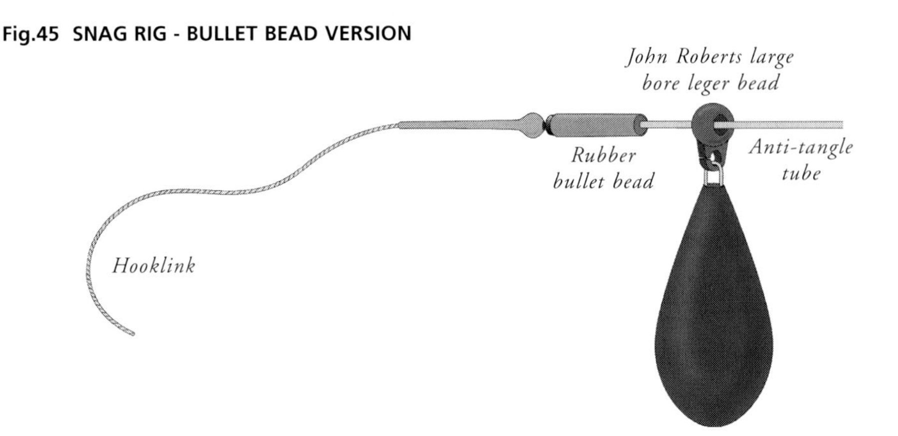

If it is being used with braid or mono, I incorporate anti-tangle tube, which is inserted in a Nash Bullet Bead (Fig 45). If, however, I am using Snake-Skin or Snake-Bite the anti-tangle tube may be omitted, and a Knot Bead substituted for the Bullet Bead.

This setup is particularly useful in new pits and quarries which, in addition to the usual stones, rocks etc. sometimes have bits of machinery, old lengths of rope or steel cable and other obstructions on their bed. Eventually these hazards become covered, or at least mitigated by weed and detritus; but early in a pit's development they can pose difficulties. A word of warning, though, this method of attaching a lead is only suitable for relatively light leads (say, up to 2oz), and for gentle casts - otherwise the lead might fly off with the risk that it will cause injury.

Hooklinks

I never cease to be surprised by the extent to which successful anglers can come to completely different conclusions. Take hooklink materials. Notwithstanding the various composite rigs which exist, the primary choice lies between braid, mono and proprietary combi-link products. I have used and caught a great many carp on all of them. Some are better suited to particular circumstances - but I honestly doubt that any one material is inherently superior to others. I say this despite having read plenty of references to improved results which have been attributed to a switch from one material to another. Trouble is, the "evidence" is contradictory. And when experts cannot agree, then likely there is no sound basis for agreement!

Come to that - even brothers cannot agree!

Were you to encounter me fishing, chances are I would be using braid. If not braid, then probably a Combi-Link product. If, on the other hand, you encountered brother Rick, there is every likelihood he would be using mono.

We both catch a lot of carp. Which does not in itself prove anything, but suggests - as I said earlier - that while there might be certain circumstances which favour a particular material, when viewed in the great scheme of things it probably makes little difference what we choose.

Braid

Most of my fishing is done in extremely weedy, and sometimes snaggy pits. In order to safely land big carp in such circumstances I require a hooklink of about 20lb test. Were I to use mono it would correspond to a stiff rig - and notwithstanding the success which Mike Kavanagh (its originator), the remarkable Terry Hearn and many others have achieved, it is not a concept with which I can readily come to terms. Somehow it seems alien to the underlying principles of my "delicate touch" approach. HPPE braid, by contrast, combines tremendous strength with great suppleness - so it enables me to handle big fish in demanding situations, yet still achieve the subtle presentation I seek.

Having developed confidence in heavy duty braid while fishing weedy pits, it not surprisingly remained my primary choice when I fished waters of a more benign nature.

Had most of my fishing been done in waters where I considered 10-12lb hooklinks adequate, things might have evolved differently.

Initially I assumed that most HPPE braids were virtually identical products marketed under different brand names. To my surprise I found that this was not so, and there are significant physical variations between brands. The main difference is in the diameter and number of HPPE strands incorporated in the braid, but also in the way they are woven.

All incorporate multi-filament cores, but whereas some cores are loosely woven - resulting in a very soft feel to the braid - others are tight. Generally, the tighter the weave, the thinner the diameter. Braids also vary as regards the number of cores they contain - ranging from two to four. Herewith a summary:

Merlin and Tricklink comprise a two-core twist of white multi-stranded HPPE, braided with a darker material.

Silkworm and Carpsilk are made with a three-core braid of multi-stranded HPPE with a darker material woven in.

Super-Silk consists of three-core multi-stranded HPPE, braided to give a semi-

Fig.46 DIAGRAMATIC REPRESENTATION OF CONCERTINA LINK ASSEMBLY

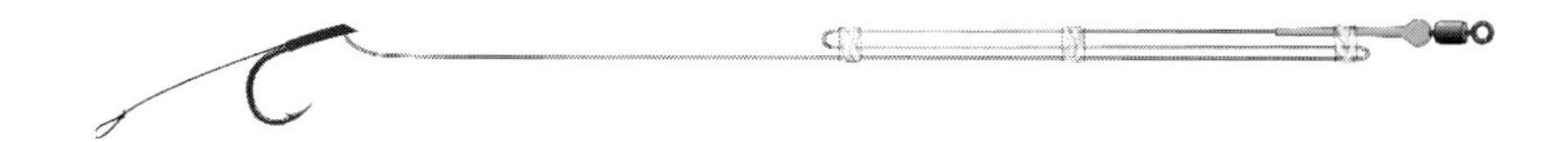

flat cross-section. The Edge appears identical with the addition of a darker material woven in.

Super Nova is very difficult to tease out, but when separated reveals a four-core multi-stranded HPPE twist with a darker material woven in.

The terms "twist" and "braid" are not used merely to avoid syntactical repetition, incidentally, but to indicate the different means by which the multi-stranded material is woven.

I do not know what the "darker material" referred to comprises, but it does not have the strength of HPPE, so makes little difference to the braid's breaking strain; my guess is that it is incorporated solely to increase specific gravity, and possibly to add colour. In relation to specific gravity - only Merlin and Tricklink, of the products I tested, lay flat on the bottom of their own accord. To ensure others do so, I weight them with two or three tiny "mouse droppings" of mouldable tungsten.

I realise many anglers catch plenty of fish on semi-buoyant unweighted braid - my brother, Martin, for one; Tim Paisley for another - but it is a confidence thing, so I shall continue to weight mine down.

My braid hooklinks are usually 45cm in length, and almost always used Concertina style.

Most anglers will be familiar with the Concertina Link, but for those who are not I should explain that it is an extending hooklink, but one which differs from most in that it incorporates no sliding elements in its construction.

To create a Concertina Link, the braid is gelled with Kryston Superstiff then, while the gel is still tacky, the upper part of the link is folded back on itself to form a long "Z". It is then hung on an umbrella spoke to dry (in hot, sunny weather this only takes a few minutes), after which the "concertina" portion is bound top, bottom and middle with Nash PVA tape (Fig 46).

If I want to use a Concertina Link without anti-tangle tube, I incorporate a 12cm length of 12-15lb mono (a sinking version like Trilene XT is best). If this is poked in the silicone sleeve with which the lower eye of the junction swivel is encased (Fig 47), and then incorporated within the "Z" and its PVA bindings, the link's stiffness is increased considerably. This Twin Strand Concertina Link, as I call

Fig.47 TWIN STRAND CONCERTINA LINK

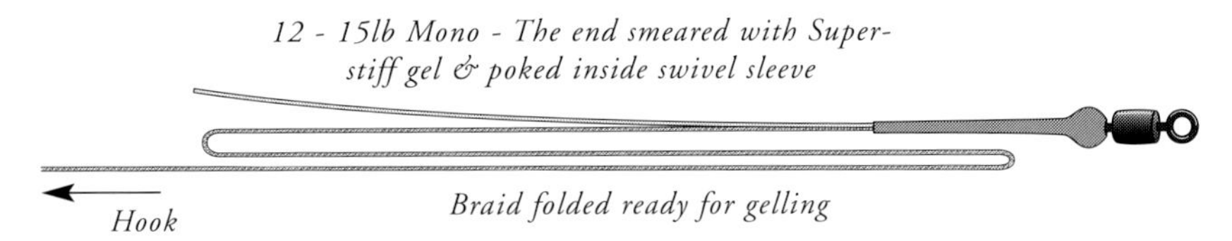

The folds of braid & the strand of mono are gelled, then bound together with PVA tape as per standard concertina link

it, is based on one of Gary Bayes's rigs, whereby a braid hooklink is secured to mono with short lengths of fine bore silicone tubing.

The Concertina Link forms what is generally termed a "confidence rig". When the PVA and gel have dissolved, the folded link allows approximately 30cm of totally unhindered, resistance free movement. It functions, in effect, like a running rig used in conjunction with a backstop - but does so far more efficiently and with much less resistance.

In addition to its extending and anti-tangle qualities, it offers a couple of other advantages; first, due to its compactness it is ideal for casting to holes in the weed, or for flicking under trees. And second, it combines the presentation advantages of a long link with the aerodynamics of a short one, thereby making it an excellent long range setup.

Disadvantages? Well, it is not particularly user friendly in that it has to be re-gelled and re-PVA'd after every cast. This is no real hassle in normal wait-for-a-run situations, but is an unmitigated pain in waters where bream and tench are a nuisance - indeed, they can render its use untenable.

Another minus is that it does not permit second casts. If the first attempt does not land accurately, it cannot be retrieved and recast before it de-gells and un-PVA's!

I did not invent the Concertina Link, incidentally, although I can fairly claim to have devised its current form. I christened it too! Dave Chilton discovered it by accident when he inadvertently spilled some Superstiff on some braid which lay on his workbench. It dried overnight and caused the braid to stick to itself. He mentioned it to Ken Townley who, in a review for Superstiff, suggested it as a possible use for the product. I was not persuaded of the practicality of the method described by Ken, but recognised that with a bit of refinement it had obvious potential. So I modified it, tried it, modified it some more, and came up with the version described here.

My braid links for those occasions when I decide not to use the Concertina Link are slightly shorter at 35cm.

Most HPPE braids are fairly conspicuous, so I use permanent spirit markers to stain them brown for use on sand and gravel, or green when fishing in weed. If I require a ubiquitous go-anywhere colour I use both together - this produces a sort of olive-khaki. All my links - other than those intended for use with a Method setup - have a 3cm sleeve of 1mm silicone which encases the lower eye of the swivel, also the knot and the upper part of the hooklink (as shown in Fig 47). In addition to being an anti-tangle measure, this sleeve is colour coded so I can tell at a glance the breaking strain of my link. I use green for 10-12lb, brown for 15lb, and black for 20-25lb.

Fig.48 PROTECTING COATING WHEN HOT-DIPPING SNAKE-BITE & SNAKE-SKIN

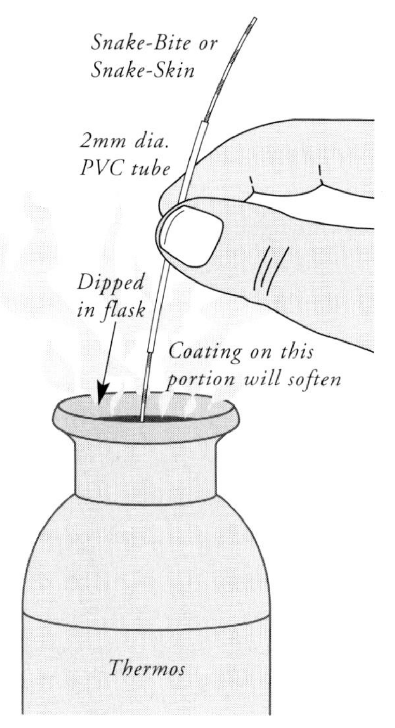

Combi-Links

Snake-Skin and Snake-Bite have sufficient inherent stiffness to enable their use without anti-tangle tube. I employ Harry Haskell's original combi-link principle which involves having a flexible portion adjacent to the hook. This is achieved by removing a short section of coating. The best means of doing this is to dip the length to be stripped in very hot water for a few seconds (I use a small vacuum flask to keep the temperature sufficiently high), after which it can be peeled off with a finger nail.

To construct my combi-links I cut a 48cm length of Snake-Skin or Snake-Bite and strip 10cm of coating from one end. To protect the coating beyond the 10cm portion from steam, I poke the material through a short length of 2mm PVC tube (Fig 48).

The hook is tied on with a Knotless Knot (Fig 49). To attach the swivel I use a twice-through-the-eye 5-turn Clinch (Fig 50). If these dimensions and knots are adopted, the completed link will be 35cm in length, with approximately 5cm of exposed core adjacent to the hook.

Snake-Skin is the more difficult of the two products to use. It is essential that the floss strands are kept under even tension when tying on the hook - this is best

Fig.49 KNOTLESS KNOT

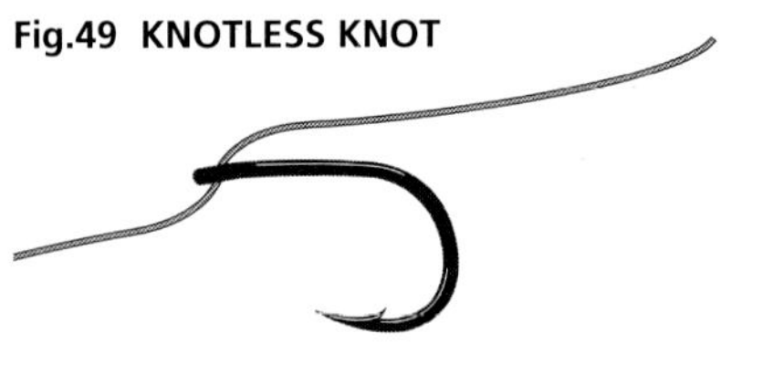

1. Pass hooklink through eye of hook.

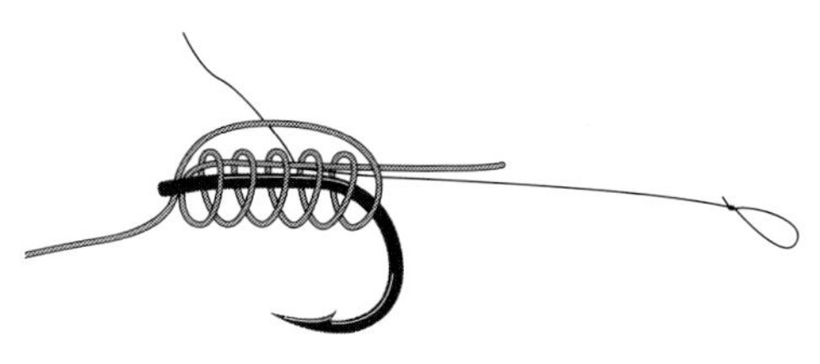

2. Wrap hooklink 10 times around shank (only 6 turns shown here for clarity) then pass it through hook eye. Secure hair beneath rear 3 turns.

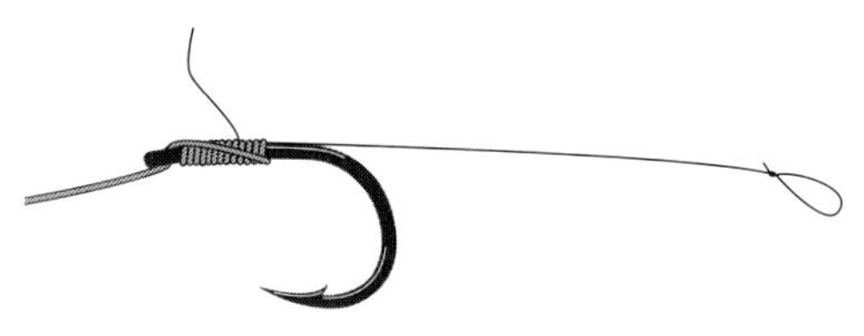

3. Pull tight, trim off tag end, tag end of hair trimmed off, (or better, use it to tie a whipping knot), Secure with superglue or Bondage.

achieved either by wetting the strands, or by temporarily bonding them together with Superstiff gel. Failure to do this will result in individual fibres being placed under excess load, which may cause them to break. The plasticised coating is rather easily damaged too, so great care must be taken when the swivel is attached.

If the stripped portion is gelled prior to casting, it eliminates the risk of it becoming wrapped around the main line in flight. In truth, Snake-Skin is not a user friendly material, but it is worth the effort and inconvenience because it enables extremely subtle presentation.

Snake-Bite is much tougher, so its coating is less easily damaged when knotted. The core is not HPPE, but is a Quicksilver-like material (I suspect it is Dyneema), so it offers high resistance to abrasion and shear. This makes it an obvious choice for fishing in the vicinity of bars, ridges, sharp stones or mussels.

Initially I used Snake-Bite with my standard 5cm

Fig.50 TWICE THROUGH THE EYE 5-TURN CLINCH KNOT (ALSO SUITABLE FOR BRAID & MONO).

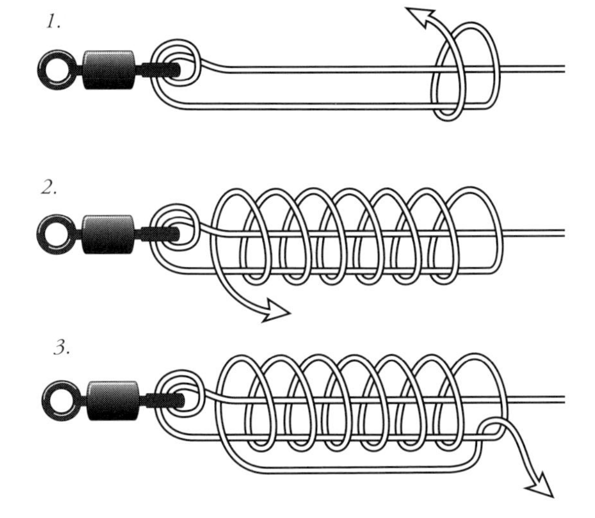

Fig.51 SNAKE-BITE CONCERTINA LINK WITH INTEGRAL STIFFENER

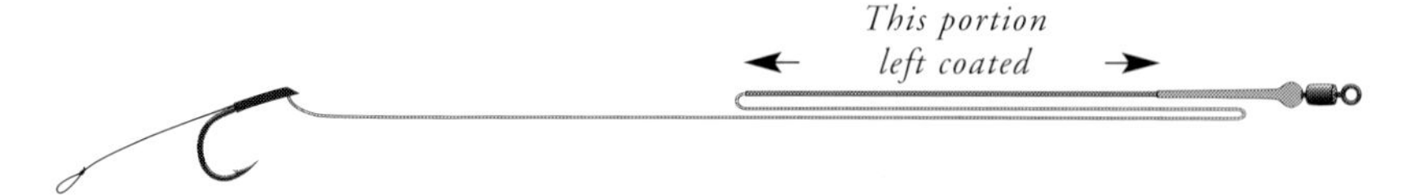

of core exposed, but I subsequently experimented with as much as two-thirds exposed and found it resisted tangles most effectively - even without the aid of gel or anti-tangle tube.

If only one-quarter of the plasticised coating is left intact, it forms an effective stiffener when incorporated in a Concertina Link (Fig 51); this works on the same principle as the Twin Strand version described earlier.

Rick experimented in the other direction, and stripped just sufficient to create a tiny hinge adjacent to the hook - thereby creating, in effect, a hinged stiff rig. It proved very successful.

Reverting to Snake-Skin, for a moment. It is unsuitable for use in waters where small fish continually peck at the bait, or where crayfish are a problem - they cause the stripped floss section to ball-up and tangle.

Mono

Prior to Dave Chilton's introduction of HPPE, the choice lay between mono and dacron. Dacron was extremely popular, but I felt that any advantage afforded by its suppleness was greatly outweighed by its poor abrasion and shear resistance. So I continued to use mono. Nowadays, however, I rarely use mono other than when I need to present baits on a mattress-like bed of bottom weed - as described in Chapter Six - or when I am compelled by club rules to use barbless hooks.

On which subject... A few years ago - in an endeavour to reduce the problem of hookpulls when fishing barbless - I devised a special shock absorbing hooklink based on Kevin Maddocks's Power Gum Rig. It worked well, but it was a somewhat complicated setup to tie and, to be truthful, was a bit cluttered with ancillary items for my taste, so I abandoned it in favour of a 45cm hooklink made from a stretchy brand of mono such as Maxima. This stretches sufficiently to absorb sudden lunges, and contracts a little when load is decreased, thereby maintaining pressure on the hook. In conjunction with stretchy mono main line, and a light lead, it works quite well. Leastways, it does in open water. In weed, or when used with a heavy lead, it does not. When compelled to use barbless hooks in weedy water I accept with as much equanimity as I can muster that a high proportion of fish will be lost.

Length

You will notice that my links are longer than usually recommended. There is a school of thought which holds that short links (sometimes as short as 10cm) reduce the risk of ejection by causing the hook to prick the carp's lip immediately the bait is picked up. Most of us, no doubt, have seen drawings illustrating how a carp, on righting itself after picking up a bait, draws the short hooklink tight when, wham! (yes, the caption to one such drawing actually included the word "wham"!) the hook is pulled into the fish's lip. The flaw in this otherwise immaculate argument is that carp do not right themselves after picking up a bait - if they did, the poor things would get dizzy as they bobbed their heads up and down like rear window nodding dogs! When carp feed they adopt a posture somewhere between 30 degrees and vertical, and maintain it until they finish foraging.

Ultra short links can be effective - I have caught carp on straight-off-the-lead breadcrust on links as short as 5cm, and on particles used in conjunction with 10cm links. But notwithstanding such experiences, I prefer a long link because I think it enables the bait to behave in a similar manner to free offerings, and also provides no impediment to a cautious carp which tentatively sucks and blows the bait before taking it properly.

Hooks

Was there really a time when, in order to obtain hooks suitable for carp, some of us resorted to cutting and solder-blobbing long shank salmon hooks? Such a situation hardly seems credible now, when we have a vast choice of excellent patterns from which to choose. As an aside, I think we have Owner spade-ends to thank for this renaissance because many current patterns exhibit what looks like a strong Owner influence - or perhaps it is merely a case of convergent evolution..?

Most of my fishing, as previously stated, is in heavily weeded pits. Hooks for weed fishing must be strong. My current choice is Nash Fang size 6, Owner spade-end size 10 (which corresponds to a conventional size 6) and Fox Series Three or Gardner Talon Tip in size 8. Where weed is patchy I like Fox Series Two size 6, Owner spade-end size 9 and 8 (7 and 8 equivalent), and again Gardner Talon Tip size 8.

From my frequent references to the Owner spade-end you will correctly conclude that it is a pattern I hold in very high regard - indeed, ten years on from when Dave Merrett and Peter Springate first recommended it to me, it remains my favourite all-purpose, all-water hook.

Where a "barbless" rule applies I will, if permitted, use Nash Pattern One. Although not a true barbless hook, its barb is so minuscule that it comes within a micro-notch of being so; its use is therefore sanctioned in some "barbless" fisheries. If the "barbless" rule is strictly applied, my choice is, yet again, Owner spade-end, but in the barbless version. It looks very similar to its barbed counterpart, but it has a silver rather than a black finish - I think it might be a tad thicker in the wire, too.

Modern hooks, in my opinion, are sharp enough to be used straight from the pack. Kevin Nash and Gary Bayes disagree, and touch up their hookpoints to get them even sharper. Kevin takes this to its limit and has a jeweller sharpen his hooks, thereby producing a point so keen that it is almost impossible to tie rigs without the hook catching in his skin - which prompted a friend to describe them as "sticky hooks"!

Kevin and Gary eliminate the risk of oxidation by lightly coating the exposed bare metal with Vaseline or line grease.

When I think a hookpoint might benefit from a light touch-up I use a sapphire nailfile, or better still, an electronics engineer's microfine contact cleaner (another of Dave Merrett's recommendations). I never try to sharpen a hook to ultra sharpness, though, because I think an excessively fine point turns over too readily.

Some writers recommend changing the hook after each capture. But why? I examine the hookpoint to see if it has dulled or turned over; if it looks and feels okay, I use it again. If I decide it is unsatisfactory, I replace it.

Size

You will recall how, at the beginning of this chapter, I said that hookbait rejection, in situations where freebies are being eaten, is due to poor presentation. Some of the setups illustrated in "advanced rig" articles are so crude that, far from being surprised that hookbait rejection happens, I am astonished that any pickups occur at all. Ever! The most common fault - in addition to cluttering up the rig with ancillary jumble - is using so large a hook that it overwhelms the bait.

Carp often live in weedy or snaggy waters where they have to be played hard. Even in open water they are best played firmly because protracted fights can lead to hooks working loose. We cannot, therefore, use ultra small, fine wire hooks. Which is unfortunate, because I have absolutely no doubt that they would result in many more pickups. So we have to strike a balance. We want a hook which is strong enough to safely land big fish, but sufficiently light to enable subtle presentation. The most effective compromise, I feel, is to use a relatively heavy wire hook, but in as small a size as is practical. Herewith my rule of thumb guide:

Size 6: single 20mm boilie, single 18mm boilie, double 15mm boilies, double 10mm cubes.

Size 8: single and double 15mm boilies, double/treble 10mm minis, double 10mm cubes, particles, naturals.

Attachment

To attach my hooks - other than spade-ends - I use the Knotless Knot; over which I sleeve a Line Aligner (Fig 52). The primary function of the aligner is to cause the hook to revolve on its axis and penetrate the tough tissue of the lower lip. In addition to providing a secure hookhold, this minimises the risk of mouth damage.

Whenever possible I use 1.6mm heat shrink - the 2.6mm version is saved for large-eyed hooks and heavy braid. My preference is for relatively thick-walled heat shrink which is obtainable from electronics spares shops like Maplins.

I use steam from the spout of a boiling kettle to shrink my aligners - but take care, steam is potentially dangerous and can cause serious scalds.

Many anglers have stated that the Knotless Knot obviates the need for an aligner. This is only true to a degree because its ability to cause the hook to revolve on its axis depends on the configuration of the hook's shank and eye. Hooks with a curved "shrimp-back" shank, combined with a down-turned eye - like the Fang - function extremely effectively with the Knotless Knot. Straight shank, straight eye patterns work best with an aligner.

Fig52 LINE ALIGNER FORMATION

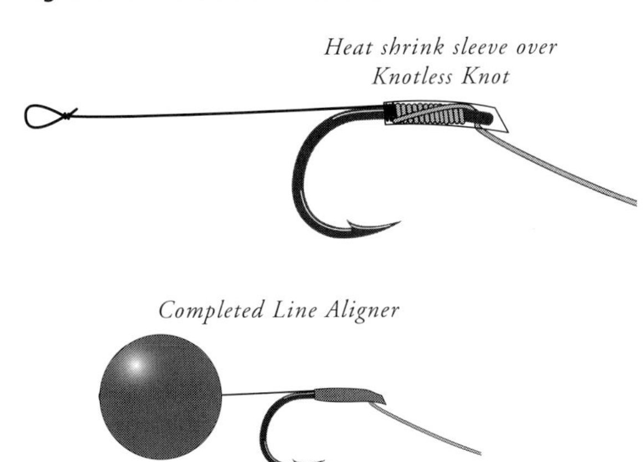

Mono works equally successfully in conjunction with a Line Aligner or the Knotless Knot, almost irrespective of the hook pattern. On initial examination this does not make sense because mono's stiffness prevents effective rotation. So how does it function? I cannot be sure, but I suspect the aggressive posture adopted

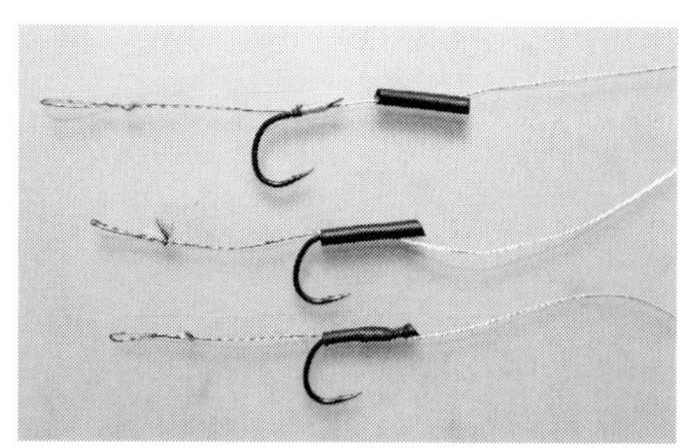

Line Aligner construction sequence.

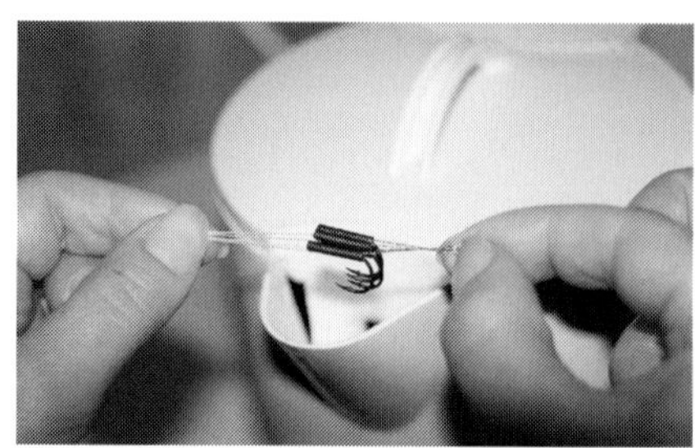

I use steam to contract my heat-shrink aligners (N.B. Steam can cause serious scalds).

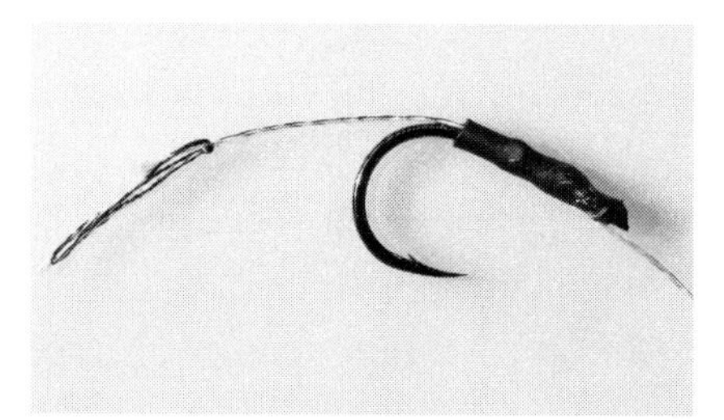

Line Aligner close up.

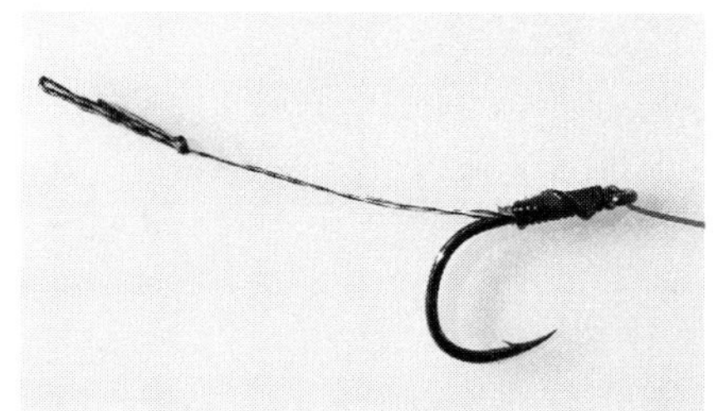

Knotless Knot with mono link and braid hair.

by the hook (an inevitable consequence of the angle of the emerging mono) is extremely efficient at finding purchase in a carp's mouth. A disadvantage is that hookholds are likely to occur anywhere, which might result in their being slightly less secure. Of more concern is the possibility that hookholds achieved in the thin tissue at the side of the mouth heighten the likelihood of damage which can lead to ulceration, and eventually to ugly "parrot mouth" deformity.

Secure bottom lip hookhold demonstrates that the rig worked as intended.

Hairs

Observation suggests that most anglers utilise the hooklink tag-end for their hair. I doubt that this is the best means of enabling a hookbait to behave like a free offering, so prefer to use a fine hair - as per the original Middleton/Maddocks concept. In conjunction with size 6 hooks I use 4lb breaking strain

Fig.53 SECURING THE HAIR

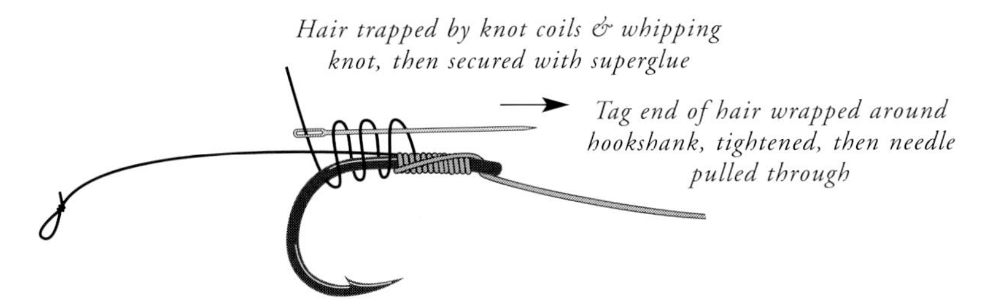

Silkworm or proprietary hair braid. For size 8 hooks I prefer Drima polyester sewing thread, which breaks at about 2lb.

I use the wraps of the hook-knot to trap the hair (Fig 53), and ensure it is held secure by finishing with a Whipping Knot and a tiny dab of Superglue or Kryston Bondage.

From spring through to early autumn I have approximately 10mm separation between my bait and the bend of the hook. Late autumn, and throughout the winter I reduce this to 5mm. I said "approximately" because it depends on the size of the bait. Very small baits - 10mm minis, for example - do not look right with 10mm separation; something nearer 5mm looks better, so I adjust accordingly, even in summer.

When attached to an ultrafine hair, which is in turn connected to a small hook, and where appropriate to a supple hooklink, the bait behaves sufficiently like a free offering to reduce, and probably eliminate, the risk of it being singled out and rejected. This forms the basis of most of my fishing, especially from spring through to autumn when my hookbait will most likely be fished among quite a lot of freebies.

From spring through to autumn I like about 10mm separation between bait and hook.

Knots

The Knotless Knot for hook attachment, and the Clinch Knot for swivels, have already been illustrated. These serve my purposes admirably, and I am satisfied that when carefully tied, and secured with Superglue or Bondage, they retain 100% of the breaking strain of mono, braid and floss. The only other one I use is the Overturn Whipping Knot (Fig 54), which is by far the best knot for spade-end hooks.

Fig.54 OVERTURN WHIPPING KNOT FOR SPADE-END HOOKS

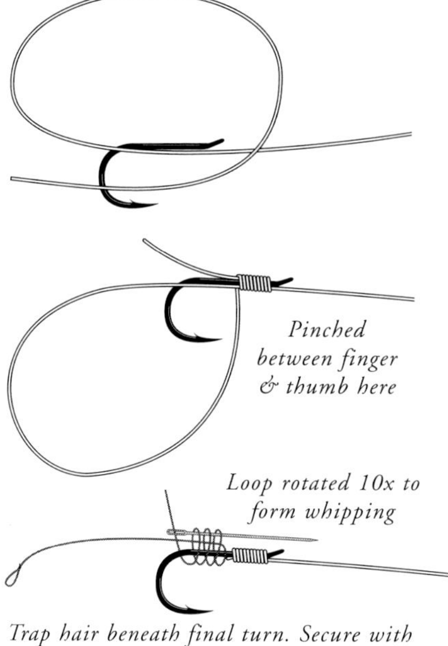

Trap hair beneath final turn. Secure with whipping knot using sewing needle. Finish with Superglue or Bondage

Never be in a hurry to tie a knot. Take it slowly, and lubricate it with either saliva or vegetable oil to eliminate the risk of friction-burn and to ensure that all the coils butt neatly together. If you use oil, wash the knot with warm, slightly soapy water, rinse it and allow it to dry thoroughly before applying glue.

Just occasionally you are likely to come across an author who says something like, "Those of us who have confidence in our knots do not need to resort to Superglue." They are missing the point. Superglue does not merely prevent the coils loosening - it eliminates strangulation. And strangulation is what can cause otherwise secure knots to fail.

That said, some knots - single and double Overhand Loop Knots for example - gain no benefit from being Superglued. I do not know why this is so.

In Conclusion

Many carp anglers equate complexity with sophistication. They are convinced that an elaborate new wonder-rig will revolutionise their fishing. I wish them luck in their quest - but I have to tell them that they are almost certainly destined for disappointment. Rigs do not catch carp. Anglers do.

One of my favourite setups - Concertina Link used in conjunction with 1.5oz inline, anti-tangle tube, PVA sheathed hook and four-bait stringer.

Chapter ten

Bait

For many carp anglers, the words "bait" and "boilie" are interchangeable. They use nothing else. Even those of us who do use alternatives rely on boilies most of the time.

The history of the boilie from its inception by Fred Wilton to its present form has been extensively documented so I shall not repeat it here.

Nor shall I discuss the HNV hypothesis, nutritional recognition, long and short term baits etc. because while debate on such issues is interesting, it is no substitute for empirical evidence.

Fact is, there are good baits, indifferent baits, and poor baits. Good baits will always be good baits - they start that way, and continue to be so. I suspect they are effective because they are stimulatory, highly palatable and pass readily through a carp's gut. In anthropomorphic terms we can say that carp "like to eat them". They might also embody certain physical characteristics - temperature tolerance, for example, which makes them slow to sour in warm water. And given the choice, I think carp favour a crunchy rather than a rubbery texture.

Home made

Commercial baits are so good that I see no point in giving a batch of DIY recipes. Nor do I think any useful purpose will be served by providing a conventional "how to make boilies" guide because most of us rely on factory made frozen readymades or have commercial readymixes rolled by one of the boilie-rolling firms which have sprung up in recent years. But home bait making still has a role to play because it enables the production of non standard shapes such as cylinders and cubes. I particularly like cubes due to their ability to hold position on a margin slope. Rick reckons their shape fools boilie-aware carp; I am not convinced of that one, but am happy to put it down as a "maybe".

There are a number of ways of making boilie cubes. My original method - which I first described in Big Water Carp - is the one I use when I want to produce baits which effectively withstand the ingress of water and so take a long while to soften.

- **A tennis ball size piece of boilie dough is rolled out to the required thickness. I find it helpful to use a couple of wooden guides - 10mm square strips being my usual choice. These enable production of nice, even thickness slabs which when diced produce 10mm cubes. A light dusting of dry mix will prevent the dough from sticking to the base board or the rolling pin.**
- **The rectangular slabs are placed in a freezer for 15-30 minutes to stiffen them sufficiently to enable them to be cut into cubes without their distorting or sticking to the knife.**
- **The cubes are boiled for about two minutes.**
- **Finally they are laid out to dry - then bagged in 500gm packs and frozen.**

Another method produces cubes which have a cooked skin top and bottom, but have cut surfaces on the four remaining sides, thereby enabling the taste and smell of the bait's ingredients, additives and attractors to leach out more readily.

- **Slabs are rolled out as before.**
- **The slabs are placed intact in boiling water and boiled for about four minutes.**
- **The slabs are laid out to cool and dry - then cut into cubes, bagged and frozen.**

The disadvantage of this method is that the cut surfaces allow the ingress of water as well as the egress of attractors. This results in the cubes softening rather more quickly than do those which have an all-over skin (they last about half as long, on average).

Home bait-making enables non-standard shapes to be produced.

A variation on the previous method is to individually wrap the slabs in clingfilm which is clipped shut with stationery staples. The advantage of this procedure is that additives which are put in the mix, stay in - nothing boils out.

The technique just described is similar to the boil-in-the-bag "bricking" process devised by Dave Preston. This involves making a brick-shaped lump of dough about 10cm long, 5cm wide and 5cm deep, which is wrapped in a pin-pricked poly-bag (freezer-bags are best) from which the air has been expelled.

Extended boiling times are required for boilie bricks because it takes a long while for the heat to reach their centre - 20 minutes is about right for the size of brick I have described - larger ones will require correspondingly longer.

When the bricks have cooled, they can be diced. The cubes differ from those made by the slab methods in that they have more cut surfaces so they are the quickest of all to soften. They are, however, ideal for the quick and easy mass production of large quantities of cubes for freebie baiting.

Boiled slabs are cubed prior to being frozen.

Attractors

The taste and detectability of a base mix can be improved by the inclusion of attractors such as powder and liquid flavours, essential oils, Sense Appeals and sweeteners.

There are other additives which, it is claimed, work directly on a carp's chemoreceptors to evoke an instinctive feeding response. Amino blends, predigested products and hydrolysed proteins fall into this category; but the most widely used is betaine (trimethylglycine) which is obtainable from bait dealers, or as Finnstim from animal feed suppliers. Whether or not these work as generally claimed is uncertain - Finnstim, for example, is used by trout/salmon pellet manufacturers to increase palatability; so whilst it may stimulate feeding, it does so indirectly.

Most alcohol-based flavours taste bitter to my palate. I have no way of knowing if they taste bitter to carp, but I prefer to play safe - so if I am using such a flavour, I add it to boilies after they have been made. 500g of boilies shaken in a poly-bag with a few millilitres of flavour will result in a thin coating being absorbed into the skin of each bait. It does not penetrate far - only to a depth of about 1mm - which enables it to perform its role as an attractor but without having an adverse effect on taste.

Nowadays, however, I rarely use alcohol-based flavours. I prefer oil palatants. Nashbait produce an excellent selection in their Supasense range; my personal favourites being Red Liver, Peach and Strawberry.

I like powdered natural extracts too - notably liver, shrimp and squid.

Until four or five years ago I had no great regard for essential oils, having had little success with them. Among those I tried were garlic, juniper berry and geranium. Garlic seemed to deter tench - which information was logged away in case I encountered a water where they were a nuisance - but other than that, I received little encouragement to persevere with essential oils. Then my French friends, Michel and Philippe Mahin, recommended asafoetida - especially for winter fishing. I tried it in an Essex pit where, to my mild surprise, it held its own against Peach and Strawberry Palatants.

No sooner had I acquired confidence in one essential oil, when along came another - Nashbait's Sting Oil. The name is somewhat misleading because it suggests a connection with the Sting mix, but such is not the case. Sting essential oil is actually a blend. I do not know what its exact constituents are, but whatever it comprises, it works particularly well in conjunction with birdfood. The original recipe was devised by Shaun Harrison - who also, incidentally, put Nashbait onto their startlingly successful Whisky additive. Shaun obviously has what is known in the perfume industry as a "good nose".

Intense sweetener is incorporated in most of my baits, even savoury ones. We may see an incongruity in a sweet fishmeal bait, but carp have no such hang up! The reasons usually given for incorporating sweetener are to "round off" the taste of the bait - whatever that might mean - and to counteract the bitterness of artificial flavours. I include sweetener to increase palatability and because I believe carp like it.

Any bait firm's catalogue will carry enough base and attractor combinations to last a lifetime - I shall not try to compete, but will list my personal favourites.

The additive levels are for use with four large eggs.

Amber Attractor
5ml Strawberry Oil Palatant
½tsp Fruit Powdered Palatant
1ml Intense Sweetener

Amber Attractor
5ml Peach Oil Palatant
½tsp Fruit Powdered Palatant
1ml Intense Sweetener

Amber Attractor
8 drops Sting Essential Oil
1ml Protaste

S-Mix
3ml Scopex No.1
5ml Red Liver Oil Palatant
1ml Intense Sweetener

Sting Fish
Success Pack (as per instructions supplied with product)

Five or six years ago I caught this fully-scaled Essex mirror. Virtually every other carp in the pit has since fallen to the same bait.

I would happily take any of those baits to any water and be confident of catching. Contrary to received wisdom on the subject, I do not think it is necessary to use something similar to everyone else. Most times, in fact, I have no idea what others are using because I "do my own thing". Sometimes I subsequently learn that I have used birdfood baits on waters which were, quote, "dominated by fishmeals", and vice versa.

Some anglers believe that particular bases are best suited to certain circumstances. Kevin Nash, for example, has expressed the opinion that baits containing fishmeal absorb odours so readily that they are best avoided when fishing over silt or among weed. Under such circumstances he recommends a bait with a birdfood base. While not doubting the accuracy of Kevin's observations on the waters he fishes, I have to say that in my experience base mixes can be chosen irrespective of weed or silt.

My choice of boilie depends more on whim than logic. I vacillate between Sting Fishmeal, Amber Attractor Birdfood, the S-Mix (essentially a fishmeal mix) and an own-recipe birdfood/fishmeal/cereal combination which, due to it being a bait developed with brothers Rick and Martin, is not for publication.

Until three or four years ago I drew a distinction between summer and winter baits. That distinction has now become somewhat blurred - but detailed discussion on the subject is best undertaken in the chapter on winter fishing.

Bait size

Size does matter...

As stated elsewhere, I am primarily a daytime angler. I reiterate that point here because I suspect it has a bearing on my preference for small baits. For a given weight of bait, the number of units will increase as the size of the bait decreases. That is obvious, but what might surprise

For my home bait-making I am geared up for mass production.

some readers is the extent to which this is so. I recently weighed out three different sizes of boilies into 100gm batches. I found that twenty-five 20mm boilies weighed 100gm, but the number increased to forty for 15mm baits, and an incredible one hundred and forty-four for 10mm minis! If the aforementioned 100gm clusters had been used to bait a swim, I believe that in daylight, in clear water, the massed minis would be the most stimulatory. At night, or when water is discoloured, sight probably becomes less important and I would expect fewer but larger baits to be equally effective.

Another factor to be taken into account is the carp's natural diet. If - as in an increasing number of southern pits - their diet comprises large food items such as crayfish, adult snails and possibly mussels, it seems reasonable to suppose that the transition to big boilies is easily made. But consider those waters where carp feed predominantly on insect larvae, or tiny hempseed size snails - a category into which most U.K. gravel pits fall. I doubt that a carp which had hitherto eaten nothing larger than small crustaceans would initially recognise 20mm boilies as food; but 10mm minis, which more closely resemble the size of food items to which it is accustomed, might prompt it to make the experiment. As it learns to eat baits which are a bit larger than its natural food, it may become more likely to accept the next stage up. So a fish which is weaned onto 10mm baits will learn to accept 15mm baits - and so on. I am sure this happens, but I believe the degree to which it happens varies from one carp to another, and depends on the extent to which individual fish retain reliance on natural food. I recall Duncan Kay telling me that when carp are stocked into a water they divide approximately into thirds; there is the third which get caught regularly, the third which get caught occasionally, and the third which get caught hardly at all. If we translate this into bait terms, it seems probable that carp which get caught only occasionally, or hardly ever, rarely extend their diet beyond natural food.

Notwithstanding my preference for small baits, I acknowledge that there are circumstances when their use is impractical, such as when freebie baiting at long range.

Then there are nuisance species to consider. I have encountered waters where bream, and occasionally tench, eels and crayfish have made the use of small baits untenable. In a couple of coastal pits I fish, shrimps can be a problem! Of them all, crayfish are the worst because they will demolish even large, rock hard baits. If you doubt me, ask those who fish Arena Essex - they will tell you about crayfish..!

Dried baits

Back in 1990, or thereabouts, I wrote about my experiences using air-dried baits for the Carpworld Yearbook. My interest in them at that time was due to their long-life properties which made them particularly suitable for overseas trips. I noticed too that, being hard, they offered some degree of immunity to nuisance fish.

Some anglers - and Rick is slowly coming to this view - believe that air-dried boilies are worth using not merely because of the aforementioned benefits but because they are, quite simply, better baits. While I have caught sufficient carp on dried baits to use them with confidence, I cannot honestly say that I have found them to be more effective than fresh ones. It is an interesting hypothesis, though, and clearly is worthy of serious consideration.

Air-drying is not the only means by which baits can be dehydrated. Rod Hutchinson recommends packing them in sugar, whereupon osmosis will do the rest. The sugar should be replaced when it shows signs of becoming damp. Rod uses this procedure for his overseas trips and reckons baits so treated will last for several weeks.

Salt works on the same principle, but I would be concerned about the taste of the baits being adversely affected.

Chilly fresh

From spring through to autumn I keep my baits fresh in an insulated cool-bag. They go in the bag while still frozen. I do not add a freezer-pack, but include one or two "bricks" of solidly frozen particles. As the day wears on the baits will slowly thaw, but they remain cool and fresh right through to evening.

Popups

Cork-ball or polystyrene inserts enable us to adjust the buoyancy of hookbaits to produce popups or neutral density sinkers. Alternatively - and this is the method I prefer - ordinary sinkers can be customised on the spot by the addition of buoyant foam.

I am not an habitual popup user. It is a tactic I reserve for those occasions when I am fishing over a thin layer of bottom weed, or when the bottom is covered with a lot of "twiggy" debris.

The snowman presentation (combination sinker and poly-ball/cork insert popup) is another matter, and I have caught countless carp on such baits.

Of microwaved, grilled and fried popups I have little experience. They obviously work, as is evidenced by the number of anglers who use them extremely successfully, but I have a bit of a mental block about them.

Boosters and dips

Many successful anglers double, or even treble the flavour level in their hookbaits.

Others recommend bait-soaks, or dips as they are alternatively known.

My experience with over-flavoured baits - whether incorporated within the bait or via a dip - has been disappointing, and I have been far more successful with hookbaits carrying flavours and other additives at or below recommended levels.

Particles

The first particle bait to achieve widespread use for carp was sweetcorn. But particle fishing has a much longer pedigree than most anglers realise. A contemporary of Izaak Walton wrote about the use of cooked beans for carp; and J. H. Keene, writing in "The Practical Fisherman" (1881) recommended peas and maize as carp baits. As an incidental aside, he also suggested the use of paste flavoured with asafoetida!

Modern carp anglers did not, therefore, invent particle fishing. They rediscovered it.

The first contemporary reference I can recall was made by Fred Taylor when he described his experiences with fermented maize in the USA. Why we failed to pick up on that gem of a snippet I do not know - we must have been terribly blinkered.

Had I the wit to recognise it, I could have secured many years head start on the use of hemp as carp bait because friends and I, fishing along a stretch of bank which we dubbed "Hemp Straight" in a local park lake, hooked a number of wildies while roach fishing. We assumed "our" carp were behaving in a totally uncharacteristic manner. Mind you, I was only about twelve at the time!

In hindsight it is clear that the evidence was there - in abundance, too. But no one made the necessary connection.

Enter Rod Hutchinson!

What the rest of us missed, Rod recognised. His early articles on the subject were a revelation. The particle era was born!

My friend, Len Burgess, and I got to know Rod before he became famous. This was a consequence of Rod contacting me to see if I could recommend "a neglected pit with big carp in it." I suggested he try Johnson's Lakes. He came, he saw, and he conquered!

Perhaps in gratitude for having introduced him to the pits, Rod revealed to us the key to his success (apart, that is, from being a brilliant and instinctive angler). Black eyed beans! These became our secret weapon, and we proceeded to catch a number of Johnson's carp - we even made several multiple catches. All of which, I would add, caused consternation among the small band who were fishing unsuccessfully with the yet to be disclosed HNV baits!

In order to conceal our bait's identity, Len and I referred to them by the code name "Suzies" (Oh my pretty little black eyed Suzie..!)

Grown men too!

We prepared our black eyes according to Rod's original recipe - in double strength tomato soup. This involved using two packets of tomato soup powder in the quantity of water recommended for one pack. Half a pint of dry beans were soaked in a pint of concentrated soup for approximately 12 hours, then brought to the boil and simmered until they were sufficiently soft to be crushed between finger and thumb, but not so soft that they went "mushy".

Talking of whom - Rod and Len, that is. One of their joint sessions on Larkfield Two inspired them to poetry. I have related this story before, but it is good enough to justify retelling!

Seemingly a rat managed to get inside Rod's bivvy, whereupon he set about it with a bankstick - like you would - and after depatching it he threw the bloodied, battered corpse up the bank. But to Rod and Len's amazement, the "corpse" recovered! It shook what remained of its head and scuttled off. So touched were they by this poignant event that they were moved to record it in verse:

Returning one of my Johnson's Lake mirrors.

Hey little rat, scurrying by,
How come you've only got one eye?
Running past at such a pace,
Where's the other half of your face?

Call me a sentimental fool if you will, but I think those words are truly beautiful!

Back to the plot! Shortly after this, Rod's name started to appear fairly regularly in magazines as he disclosed information on other successful particles. Len and I tried most of them - none were quite as successful as were the original black eyes, but chick peas and maple peas ran them a pretty close second. The main difficulty on the pits we fished was that tench liked particles as much as did carp. Tench were slower to "get on them" than were carp, but once they acquired a taste for any given particle we were forced to move on to something different.

Tench were also the reason we did not use sweetcorn to any extent. We caught carp on it, including one Len had from the mega difficult Johnson's Railway Lake (it held fewer carp then than now), and an early morning brace which I caught from Johnson's Island Lake - one of which took a bare hook. Perhaps I had better explain! I had waded out on a long, shallow bar in order to catapult some sweetcorn. On returning to the bank I cast out my unbaited rods in order to soak the lines and reduce their springiness. Within a couple of minutes I became aware that one of my reels was spinning like a food whisk! Obviously the carp - a low double figure common - had been feeding over my newly applied bed of sweetcorn and inadvertently sucked in my hook. A carp on a bare hook - at Johnson's of all places!

The next major development arose from the discovery that carp like peanuts. They were extremely successful, but problems arose. Waters were overbaited; carp became preoccupied and in some instances suffered loss of condition. Then came examples of misuse when anglers used uncooked nuts which, according to anecdotal evidence, swelled inside the fish and set like concrete to occlude the gut. The final straw came when it was revealed that some peanuts carried a toxic mould. Clubs reacted and peanut bans became widespread.

Then followed the discovery of what I, and many others, regard as the best carp bait of them all. Tigernuts! Who was the first, I wonder, to take a handful of tigernuts and think to himself, "I reckon carp will eat these." Whoever he was, he made a leap of faith which boggles my brain. Tigernuts, even after a 24 hours soak and 30 minutes boiling, remain rock hard. Who, in their right mind, could possibly imagine that carp would give them a second glance? But someone did. Anonymous he may be, but so far as I am concerned his name belongs up there with Wilton, Diedrich, Winkworth, Hutchinson and the Premier boys when the history of carp baits comes to be written. The man was a genius!

Particle preparation

At this juncture, a few details on particle preparation seem in order. I shall not attempt to be comprehensive, but will confine my comments to those I actually use. Information on others is obtainable from Hinders who supply a Particle Preparation Guide free with orders.

The best carp bait of them all?

BLACK EYED BEANS: As per Rod's method described earlier.

CHICK PEAS: Soak for 24 hours; bring to the boil, then simmer gently for 20-25 minutes. Remove from the heat, drain through a colander and allow them to cool.

Although I generally use chick peas in their natural, unflavoured state, they take flavours and dye extremely well. I suggest that the amount of flavour and/or sweetener recommended for a 4-egg boilie mix be added to each litre of water in which the peas are to be soaked. They should be cooked in the same water.

MAPLE PEAS: Soak for 24 hours; bring to the boil and simmer very gently for 10 minutes, then take out a few peas every minute and test them between finger and thumb. If they pop from your grasp and fly across the kitchen, they are not cooked enough! Eventually you will find that they can be crushed while still remaining firm. They should then be removed from the heat, tipped into a colander and allowed to drain and cool.

There is, unfortunately, no way of shortcutting this somewhat arduous procedure because the dividing line between underdone and overdone is critical - finer even than the point which divides too hot and too cold on a shower unit! Which makes it, unquestionably, the smallest, finest dividing line known to modern science!

TARES: Another critical one. Soak for 12 hours; bring to the boil and simmer gently for 10 minutes. Then test between finger and thumb every minute.

MAIZE: Soak for 24 hours; bring to the boil and simmer for 30 minutes. Drain and allow to cool.

HEMPSEED: Soak for 12 hours; bring to the boil and simmer until white shoots appear (usually 20-30 minutes). Drain and allow to cool.

TIGERNUTS: Soak for 24 hours; bring to the boil and simmer for 30 minutes. Drain and allow to cool.

After my boiled particles have cooled I bag them in 500gm batches and store them in my freezer until required.

Pellets

Salmon and trout pellets make effective baits. Custom made pellet bands can be bought, but I prefer to bore my pellets with a nut-drill and thread them on a hair in the conventional manner.

Something to consider is that carp in most waters are familiar with pellets because they are widely used as feed, but only rarely does anyone use them as hookbait - which means that every pellet a carp eats is safe. A relevant point, I think.

My son, Peter, fished a syndicate lake in Sussex where 14mm salmon pellets outfished boilies and particles by something like five to one. A friend of his used them throughout the spring and early summer on Aveley, and at least held his own with the baiting teams who were putting in prodigious quantities of boilies.

Their disadvantage is that they break down in water much more rapidly than do boilies. In summer water temperatures 8-10mm trout pellets last about four hours; 14mm salmon pellets perhaps six hours.

Further information on pellets will be found in the next chapter, in which I discuss baiting and feeding.

Naturals

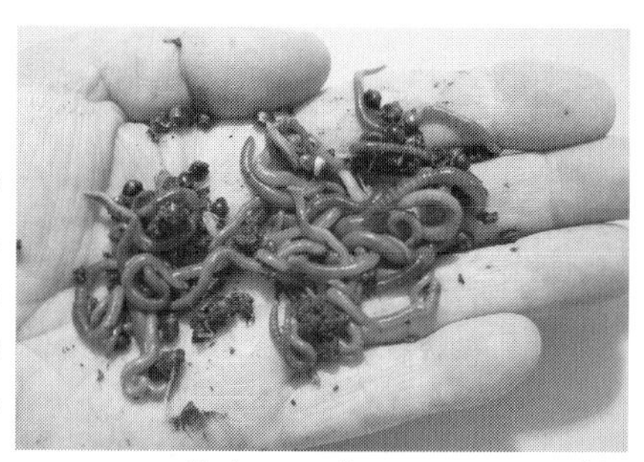

Redworms from my compost bin.

The next category of baits are those which might loosely be termed "naturals". They are not natural in the sense that they form part of a carp's normal diet, but simply that they are unadulterated.

The most useful of these are worms. Redworms are my favourite. I have a compost bin in my garden in which I place vegetable waste (cooked and uncooked), also autumn leaves, unused cereal groundbait etc. When we had pet rabbits and guinea pigs, I added their soiled straw. The occasional torn corrugated cardboard box, too. Grass cuttings go in occasionally, but not too often lest they raise the temperature to a level which is unsuitable for redworms. If that happens the wormery will become tenanted by brandlings which are useless for bait.

Redworms colonise a compost bin quite naturally, and if left undisturbed will breed prolifically. On no account, incidentally, should compost accelerators be added.

Back in my Bysingwood winter carp era, when I fished there with Gerry Savage, we impaled two or three maggots on our paste baited hooks in the hope that their movement would attract the attention of carp. We caught lots of carp - whether we would have caught as many had we omitted the maggots, I cannot say.

Casters, I am convinced, would make excellent feed items. In pre-pole days when matchmen fished caster and hempseed in conjunction with waggler tackle, they frequently hooked carp. Many were lost, of course, but it demonstrated the potential of the bait.

The aforementioned Mahin brothers fished a Loire Valley pit where boilies and particles were consistently unsuccessful. The water contained countless snails which, Michel and Philippe concluded, were probably the primary food source. So they collected snails by the bucketful, baited heavily with them alongside an island, and fished de-shelled snails on a standard hair rig. This enterprising tactic worked extremely well and produced carp to over 40lb.

Cockles can be effective. I said "can be" because they are an inconsistent bait in that they work well in some waters, but are virtually useless in others.

I recall reading in an old BCSG magazine that whelks were the favourite food of carp which lived in someone's garden pond. I have used them chopped as feed in conjunction with cockles or worm on the hook, but never as hookbait.

Some readers may wonder why I am devoting space to a subject which is very much a minority interest. It is due to my increasing conviction that naturals provide us with the best chance of catching those carp which rarely, if ever take standard baits. This belief was recently reinforced when I used natural baits to catch several carp, each of which had a pristine mouth and an intact palate veil. The significance of this observation being that the pit from which they came has been very hard fished and blitzed by boilies for many years (particles are banned). Which suggests - and I put it no stronger - that those fish had evaded capture due to their never having become boilie eaters.

If my interpretation is correct, it raises some very interesting possibilities.

Chapter Eleven

Feed and Feeding

Feed will not by itself persuade carp to move into a swim. And contrary to the creed which holds otherwise, it will not detain them for long once they decide to leave. So, if feeding will not attract carp, and will not hold them, why do we do it?

My belief is that the primary purpose of feed is to stimulate a food-search response. It achieves this by appealing to the carp's senses of sight and smell - but only if the distribution, density and content of the feed is correct.

To take an extreme case; if we spread 20 boilies over a tennis court size area, carp could easily swim through without coming across any. We could eliminate this risk by using sufficient boilies to give close coverage - but the quantity required would reduce the chance of the hookbait being picked up before carp had their appetite sated. So we need to gauge how much feed we can safely use, and how widely that feed can be scattered without causing it to be spread too thinly. My rule-of-thumb guide - range permitting - is to have a sprinkling of feed approximately the area of a dining-room table around each hookbait. The amount of feed used to achieve this effect will depend on the size and number of fish in the water, but from late spring through to early autumn 150-200gm (5-7oz) per rod is my usual starting point. Late autumn and through the winter, quantities are significantly reduced.

The presence or otherwise of other species is a consideration too. Cormorants have virtually eradicated roach and skimmers from most waters, so only rarely do they come into the reckoning. In pre-cormorant days things were very different; skimmer-bream were a nuisance in many pits and gave constant rod-top knocks and buzzer bleeps. Nowadays, only bream sufficiently large to be safe from cormorants - say, over 2lb - remain a problem. They will consume large quantities of feed and have on occasions made me so exasperated that I have stopped feeding altogether, and relied on hookbaits only. I tried the alternative tactic - feeding very heavily - but it merely served to increase their enthusiasm!

In some pits tench can be troublesome, especially during the May/June period. Only rarely, though, are they as annoying as bream - besides, I have a soft spot for tench, and unless they are small, persistent and piranha-like, I welcome their uninvited presence in my swim.

Mixed size trout pellets - my favourite feed items.

You will notice that I keep using the word "feed", rather than "boilies". That is because the crux of my approach is to use a variety of items. The conventional bed of boilies works extremely well in some circumstances, but more effective stimulation - especially in waters which have been subjected to a lot of boilie pressure over the years - is achieved by using items which vary in size, taste, smell and colour.

The main benefit of multi-item feeding is the sheer number of units. I touched on this in the previous chapter when I expressed the opinion that in daytime, in clear water, lots of small items are more stimulatory than the same overall quantity of food presented in fewer but larger units.

My standard procedure is to feed the swim with both whole and halved boilies, chopped boilies (comprising cubes ranging from approximately 3mm to 10mm cut from a boilie brick), mini (2.6mm to 5mm) and 8.5mm trout pellets, 5mm and 8mm Nash pellets, sweetcorn, maize, maple peas, tares and hempseed. In waters where seed baits are not permitted, I substitute Micromass. The total amount of feed - in weight terms - is not very great; but numerically there are a lot of individual items.

This, I believe, creates a situation whereby carp which may not immediately respond to standard size boilies might have their feeding instincts aroused by smaller items such as hempseed, boilie bits or the mini pellets. In addition to visual stimulation, there will also be the water-borne scent of attractors leaching from the Nash pellets and the cut surfaces of boilie halves and cubes. As the trout pellets slowly disintegrate, tiny oil droplets and pellet fragments will be held in suspension.

I believe hempseed stimulates small-item feeders into a food-search response.

The viability of loose feeding depends on the range.

The level of visual and olfactive stimulation provided by this sort of multi-item feeding is high. Carp are creatures of instinctive responses; if their food-search senses are bombarded by stimuli, I think they find it difficult to hold back. My objective is to evoke investigative samplings - when that is achieved, I am confident it will lead to more purposeful feeding.

Sometimes a very short period - just a few minutes - elapses from initial stimulation to the first run. Other times it takes much longer - perhaps several hours - with numerous stops and starts along the way. It is not unusual for fish to leave the baited area for a while - maybe for half an hour or more - then return for another brief period of sampling before leaving the area again. And so it continues. But once stimulated, carp rarely lose interest - unless something spooks them, of course.

Catching a fish will inevitably disturb the swim, and there is a high likelihood that other carp which were over the feed will move away. But hopefully they too will have been stimulated; and providing they have not become excessively frightened they are likely to return and, after a bit of nervous hesitation, will resume the sampling procedure.

To ensure the complete assortment of feed items remains available, I top-up after each capture.

Mid-range

Loose feeding such as I have just described is only possible at relatively close range because the lightest, least aerodynamic items cannot be catapulted more than about 15 yards. By omitting hempseed, mini pellets, sweetcorn and the smallest boilie bits, I can push the range to 20-25 yards; but this reduces the effectiveness of the tactic. If I want to retain all the feed items, I need to employ either a spod or groundbait.

Neither of these are as discreet as loose feeding, and their use is likely to spook carp. So what to do?

If I think fish are already in the swim or close by, I dispense with the smallest items and rely on loose feeding. Better, I feel, to compromise the feed situation - with the risk that its effectiveness will be reduced - rather than scare the carp away.

If, however, the water has predictable feeding times, and I am in position two or three hours ahead of schedule, or if I am hoping to intercept patrolling carp, I will retain the full spectrum of feed items, and deliver them by means of a spod or a ball of groundbait.

"Noisy" surface water - such as produced by wind and waves - camouflages the splash created by a spod or groundbait, and probably mitigates the scare factor. Deep water, likewise.

Distance is taken into account, too - I think carp are more tolerant of disturbance, and recover more quickly from it, if they are a long way from the bank.

The foregoing comments apply to waters where spods and groundbait balls are rarely used. When feeding by either of these means becomes standard practice, there is little doubt that carp learn to associate heavy splashes with food. I remember watching the match anglers who specialised in catching the carp on Layer - they would fire out a maggot and caster laced groundbait ball, then cast their Zoomer float tackle right into the centre of the spreading rings. Takes usually came as their hookbaits sank amidst the groundbait cloud. I understand too that in waters where a lot of Method fishing is practised, it is not unusual to get takes while groundbait balls or spods are splashing down directly over the top of baited end-tackles.

Spodding

For mixed-item feeding I like Gardner's Pocket Spod. It has a wide diameter relative to its length; a feature which helps it discharge its contents. Small items, especially light, irregular shaped ones like maize and sweetcorn, tend to jam in longer, narrower models.

The best method is to two-thirds fill the spod with feed items, then top it up with water. This prevents the feed compacting and becoming wedged in place.

Fully loaded the Pocket Spod weighs about 2.5oz, so does not require a special heavy duty spod rod - certainly not at the mid range distances I am talking about here.

The Pocket Spod floats; so after it has emptied it can be left in place for a few minutes and - with allowance made for drift - used as a casting marker for the baited end-tackle(s). I clip-up when spodding, incidentally, thus ensuring every load goes the same distance. By casting towards a far bank marker, baiting can be kept quite tight.

Groundbait

As an alternative to spodding, I use groundbait. The popularity of Method fishing has led to the development of numerous proprietary groundbaits, and most of the big bait companies produce their own versions. I have tried several of these, but most times I use a homemade blend which comprises equal parts (by volume) of white breadcrumbs and layers mash. To 5kg of the mixture I add 500gm of roasted, kibbled barley (made by giving barley grains a quick whirr in a grinder, then cooking them under the grill until they darken). Finally I add 500gm of either fishmeal or birdfood - depending on what boilies I am using. An alternative, but more expensive means of achieving the same end, is to add a generous measure - about 1kg - of boilie base mix.

At the waterside, after dampening the mixture, I cram in the aforementioned feed items. I may, depending on whim and availability, also include a few maggots, casters and worms. To my water filled spray bottle - with which I fine tune the dampness of my mixture - I add a teaspoonful of liquid molasses or a Minamino-type mucosa/spleen product. I much prefer these to alcohol based boilie flavours which, in my opinion, disperse too readily in water and thereby reduce the effectiveness of groundbait by "scrambling" the carp's chemoreceptors.

In deciding how much groundbait to use we have to achieve the correct balance - too little and there will be insufficient stimulation to induce enthusiastic feeding; too much and the "blade of grass in the meadow" syndrome applies and we may decrease the chances of our hookbait being taken.

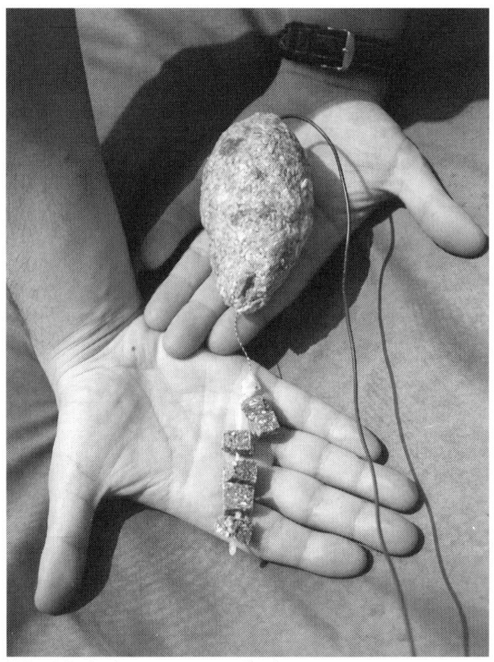

The Method concentrates feed items near the hookbait.

If the range is hand-throwing distance (a high, full toss, cricket-style bowling action is best, incidentally), I lob three smallish grapefruit size balls in the vicinity of each hookbait. Ideally I like one ball to land adjacent to my hookbait, and the other two a yard or so beyond. This reduces the incidence of line bites - which are best avoided if possible or there is a risk of the end-tackle being pulled out of position and into weed. I also worry about the hook being dragged along the bottom whereupon the point might become masked with rotting leaves or other debris.

If the range is beyond my ability to throw by hand, I decrease the size of the groundbait balls a little, and use a Cobra baiting spoon. For distances up to about 40 yards it is a very effective tool - I cannot understand why I see so few in use.

For distances farther than those achievable with a baiting spoon, I make smaller balls - about golfball size - and use a Drennan Whopper Dropper groundbait catapult. The overall amount of groundbait and feed remains the same, only the ball size varies.

When using groundbait to deliver feed, I usually combine it with a Method approach. To date I have not used the special caged or vaned leads designed for Method fishing because I have found elongated inlines to be preferable. My Method rig, therefore, comprises my standard inline setup, utilising a 1.5oz or 2oz "Distance" Korda or Zipp. With 15-18lb line I am happy to lob a fully loaded Method rig up to about 40 yards; for greater distances I use 12-15lb line in conjunction with a shock leader.

My link is 45cm in length, and is folded back, concertina style, inside the groundbait ball (Fig 55). It is not possible to achieve the neat "Z" which is obtained with the standard Concertina Link, so I omit tungsten "mouse droppings" for fear they might snag and thereby interfere with the link's ability to

Fig.55 HOOKLINK FOLDED CONCERTINA STYLE INSIDE METHOD BALL

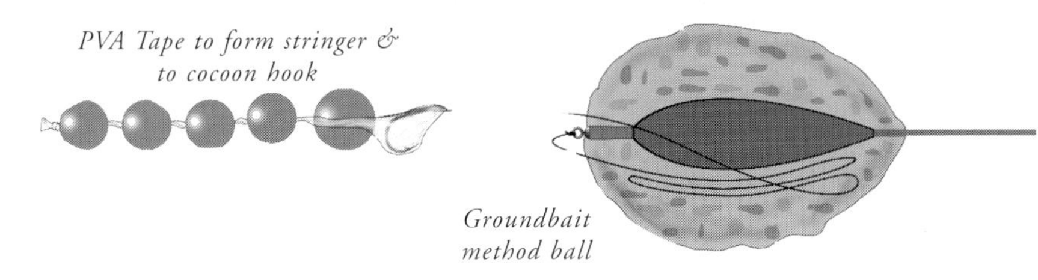

straighten. An unadulterated link, even though it might be crammed somewhat untidily inside the Method ball, straightens perfectly when a take occurs. The smooth shape of the elongated inline helps in this regard, too.

To enable me to dispense with putty weight, I use Merlin or Tricklink for my Method links - both of which lay moderately flat of their own accord. The colour-coded silicone swivel-sleeve I incorporate in my standard hooklinks is omitted from the Method versions because it impedes folding back.

Some readers might be surprised by my choice of a 45cm link, which is much longer than usually recommended for Method fishing. I tried shorter versions,

'Geordie' Mike lobs out a Method rig.

but with bottom baits got a higher proportion of dropped takes and twitches - a few hookpulls too.

Brothers Rick and Martin often press their hookbait into the Method ball - and clearly it works well because they catch a lot of carp while doing so - but I prefer to have a few centimetres of link hanging clear. I rig my hook with a stringer, too.

On the infrequent occasions I use popups in conjunction with a Method setup, I reduce the length of the link to 35cm. Popups are taken differently to bottom baits, and less leeway is required. I still use braid, however, and fold it back inside the Method ball as previously described.

Before leaving the subject of Method fishing - herewith a few tips.

- **Anti-tangle tube should emerge from the Method ball dead centre. This minimises the risk of the groundbait disintegrating in mid-cast.**
- **Slow the casting action so it becomes more of a lob - and aim somewhat higher than usual.**
- **The groundbait ball, while heavy in air, reduces the specific gravity of the end-tackle; this can result in it being pulled out of position by over zealous tightening. I sink and straighten the line very gently by hanging a small weight (a quick-release backlead) on the line between a couple of rod rings. It is removed when everything is configured correctly.**
- **In order to build up the feed area, all casts should go to the same spot. Accuracy is easily achieved by means of clipping-up (I use my Power Gum harness system). This has the additional advantage of ensuring the Method ball sinks on a tight line which reduces bellying in a cross-wind (if I am not clipping-up, I trap the line against the spool as the rig sinks).**
- **If fishing at close to medium range, especially if the water is deep, the line will rise at a steep angle. I think it pays to incorporate a small backweight to ensure the anti-tangle tube lays flat. The proximity of feed makes line bites unavoidable, but these are reduced if the end-rig lays flush to the bottom.**
- **Still with line bites; a semi-slack or droopy line, coupled with a long drop on the indicator, will absorb line bites to a degree. They still occur, though, so I ignore all indications other than runs, or lifts which pull tight and hold.**

An approach closely allied to Method fishing is that involving the use of trout pellet paste instead of groundbait. Julian Cundiff has written of his winter success with this tactic at Catch 22; and I understand it is widely used on Horseshoe and Arena Essex.

To make trout pellet paste, the pellets are scalded in hot water, left to stand for twenty minutes or so, then kneaded. Cold water may be substituted for hot if granule-size fry feeds are used. Just sufficient water is added to dampen the granules, whereupon - as before - they are left to stand for a while. My erstwhile trout and salmon pellet hookbait paste was made by this means.

Stringers

Very rarely do I cast a hookbait without first attaching a stringer. I like the notion of there being a few safe baits immediately adjacent to the hookbait. Often I read and hear references to carp in some waters becoming wary of little clusters of bait, but I see no evidence to support this view.

Some anglers worry that carp associate the smell of PVA with danger. I fish many different pits, including some which receive intense pressure, and I have yet to detect the merest hint that my results are adversely affected by my use of PVA.

To create a stringer I much prefer PVA tape to thread or string. Tape achieves three things: it keeps the baits apart, enables the hair to be bound tight to the hook so it cannot tangle in flight, and provides a means by which the hook can be sheathed to minimise the risk of it becoming caught up on weed as it sinks.

Talking of stringers... Late one winter afternoon, Rick was settling down for a few hours fishing on a small Essex pit when another angler arrived. By the time the second angler was ready to cast, it was dark, so Rick was unable to identify the reason for the unusual sounding "spudooshes" made by the new arrival's end-tackles.

Rick caught a couple of fish; and to judge from diverse splashes and bite-alarm noises, he assumed the other guy had done so too. When Rick packed up he stopped by to speak with the other angler, whereupon they discussed their respective results. When they got round to the subject of feed, the angler commented, "I don't use freebies in winter - just hookbaits and a 30-bait stringer."

The strange "spudooshes" had been identified - and a new definition of "no freebies" entered our lexicon!

My preference is for two to six stringer baits. Most times I use four. This is because I nearly always use

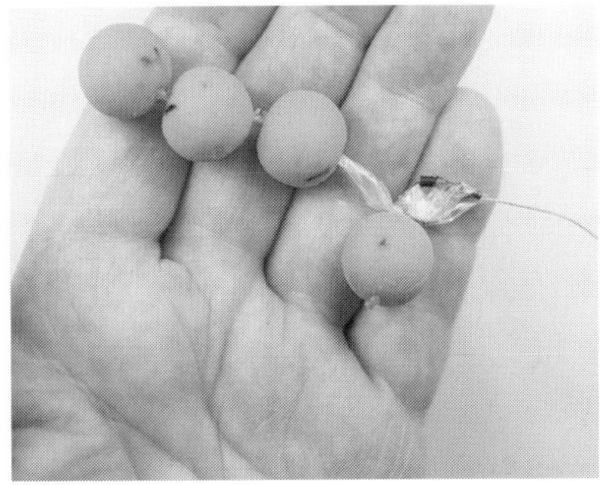

I almost always incorporate a stringer.

two baits on the hair; and two hookbaits plus four stringer baits makes six. And six is my lucky number. No, that is not an example of superstitious nonsense. It is impeccable logic. I do not have a superstitious bone in my body - indeed, I am a typical Taurus in that I only believe what I can see, hear and touch - or I would be a typical Taurus if I placed any credence in astrology, which I do not.

As I said, I am not superstitious!

PVA Bags

PVA bags are excellent for dry items like pellets.

PVA bags are of limited use for mixed-item feeding because they are unsuitable for wet constituents such as hempseed, sweetcorn etc. For pellets, Micromass and boilie bits, however, they are excellent.

Latterly, in conjunction with popups, I have been experimenting with dry groundbait and powdered trout pellet in PVA bags. The effect produced by dry powder is interesting, comprising a cloud which ascends and spreads as the fragments slowly absorb water. In calm conditions the cloud remains in suspension for quite a long while - at least half an hour - but it is rapidly dispersed by wind induced undertow.

Further Still

As the range increases, mixed-item feeding becomes progressively less viable. I have never measured the maximum distance I can catapult groundbait balls or cast a particle spod, but I very much doubt if it is more than about 60 yards - maybe 70 yards in a following wind. I have heard tell of particle spods being cast 100 yards plus, but I have yet to witness it. While in France I saw particle-laced clay-balls fired 100 yards or so by means of an impressive ground-mounted catapult. The elastics comprised bungee rubbers (the type used to make luggage retainers), and the tripod legs were made from scaffolding poles! It was an awesome item, but hardly the sort of thing I would want to lug around the average pit!

For all practical purposes, 70 yards or thereabouts is maximum range for particle spods and groundbait balls; baiting at greater distance - dinghies and toy boats aside - is restricted to boilies and ball pellets.

I have used ball pellets a good deal - in fact I obtained a pre-production batch from Clive Diedrich almost a year before they went on general sale. I particularly like those which contain fishmeal. They are most effective, I find, when used in the proportion of two ball pellets to every free boilie.

An alternative approach, and one which is currently producing a lot of fish in the Lea Valley, involves fishing hookbaits over an area heavily and solely baited with ball pellets. No freebie boilies are used at all - or at most, just a few. Seemingly the winning combination at present is Mainline Activ-8 boilies used in conjunction with dedicated Activ-8 ball pellets.

Nashbait and Nutrabaits - and doubtless others - produce dedicated combinations of boilies and ball pellets, so this is doubtless a tactic about which we will be hearing more in the future.

Throwing sticks and boilie spods are the tools for medium to long range baiting with boilies and ball pellets - but I have discussed these in some detail in the chapter on long range fishing so will not repeat myself here. The only comment I would add is that most ball pellets are less robust than their rock-hard texture would suggest, so they do not permit a real "whack" with a throwing stick. For maxi range, therefore, a boilie spod is better.

In pre-Cobra days, wrist-rocket catapults were popular. I still have a Black Widow and a stock of unused power bands, and although I have not tried it for ball pellets, I have no doubt that it will prove effective. Trouble is, when used for heavy baiting the power bands do not last very long, and frequent replacement works out expensive.

Prebaiting

Most of us, at one time or another, have embarked on prebaiting campaigns. And most of us, I suspect, have been disappointed with the outcome.

So, is prebaiting worthwhile?

On balance, I think the question deserves a "Yes." Well, more of a hesitant "Mmmm, perhaps, maybe" rather than an outright "Yes." And only then if we have realistic expectations. If carp could be "bought" by the simple, albeit expensive procedure of piling in vast quantities of bait, there would be far more successful anglers about than is actually the case!

An important fact to be borne in mind is that prebaiting works best in waters which receive only light angling pressure. Mass baiting by a number of different "teams", all of whom are using different baits, may help make the carp population as a whole more boilie aware, but makes it difficult for any one angler, or group of anglers, to derive significant benefit. So if others are baiting heavily, I doubt that it is worth trying to compete by "outbaiting" them. Better to rely on the intelligent application of feed while actually fishing.

Baiting Tips

To those readers who, after weighing up the pros and cons, intend embarking on a prebaiting campaign, I offer the following advice.

- Only in exceptional circumstances will prebaiting create a "hotspot"; we should therefore confine our efforts to areas which the carp visit of their own accord.
- It makes sense to apply the same location principles when prebaiting as when actually fishing, and scatter the bait where carp are seen jumping or rolling; near snags and weedbeds; in the vicinity of islands; at the downwind end of the lake etc.
- Prebaiting is best confined to the sort of weather conditions when we can reasonably expect it to be eaten. It is a waste of bait, time and money to prebait if feeding is inhibited by excessively high water temperature, a bitterly cold wind, or when the dissolved oxygen level is low. In the last instance, heavy baiting can exacerbate the water's problems.
- High levels of alcohol based flavours can, I believe, make baits unpalatable if large numbers are eaten; it is therefore advisable to use relatively low flavour levels (half that recommended by manufacturers is a good guide) when high volume baiting is undertaken.
- If there are a lot of bream or tench in the water, it is advisable to use boilies of 20mm plus for prebaiting purposes, even though smaller versions might be used when fishing. Large baits are less readily taken by nuisance fish, thereby increasing the likelihood of their being found by carp.
- Tufties likewise - large baits afford a degree of immunity.

Talking of which... If, as many anglers believe, boilies are the primary reason for carp being larger nowadays than they used to be; how come the tufties on some of the pits I fish are not the size of ostriches?

I like variety, so I fish a number of different waters - prebaiting is not, therefore, a viable proposition. Instead, I content myself with scattering leftover baits in my swim, or adjacent areas where I have seen carp activity, when I pack up. Most times, I would guess, this amounts to about half a kilo. Trickle-baiting on this level can only hope, at most, to give a small number of carp a taste for my bait. In real terms, though, I doubt that it makes any difference - a view supported by the fact that I often catch first time out on a bait which has never been used in the water before.

In autumn I reduce my loose-feed quantities - here is the result.

It is just possible, I suppose, that the little-and-often application of safe freebies might offset the bad experience of being caught, and thereby prolong the life of a bait. It is a tempting notion, but with so many different baits going into most waters I doubt if carp are capable of making the connection between a particular bait and the experience of being caught. I know anglers talk of baits having "blown", but empirical evidence does not support this. In recent years I have used Nash Sting and a homemade birdfood/fishmeal bait to take practically every fish in one particular pit - indeed, I stopped fishing there because I was getting too many repeat captures. Likewise, Rick and his friend Steve Lindsell caught a stack of fish from an Essex gravel pit on boilies made from Solar's Dairy Pellets, and again experienced no signs of a slowdown. Last year, on a syndicate fishery, Rick took a colossal number of fish on Nashbait S-Mix. Again, no signs of a slowdown. Were I inclined to do so, I could quote many more examples - but all would demonstrate the same thing which is, quite simply, good baits do not "blow". They might if everyone used the same base and same attractors - but all the while a varied selection of baits goes in a water, I doubt that carp are able to identify which are dangerous.

In a nutshell, then - in most waters, prebaiting is unnecessary. Which is not to say it is a total waste of time because, if nothing else, it might enable us to fish with a bit of extra confidence. Besides, from spring through to autumn, providing it is not overdone, it is most unlikely to do any harm. Winter is another matter, and I have seen fishing rendered completely ineffective by excess baiting - a subject I shall return to when winter fishing is discussed in detail. Periods of low oxygen and/or high ammonia levels (early autumn is the most likely time for this to occur) should be avoided too. Indeed, when this circumstance arises, I think it better if the affected water is closed completely.

Pellet Facts

In this, and other chapters, I have made frequent reference to trout pellets. During the course of the past year or two there has been a considerable amount of discussion in the angling press regarding the safety of trout pellets, and this has resulted in some clubs instituting pellet bans.

Time, I think, for a rational look at the subject.

Fact. On some heavily stocked, highly pressured match-oriented commercial fisheries carp deaths have occurred which have been attributed to anglers' excessive use of trout pellets.

Fact. In ordinary carp waters - the pits, estate lakes, canals, rivers etc fished by carp anglers - there have been no deaths which have been reliably attributed to trout pellets.

Now, I do not claim formal qualifications in freshwater biology or fisheries management - but the conclusion to be drawn from the foregoing strikes me as obvious.

We are not talking rocket science here, are we?

The problem lies not with trout pellets, but with small commercial fisheries which are stocked with a biomass of carp beyond that which they can sustain. This results in natural food supplies becoming depleted to the extent that carp are compelled to place disproportionate reliance on anglers' baits. The dietary imbalance thus created leads to ill health; a situation exacerbated by excessive demands being placed on the water's dissolved oxygen content. High phosphate and dissolved ammonia levels make matters even worse, with the predictable consequence that the carp's immune system becomes affected - an early sign of which is the development of sores and ulcers. Subsequently they die.

Only a fool would attempt to deny that pellet-related problems have arisen on these synthetic fishing facilities. But then again, only a fool would be surprised at such an outcome. I repeat; there have been no health problems or premature

Son, Peter, was on hand to photograph this beautiful Kent common for me - and a lovely job he made of it, too.

Pretty scale pattern on a clay pit mirror.

It looks like France, but it is actually a Kent reservoir.

Brother Martin with a fabulous common from a deep Essex pit.

Sunset over Stonar.

Method rig ready to go.

mortalities arising from the use of trout pellets in waters which contain a naturally sustainable population of carp. Via correspondence in Coarse Fisherman magazine, I asked for evidence which would refute this observation. No such testimony was received. Likewise Doctor Bruno Broughton's 1999 report on the use of pellet feeds in coarse fisheries - it contained no verifiable instances of pellet problems occurring in any waters other than grossly overstocked and overfished commercial facilities.

But will common sense prevail?

Will it hell!

Notwithstanding the overwhelming weight of empirical evidence which makes it obvious that there is no justification for banning the use of trout pellets, the "ban dynamic" is now up and running - and no matter how misguided, nothing will stop it.

Inside Information

As an antidote to the silly "Shock! Horror!" headlines and ill informed comments which have appeared in some sections of the angling press, I would like to subject pellets to careful, dispassionate scrutiny. Exact formulations are likely to vary from one manufacturer to another, but most trout and salmon pellets contain the following ingredients:

Fish Meals, Fish Oils, Wheat and Wheat By-Products, Soya Meal, Whey Products Binders, Antioxidants, Vitamin Supplement, Mineral Supplement, Betaine and Astaxanthin (a synthetic product which is nature-identical with the carotenoids from which wild salmon and trout develop their pinky-orange flesh).

The palatability of some pellets is enhanced by the addition of liquid molasses. This is what gives them their dark colour.

Fry feeds are obtainable in powder and granular form - but our freebie baiting purposes are best served by pellets ranging from 2.6mm - which are about hempseed size - to 8.5mm. I like to have a selection comprising 2.6mm, 5mm and 8.5mm - with a few 14mm for longer range.

Breakdown times vary according to oil content, the extent to which the ingredients are compressed, and water temperature (the warmer the water, the faster they disintegrate). In summer, 2-6 hours is usual; although I once obtained some 14mm pellets which lasted almost 8 hours.

The foregoing comments apply to sinking pellets, but floating versions are also available. These are excellent for loose feed to encourage surface activity, but soften rather too quickly to make suitable hookbaits.

Compared with boilies, pellets are inexpensive. If bought in small quantities they cost about £2 per kilo. They are even cheaper if bought in bulk - depending on the type, expect to pay £20-£35 per 25kg.

The shelf life of pellets depends on how they are stored. If kept somewhere cool, dark and dry they remain in good condition for several months. A mistake many anglers make is buying in bulk to keep costs down, then finding themselves with more bait than they can use. My advice is to be realistic - estimate your requirements and buy accordingly. If you think 25kg may be too much for your personal use, either bulk-buy with friends, or obtain smaller amounts.

Their relative cheapness encourages some anglers to use pellets to excess. While this is unlikely to cause health problems in a normal gravel pit, it makes sense to act responsibly and err on the side of caution.

Carp Pellets

Animal feed suppliers also stock carp pellets and general coarse fish pellets. These have a lower protein level than trout and salmon pellets; a lower oil content, too. I cannot comment on their effectiveness because I have yet to try them.

The popularity of trout and salmon pellets has prompted some bait manufacturers to produce versions which, they claim, are formulated specially for carp. It is difficult to substantiate these claims because, unlike animal feed manufacturers who produce superb technical literature, most bait makers tend to be somewhat coy about disclosing information. Nashbait are a notable exception; they provide comprehensive product details on all their range. I have in front of me a label from a bulk bag of Nashbait pellets; it reads as follows:

Oil 6%, Fibre 4%, Protein 20%, Ash 8%, Vitamin A 9900 IU/kg, Vitamin D3 300 IU/kg, Vitamin E 100mg, Vitamin C.

Contains: Cereals, Derivatives of Vegetable Origin, Meat and Animal Derivatives, Oils and Fats, Vitamins and Minerals.

The label also gives storage advice and information regarding the shelf life of the vitamins within the pellets.

At the time of writing Nashbait pellets are obtainable in 5mm and 8mm - and in several flavours. I have incorporated the Scopex version in my multi-item feed approach, in conjunction with Scopex Squid 10mm mini boilies, and had some good results.

Summary

Trout, salmon and carp pellets are excellent feed items. Carp obviously find them highly palatable, so they eat them enthusiastically. Pellets have the further advantage that, being small, they can be used in visually stimulating quantities. It is important not to overfeed, though. Their purpose is to induce excitation, not preoccupation. I said earlier that I normally put about 170gm of feed around each hookbait - under normal circumstances that total will divide roughly into thirds: a third boilies and boilie bits, a third particles, and a third pellets.

Used sensibly, none of the pellets currently available do any harm whatsoever to carp; indeed, as a supplement to a mixed diet it is difficult to see how they can do other than good.

Chapter Twelve

Off the Top

Back in the '60's and '70's, and possibly into the early '80's, I caught about one third of my summer fish on floating baits. After dark they came from the margins; during the daytime they were stalked from reedbeds and lilies, or taken on anchored crusts well out from the bank. But things have changed. Now, most years, I catch relatively few fish off the top. Some years, none at all.

Observation suggests that I am not alone. Only rarely do I see anyone fishing topwater baits. This lack of attention is reflected in magazines - they contain innumerable articles on conventional bottom baits and rigs, but hardly anything on floater fishing. So why has a method which was once so popular fallen into disuse? Fashion is undoubtedly part of it; but the main reason, I suspect, is birds. Not only water birds - mallards, swans, coots etc - but gulls too. Birds have always been a problem in this regard, but nowhere near as bad as they are nowadays. I do not have any figures to hand, but I would be surprised if ducks in general, and mallards in particular, are not far more plentiful than they used to be - perhaps, like cyprinid fish, they have benefited from pits becoming weedier as a result of eutrophication? And as for gulls - in ecological niche terms they are airborne rats which thrive on the edible detritus which we, as a species, discard in streets, parks, public places and landfill sites.

I know of no pit where birds do not make floater fishing difficult; in many they render it well nigh impossible. At the first sign of free baits, the sky becomes full of wheeling, squealing gulls, and the water surface is furrowed by determined armadas of mallards.

God, I hate the damn things!

All of which is unfortunate because, where it is viable, floater fishing is a tremendously exciting way of catching carp. I defy any angler, no matter how many carp he has caught, to remain calm at the sight of a bow-wave stopping just short of a floater; you just know the fish has seen it... Will it take? Will it..? Then a pair of orange lips engulfs the bait, the water boils and the line draws tight... Marvellous stuff!

On its day, floater fishing can be extremely productive, too. Indeed, I go further, and say that there are circumstances when it will far outfish conventional bottom tactics.

Water, Weather and Season

There is no such thing as a no-hope floater water. There are many which have that reputation - but that is another thing entirely. It is true, however, that carp vary in their enthusiasm. While this may be explained in part by genetic factors, it is not the whole story because there are plenty of instances of fish from the same batch going in separate waters, and subsequently reacting very differently to floating baits.

Puzzling, that.

Nor is there any such thing as no-hope floater weather. Yes, some days are much better than others - and given the choice I would unhesitatingly opt for a warm sunny day with a nice ripple on the water - but I have caught fish in the most unlikely conditions including cold northerlies that had me dressed almost as if for winter, and overcast days of persistent drizzle. I even caught an April fish in hail, and another during a sleet shower.

Which reminds me - I have yet to catch a carp on floater before April. I have tried quite hard in March, and while I have had a few exploratory nudges, I have not managed a single strikeable take. At the other end of the year, I have caught carp on floating baits in late October, but none in November. As for winter proper; I have occasionally tried it - the most recent occasion being two or three years ago when we had a freakishly warm mid-February period - but I have had no success at all.

April is the earliest I have caught carp on floaters (I had three or four this day, as I recall).

That carp will occasionally take topwater baits in winter, however, was demonstrated in spectacular fashion by Chris Ball when he caught a 31lb Hampshire mirror which, I believe, is the largest floater-caught winter carp on record. Anyone with visions of emulating Chris should, however, bear the following words of his in mind, "Though it is true that carp can be caught on surface baits in winter, it can, in my experience, be a very hit or miss affair and in some instances downright impossible." (Carpworld, 100). Chris demonstrated just how difficult by adding that he had caught only 12 winter carp on surface baits in 15 years of trying.

Another Chris - Chris Currie - has caught topwater winter fish too. Like Chris Ball's winter thirty-plus, they came from Hampshire. This Chris, for those unaware of the fact, is the man who popularised, and probably discovered the effectiveness of dried petfoods as floating baits. I recall him saying that in his opinion winter surface fishing was a viable tactic, providing fish were accustomed to accepting such baits via steady feeding through the warmer months.

That it is not a prerequisite to be called Chris, nor to fish down in Hampshire, in order to catch topwater carp in winter, was demonstrated to brother Rick on a series of interconnected Essex gravel pits. Rick used mini bottom baits and, predictably, caught well - but the most successful angler on the complex during the early spring period fished surface baits among the dead stalks of the previous year's reedbeds.

So topwater fishing can work well in cold water - whether it will do so universally, or only in certain waters, I do not know. Relatively few anglers fish floaters even in high summer, let alone in the late autumn to early spring period!

Single Baits

The classic floater approach involves first getting carp going on freebies. Sometimes, however, this does not work. There are days when a drifting group of half a dozen mixers might produce a certain amount of interest, but only one or two will be taken. On first encountering this situation I thought, "Simple; I'll only put out one or two." But that was insufficient to evoke a response. The clichéd "Catch 22" phrase leaps unbidden to mind! On such days I have found it best to feed freebies for an hour or so in order to get the carp semi-aware that surface food is available, even if few or none are actually taken, and then put out no more. On days like that the fish are not actively feeding on the surface, but if they come across an isolated hookbait there is a reasonable chance of a take.

There are other days, especially when it is cold and gloomy, when freebies produce no reaction at all so there is little encouragement to put out a floater. And normally I would not bother - but three years ago I went on a floater "bender", and used topwater baits no matter how unpromising the conditions. Surprisingly, even on the most unlikely days, I had the odd out-of-the-blue take. There was no prior warning on such occasions, and no sign of carp on or near the surface, just a sudden swirl followed by a warbling Delkim and a purring Baitrunner! Even more surprisingly, these unexpected topwater captures sometimes occurred on days when those using bottom baits caught nothing.

Freebies among the eel grass - a big mirror took a couple shortly after this photo was taken.

Floating Baits

You have probably read articles which advise you to use mixers or similar for loose-feed, but to have something more durable, like a corkball, on the hook. This works when the carp are in a competitive mood (when they are really "up for it", they will even investigate controllers), but I have found corkballs produce no response at all when fish are in what we might term a "normal" mood. So although mixers suffer from the disadvantage that they will not withstand repeated casting - and even when left undisturbed need changing after about 40 minutes - they are generally far more effective than a corkball substitute. Nor, incidentally, have I found floating popup boilies a good alternative. Other anglers, however, have - so I suspect I might have given up too easily on them.

You will notice that I have made several references to "mixers", but have not specified a particular brand. In the past I used Chum Mixers, but a couple of years ago they suddenly shrank in size! As a consequence of this - and possibly a different recipe or manufacturing process - they became less buoyant. This rendered them almost useless as carp baits, and prompted me to look for an alternative. Currently I am using Tesco Mixers, which are virtually indistinguishable from the original Chum version.

There are numerous other dried petfoods - modern pet "supermarkets" are a veritable treasure trove in this regard - which will doubtless catch carp. I have tried several, but thus far have found nothing which combines acceptability with longevity better than Tesco Mixers. I shall keep looking, though.

Mixers can either be used straight from the bag, or they can be "rubberised". There are several variations of the "rubberising" procedure - all of which involve pre-wetting the mixers and then leaving them for several hours in an airtight container. My preferred method is as follows:

- **half fill a Tupperware-type sandwich box with mixers**
- **pour boiling water over them**
- **tip the mixers into a colander**
- **allow them to cool and drain**
- **place the drained mixers in a poly-bag**
- **inflate the poly-bag by blowing into it**
- **add flavour, sweetener or colour if required**
- **shake the mixers to prevent them sticking together**
- **deflate the poly-bag, seal it and leave for at least two hours**

The resulting baits lose their crispness and develop a somewhat rubbery texture. They can be fished directly on the hook, or mounted on a hair without requiring that they be pre-drilled.

"Rubberised" mixers are relatively tough initially, but soon swell and soften when immersed in water. If longevity is important, therefore, it is better to use fresh and crispy mixers, straight from the pack.

In addition to mixer-type baits, I use diced floater-cake. As long ago as the '60's and early '70's - back in my Horton Kirby and Brooklands' days - I made a sort of unleavened bread flavoured with melted cheese. Unbeknown to me at the time, I anticipated the deep-pan pizza revolution! It worked well, and I caught a lot of carp on it. Then, with the onset of the HNV philosophy of the '70's I made Wilton inspired floater-cake from refined milk products. It worked well, especially when dyed yellow and flavoured with Geoff Kemp's Mellow Brandy. Nowadays I use standard boilie mixes, but with double the quantity of eggs - this produces a stiff-runny mixture, rather than a dough. Attractors are the same as used in bottom-bait versions.

To encourage the mixture to develop mini air pockets - and thus increase its buoyancy - I add one heaped teaspoon of baking powder (or bicarbonate of soda) per six eggs. I also add a level teaspoon of salt to toughen the gluten contained within the bait's cereal constituents - this makes the resulting floater-cake more durable. The mixture is poured to a depth of about 15mm into a lightly greased non-stick baking tray. If non-stick versions are unavailable, an ordinary one can be lined with aluminium foil which should be lightly coated with cooking oil or lard. It is baked in a preheated oven at 160 degrees Celsius (gas mark 3) for approximately one hour. Most mixes swell to almost twice their original thickness during cooking, thereby producing a slab approximately 25mm thick.

After being allowed to cool the slab of cake can be cubed for immediate use, or frozen until required.

Cubes cut from a slab have crust top and bottom which delays the ingress of water, and consequently slows their going soft and soggy - they remain firm (by floater standards) for about two hours. They therefore make relatively durable hookbaits.

Alternatively, floater-cake can be produced in loaf form. Loaves are made in exactly the same way as slabs, except that they are cooked in a loaf tin, and the mixture is poured to a depth of about 5cm. Cooking time will probably need to be extended - almost certainly to 90 minutes, and possibly for as long as two hours. It is impossible to be precise about timing because it depends what base mix is used, and the viscosity of the mixture.

Cubes cut from the inside of a loaf-shaped block of cake soften more quickly than do cubes cut from a slab, but they are satisfactory for freebie baiting. Cubes cut from the outside of a floater loaf have crust on one face, so they are okay for hookbaits. Then there is bread. Its disadvantage is that it softens so quickly that it is easily swirled off the hook or broken up by wave action. Carp like it though, and take it avidly, so I ensure that I always have some in my freezer. I buy a square-tin white sandwich loaf (the one with straight top, bottom, ends and sides) and leave it uncovered on the kitchen worktop for two days. It will not go stale in this time, but will firm-up a tad. I then cut off the crusts with about one inch of crumb attached, and put them in sealed poly-bags for freezer storage.

Mixers, floater-cake and bread serve all my surface fishing requirements. I tried marshmallows - having seen frequent recommendations for their use - but found they were useless. Carp showed no interest in them at all. Even mallards and swans left them alone after an initial exploratory peck! I keep meaning to try paste covered poly-balls, floating particles (buoyed up with foam) and, bizarre though it may sound, floating water snails (also utilising foam). Anyone who has an aquarium or garden pond will have seen how snails can cling upside down to the surface - as a consequence of surface tension - when water is calm. Presumably it happens in a natural environment, too? And if it does, then surely carp will have learned to sip them down? But you know how it is - when mulling over ideas in the abstract, notions such as floating snails seem quite exciting, "Yes," you think, "that has got to work." But when it comes to actual on-the-bank practical fishing, unorthodox ideas tend to remain untried - leastways, they do by me. "Fantasy fishing", I call it; which is harmless enough - except that some writers allow their fantasies to find their way into print!

Tactics

At its simplest, floater tackle can consist of a freeline. Nothing is needed on the line at all - just a hook. Where carp patrol the margins, the bait can be fished directly below the rod tip - ensuring, of course, that there is sufficient slack to enable the bait to be sucked down. This is classic margin fishing, circa 1950's and '60's. Some readers will doubtless be dismissing such a simple, rig-free approach as "old hat" - but I can assure you, it catches carp.

Freelining is also an effective tactic in surface weed, or among emergent reeds. In our formative carp fishing years Rick and I caught lots of carp this way. We crept round small Essex ponds, all the while looking for signs of carp. Sometimes the signs were obvious - reeds would shake as though a dog was blundering through them - but often only the most subtle signs would be seen, like a single stem describing a gentle arc. Baits were lowered into tiny clear spots (very rarely did they need to be cast), and we would sit, rod in hand, waiting for the bait to be engulfed. Some takes were so gentle that the crust seemed to sink of its own accord; but most times there was a gurgling slurp as the crust disappeared as though down a plug-hole!

Where the bait is required to be a bit further out, it can be cast just beyond lilies or floating potamogeton. The leaves tether the bait, thereby holding it in position. Or - and this is one of my favourite ploys - the line can be hooked over the end of an overhanging twig. This not only prevents the bait from drifting, but ensures that no line touches the water.

For greater distances, especially in an offshore wind, a controller setup is a good option. Some anglers lock the controller in position, claiming that it provides a bolt rig effect. I prefer to have it free running because I have found this results in lovely, easy-to-hit sailaway takes.

Most of my floater fishing is at 30 yards or less, so the smallest size controller will usually suffice. There are lots from which to choose - I use the Nash version, but Gardner, Gold Label and Drennan make nice ones, too. The controller is slid on the line, and stopped by means of a rubber bead, into which a short length of wooden cocktail stick is jammed (Fig 56). I leave about half a centimetre of stick protruding below the bead (not above it, or it might snag the hooklink) to facilitate its removal should I want to alter its position. Only parallel bore rubber beads - I use those produced by John Roberts - provide a snug, non-slip fit on a cocktail stick; tapered bore versions do not grip sufficiently tight.

Fig.56 CONTROLLER SETUP USING RUBBER BEAD STOP

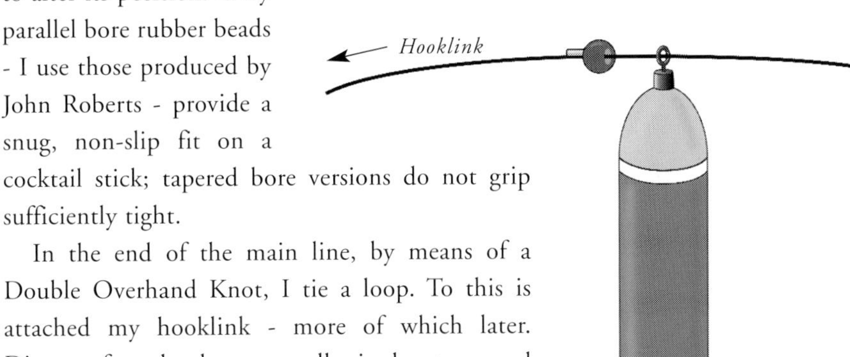

In the end of the main line, by means of a Double Overhand Knot, I tie a loop. To this is attached my hooklink - more of which later. Distance from hook to controller is about one and a half metres.

If the breeze is in any direction other than directly behind me, I prefer to use an anchored bait. My favourite setup is a running-paternoster, with a sufficiently long tail length to enable the bait to lay on the surface (Fig 57).

Fig.57 LONG TAIL RUNNING PATERNOSTER

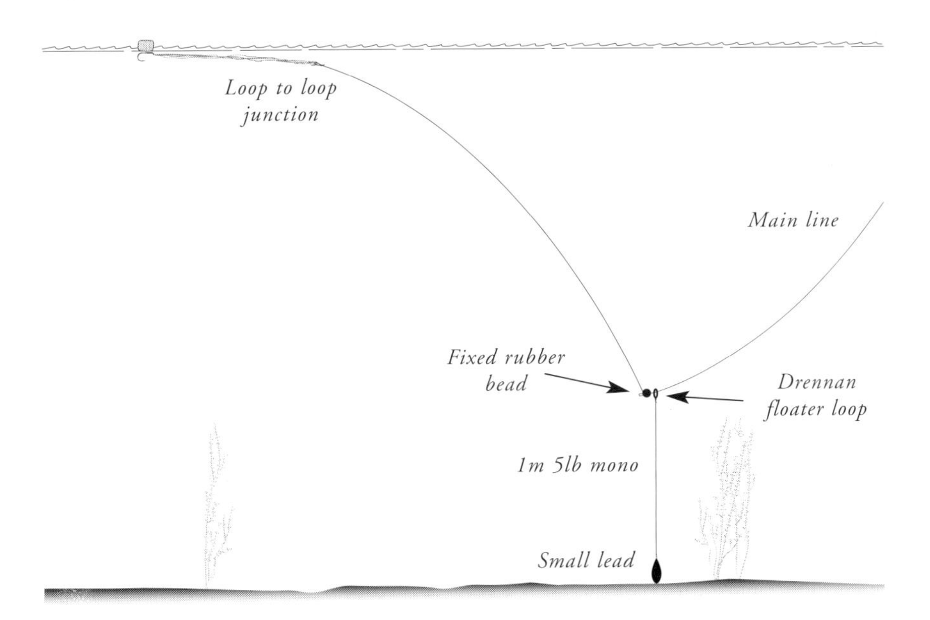

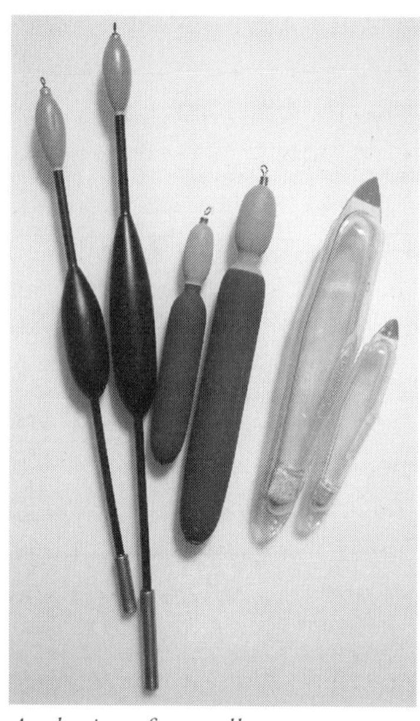

A selection of controllers.

My long tail paternoster setup incorporates a Drennan Floater Loop which is stopped by the rubber bead, cocktail stick combination. To the Floater Loop is tied a one metre length of fine mono, about 5lb test. To this is attached a small lead - usually 1/2 - 3/4oz. If the pit is weedy I use a disposable weight comprising an AA shot, over which is moulded a piece of Kryston Snag-Safe Putty or plasticine.

As with the controller rig, the main line terminates in a loop, to which is attached the hooklink. Distance from hook to stop depends on the depth of water - ideally it should be about one and a half times the depth to minimise the likelihood of underwater drag pulling the bait below the surface. The long tail paternoster is only practical in relatively shallow water due to the extreme awkwardness of casting with a tail length longer than the rod. For water over about 8ft deep, therefore, I use a modified version in which both the tail and the lead-link are about one metre in length. After casting, the bait is allowed to draw line through the Floater Loop until the bait appears on the surface. Unfortunately, mixer-type baits have insufficient buoyancy to reach the surface unaided, so they require the assistance of some sort of riser. A couple of extra mixers PVA'd to the hook will do the job, as will a piece of crust.

The disadvantage of detachable risers is that while they are effective in bringing the bait to the surface, they will not hold it there against underwater drag. This is doubtless why some anglers favour a permanent riser, such as a corkball or poly-ball, fixed to the line a couple of feet from the hook. Now, maybe it is just me, but I cannot get on with permanent risers - I find they increase the incidence of casting tangles and result in dropped takes. So if I deem a detachable riser unsuitable, I use a hookbait which has sufficient buoyancy to rise to the top and stay there, such as a 20-25mm (about quarter matchbox size) cube of crust or floater-cake.

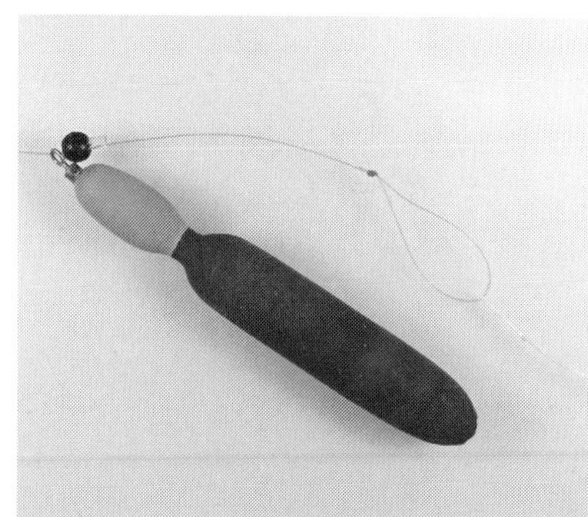

My loop-to-loop hooklink junction (in practice it is further from the controller than shown in this picture).

When a self-rising paternoster is combined with a large-ish cube of cake or crust it has the incidental advantage that if casting range or surface glare make it difficult to see the bait, a lightweight indicator can be hung on the line - one that is just supported by the buoyancy of the floater - and if the bait is swirled off the hook, or if it simply disintegrates due to wave action, the indicator drops back.

Another advantage of the self-rising paternoster is that the bait can be pulled beneath the surface when water birds approach. The frustration and confusion this causes them goes a small part of the way to mitigating their irritant quotient! Coots are particularly gratifying in this regard; they look around, completely baffled - you can almost imagine them thinking "Where'd it go? Where'd it go?" Mallards, unfortunately, quickly work out what has happened, and will try to dive for the bait if they can see it. It is therefore necessary to pull the bait beyond their reach. Young mallards can dive about nine feet. A well fed adult is too buoyant to get down that far, five or six feet is nearer their limit (you do not get useful information like that in RSPB spotter books).

If gulls are a problem, the bait can be pulled just beneath the surface and held there by putting the line in a clip. I have not found subsurface floater to be as effective as floater proper, but sometimes it is the only feasible means by which a topwater bait can be fished.

Takes on the running paternoster vary in character. Sometimes the bait is sipped down with barely a ripple; most times there is a swirl, and the bait disappears; best of all though, are the occasions when there is an almighty splash and a great V-wake cleaves the surface!

Soft Link

Earlier, you may recall, I mentioned that three years ago I went on a floater bender. Initially, as per standard practise, I tied my hook direct to the end of my mono main line (usually 10lb test). I found, however, that the proportion of strikeable takes to swirls and mouthings was not particularly good - in the region of 30-50% would be my guess. Lots of writers have mentioned this, and the consensus seems to be that the problem is due to the visibility of the line. Suggested solutions have included fluorocarbon links, suspender-type rigs, or the beachcaster setup. I was not persuaded that I needed to resort to any of these because observation convinced me that it was not the visibility of the mono hooklink which was leading to aborted takes, but its stiffness. Carp were not making last-moment refusals, but were being physically prevented from taking the

Fig.58 LOOP-TO-LOOP JUNCTION FOR JOINING MULTISTRAND TO MONO

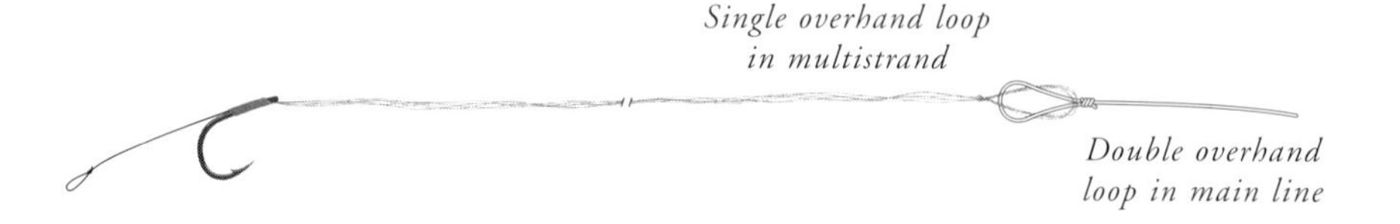

bait by the hindrance afforded by the adjacent mono. So instead of tying the hook direct to my main line, I tried a 50cm link of 15lb Multistrand.

I had expected a decrease in abortive takes, but was totally unprepared for what actually transpired which was their virtual disappearance! Not only did frustrating false-passes become a thing of the past, but takes became lovely sit-back-and-wait full-blooded runs! I was astonished at the difference it made.

Having become convinced as to the worth of Multistrand in this context, I experimented with Multistrand/mono junction knots and found, to my surprise, that the strongest was a simple loop-to-loop version (Fig 58). The loop in the end of the mono is made with a Double Overhand Knot, while a Single Overhand Knot is used to tie the loop in the Multistrand. Neither knot is Superglued - yes, I tried it, but on testing found that in these circumstances it gave no advantage. The double loop junction results in approximately 15% strength loss, for which I compensate by using stronger main line than I would normally choose for floater fishing. For open water my standard combination comprises 15lb Multistrand looped to 12lb nominal (14lb actual) Nash Power Plus, which gives an effective overall breaking strain of 11-12lb. For weedy water I upgrade to 25lb Multistrand and 15lb nominal (17lb actual) Power Plus - this provides an effective breaking strain of about 14lb.

Multistrand hooklink, double mixer and broom bristle stop.

A good take to hooking rate depends on initial pricking, followed by ease of penetration. This applies to all carp fishing situations, of course, but is especially so when using floaters because they create their own unique difficulties. Floating baits are taken differently to bottom baits, and the mechanics of floater setups (the beachcaster rig excepted) precludes the possibility of any significant bolt effect. Ultra sharp hooks are therefore essential - and I prefer straight point, straight shank patterns. In open water I like Nash Pattern Two, size 8, which has a razor sharp point and a tiny barb. In common with other micro-barbed patterns, however, it is not very good in weed - it is somewhat light in the wire for weed fishing, too. In which case I choose Ashima C310 Super Carp.

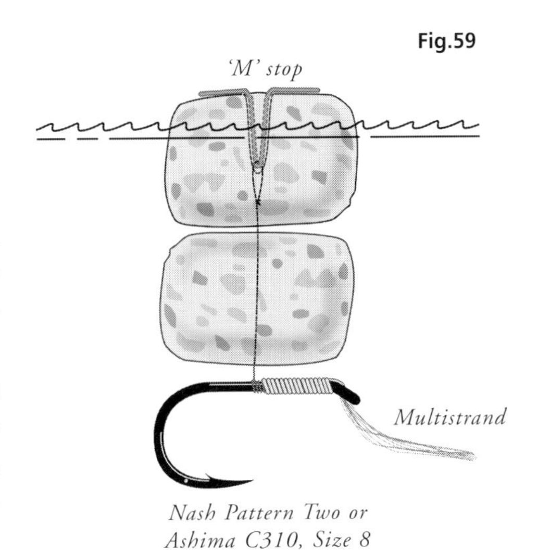

Bait Attachment

"Rubberised" mixers can be mounted directly on the hook. This is particularly suitable when freelining among surface weed for it reduces the risk of a hangup. It works well on a controller setup, too. On paternoster tackle, however, I prefer hookout bait attachment. I have tried Superglue, elasticated rings, Power Gum, tight hairs etc, but have abandoned them all in favour of a hair which emerges from the middle of the hook shank. The hair is sufficiently long to provide just 2-3mm clearance between the bait and the hook shank - in the case of double-mixer baits, for example, it will need to be about 12mm in length.

"Rubberised" mixers can be penetrated with a conventional baiting needle, but fresh, dry mixers need to be pre-bored with a nut drill or an ultrafine drill bit. Whether "rubberised" or dry, they are threaded on the hair and retained by means of an oversize nylon stop shaped something like an elongated letter "m" (Fig 59). I make these stops from nylon bristles cut from the head of a garden broom. If they are shaped with the aid of forceps, they have sufficient "memory" to retain the "m" configuration.

For floater-cake the hair length will need to be longer - 22-28mm is normal.

Crust can be attached by means of a hair - as per mixers and cake - but goes so soft and soggy that even my oversize "m" stop does not hold it in place for long. Better, I think, to mount it directly on the hook. A relatively fine wire pattern, like Nash Pattern Two or Kamasan B980, is best, and it needs be fairly large, too - at least size 6. I thread the hook in through the crumb side, out of the crust side, then push the point back in (Fig 60).

Fig.60 MOUNTING CRUST DIRECT ON HOOK

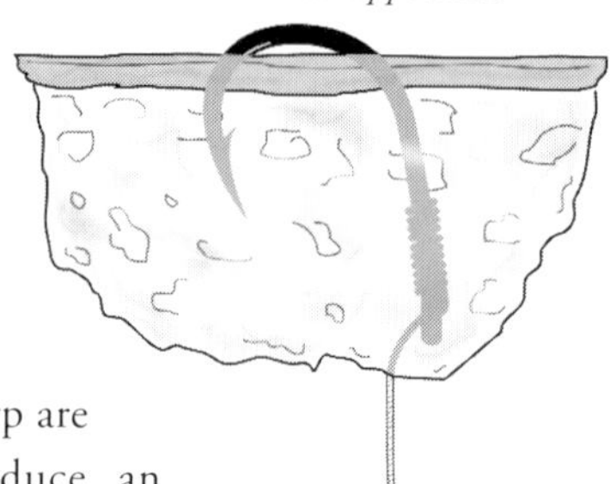

Feeding

In good floater weather, in a water where carp are topwater oriented, loose feeding can produce an enthusiastic food-search response. Care should be taken if there is a ripple on the surface, though, because fish can be lost from the area as they follow surplus baits downwind. Five or six baits every ten minutes is enough to keep the carp interested and ensure they stay in the vicinity.

When carp are swirling eagerly at floaters it is not uncommon to have them quartering the area, obviously looking for more - and not surprisingly takes are rarely long in coming. Several times, under these circumstances, I have had catches of between six and ten in a day - while my friend Carl Carlucci, who is a better floater angler than I will ever be, once took about 30! Yes, in a single day!

Effective loose feeding is only possible in an offshore or cross breeze, or if it is calm. An onshore wind presents difficulties because it results in baits spending too short a time in the vicinity of the hookbaits. I have tried bait droppers, PVA bags and stringers, and while all get freebies out there, none solve the short-stay problem.

An angler lands a carp on a controller setup.

This Essex pit fish proves that "golden carp" actually exist.

Tucked behind cover while fishing the margins of an Essex pit.

Summer sunshine and a handsome mirror - who could ask for more?

An overcast sky combined with a tree-girt swim required that this handsome common be photographed with flash.

Coastal pit common.

Late April sunshine caught me unawares and I suffered sunburn - it caught the carp unawares, too, and they took mixers with abandon!

The most effective method of freebie feeding in an onshore wind is to fish opposite someone who is using floaters from the upwind bank. Their surplus freebies drift across the pit towards you - hopefully followed by carp! It works brilliantly - but unfortunately the necessary circumstances occur only occasionally.

Early and late season (up to the end of April and after mid-September) carp demonstrate a significantly reduced tendency to follow the wind. This means that the upwind bank can be productive, which in turn makes freebie baiting easy. The optimum distance from the bank, incidentally, is usually where the sheltered calm water meets the ripple edge. How far out this occurs depends on wind strength and the height of bankside vegetation - but it is usually in the 15-30 yards range.

Birds Again...

A gorgeous mirror which sipped down a double mixer at dusk.

The disadvantage of any form of freebie-baiting is that it attracts the aforementioned gulls, swans, ducks etc. Bird blight sometimes gets me so strung-up that I am sure my blood pressure soars to dangerously high levels! One such instance prompted me to describe in a Carpworld article ("Floaters Revisited", 1996) how I arrived home one evening, still seething with frustration, and greeted Maria with the words, "This weekend, I want duck for dinner. I don't particularly like it, but I want the satisfaction of eating one of the damn things!"

The specimen on which I subsequently wreaked my carnivorous revenge was a blameless creature from Tesco's frozen food cabinet, and not one of the stupid, deficient, dim-witted nuisances which had caused me such strife.

But only fools expect justice in this cruel world!

Chapter Thirteen

Winter

Every year, it seems, we read an increasing number of references to winter fishing becoming more difficult.

An explanation put forward by Lee Jackson is that the carp's nutritional requirements are so sated by the widespread use of fishmeal boilies from spring through to autumn, that they have no need to "top up" their fat levels in winter. Harry Haskell suggested that the use of preservatives in some readymades has an adverse effect on the gut flora of carp; the outcome of which being that winter feeding is seriously inhibited. Several writers have speculated that there is too much natural food available in winter as a consequence of eutrophication and global warming.

It is true that in some, perhaps most waters, winter fishing has unquestionably become more difficult - but I doubt if this is due to any of the aforementioned reasons. In my opinion, it is simply the inevitable consequence of increased angling pressure.

I base my conclusion on the fact that I know of no water, however easy or difficult it might have been to start with, which has not become harder - and here I am not referring only to winter fishing - when subjected to angling pressure. As an illustration let me quote the case of RMC Angling's Sutton at Hone syndicate fishery in Kent. It is only a small pit - RMC reckon four acres, but I doubt if it is more than three. It holds upwards of 50 carp - most of which are over 20lb, with at least a dozen over 30lb and, at the last count, three in excess of 40lb. Not surprisingly, it is fished hard - by some quality anglers too.

When I fished Sutton in the early '80's the situation was very different; there were a couple of twenties, but the rest averaged low to mid double figures. They were quite amenable carp too. I could turn up any summer day and confidently expect to catch two or three. My best day produced six. I was not the only one to find the fishing moderately undemanding; a couple of local youngsters caught extremely well on tigernuts. Now, far from catching six carp in a day, you would be doing exceptionally well to catch six in a season!

Sutton is an extreme example because it has gone from being relatively easy to very difficult; but while the scale of change may be less pronounced on other waters, the pattern is the same.

Now, let us examine how this might impinge on winter fishing. In the vast majority of waters, it is generally far more difficult to catch carp in winter than it is from spring through to autumn. Such has always been the case. The main reason for this is the likelihood that in any given 24 hour period in winter there will be fewer carp willing to feed than in an equivalent period at any other time of the year. Furthermore, I believe that feeding spells are of much shorter duration. This decreased food requirement being due to low water temperature and its attendant reduction in metabolic rate.

This one came on a bitterly cold December day.

If we combine the reduced level of feeding which occurs naturally, with carp getting harder to catch as a consequence of angling pressure, then it is hardly surprising if winter carp fishing in many waters has become considerably more difficult.

"Not so," some readers might be thinking, "winter fishing is so unproductive on my local club water that hardly anyone does it now - so pressure can't be the reason for poor results."

That, I suggest, is too narrow a view because it fails to take account of the fact that reduced pressure in winter, when fish are less active, is unlikely to negate the accumulated wariness with which carp have become imbued over preceding months and years. A situation exacerbated nowadays by the fact that, with the abandonment of a statutory close season, many waters are open for the whole twelve months.

If I am correct, the lesson to be learned is obvious - the best winter waters are likely to be those which receive relatively scant angling pressure. And as a generalisation, it is not a bad principle to adopt. But, as is so often the case with neatly packaged guidelines, things are not quite that straightforward. A complication arises from the fact that for a given level of angling pressure, some waters offer much better prospects than others. Often this can be explained in terms of population density - the more carp there are in a water, the easier the fishing is likely to be. The "more carp equals easier fishing" equation does not, however, explain why two physically similar waters, each of which hold roughly the same number of carp, and are subjected to more or less equivalent angling pressure, should sometimes differ greatly in their level of difficulty.

Which brings me to hypothesis number two!

Carp are not native to Britain - nor even to northern Europe. Its native waters were the large rivers of Asia, and those which flow into the Mediterranean, Black, Caspian and Aral Seas. Carp are, therefore, a warm water species, and in their native environment rarely feed when the water temperature drops below about 10 degrees Celsius (50 degrees Fahrenheit). But their relatively fast growth and value as a food fish, coupled with the ease with which they could be bred, resulted in their being introduced to many other countries - the first of which were Czechoslovakia, Poland, Germany, France and Yugoslavia, where summers are shorter and cooler. Is it not reasonable to assume that over several generations a certain amount of adaptation occurred, allowing feeding to take place at lower temperatures than hitherto? Which, in case you are wondering where all this is leading, brings me to the crux of my hypothesis. Most U.K. carp have been imported from fish farms in The Netherlands, Belgium, France, Germany, Italy and, to a lesser extent, Israel. I think it is possible - likely even - that fish which come from a bloodline bred in the U.K. or northern Europe, have a genetically inherited predisposition to feed in cold water. I would not expect to find this characteristic in those which have come from warm countries like Italy and Israel.

As an incidental point, the foregoing hypothesis might also explain why some carp become almost completely torpid - a fact of which we may remain unaware until we catch them in spring and find they are heavily infested with leeches. In one of my Carpworld "Let Us Talk" columns I quoted an extreme example of this torpor which occurred in the middle lake at Murston, near Sittingbourne. Poor winter results prompted some anglers to wade out in the shallow water to see if they could discover where the carp had gone. They were found laying immobile in a reedbed and were so sluggish that they allowed themselves to be cradled in anglers' arms and lifted from the water!

Weather

In common with most winter anglers I like big, mild winds. I do not mind if the wind is accompanied by cloud and possibly light rain, or clear skies and sunshine. You will notice that I specified "light rain", because heavy rain is quite another matter and offhand I cannot recall a single instance when I have done well in such circumstances.

I like high pressure, sunny, still weather too, especially after an overnight frost - but only in November, and only in deep water (20ft plus). Identical weather during any other winter period, or in shallow water has tended to be unproductive. Strange that.

Rod Hutchinson, among others, has said that he likes the onset of a cold spell; he reckons it induces a sort of "Come on lads, let's get some food inside us before the big ice comes!" Certainly some animals seem to have the ability to predict hard weather, so maybe Rod is correct.

Hail is the kiss of death, I have found. Yet I recall Brian Mills telling me about an amazing catch he made from a big south coast pit after hail had fallen so hard that a floating layer of mini ice-cubes covered the lake's entire surface!

Snow is something of a novelty here in the south-east, and occurs too infrequently for me to be able to evaluate its influence. But providing the roads are

I like these conditions in November - but in February, when this picture was taken, I prefer big, mild winds.

An overnight sprinkling of snow only just manages to whiten the banks.

safe, I will happily fish in it. And that, I suppose, best sums up my attitude to winter carp weather - if I can get to the water, and providing the conditions are not so unbearable as to make being out too much of an ordeal, then I will fish. I used to try to pick my conditions but was wrong so often that nowadays I let the carp decide whether or not they will feed!

There is also the switch-on syndrome to consider. This phenomenon seems to occur quite independently of the weather, and refers to those brief spells when for no apparent reason a large proportion of the carp in a water become active and go enthusiastically "on the prod". It happens on most waters - even the very difficult ones. Rarely, however, does it occur more than once or twice in the entire winter. Usually the feeding periods are of quite short duration, rarely longer than a day or two, so only those anglers who fish regularly, almost regardless of the weather, stand a realistic chance of being there when it occurs. By the time word gets out that the water is producing, the switch-on period has passed and it is too late to capitalise on the situation. So my advice is to ignore everything you hear or read about the best weather for winter carp fishing; instead, "keep the faith" and just try to be there!

Location

When your winter carp fishing experience is confined to just one or two waters it is tempting to assume that location "rules" which apply there apply everywhere. Then, as more waters are fished, the picture becomes progressively more confused. In one water the most productive spots might be the deeper areas; in another it seems that the margins of distant islands are best; in yet another it might be the remains of the previous summer's lily beds, or the marshy shallows near an inlet stream... and so on. Which gives the impression that winter carp are completely unpredictable, and the only means of finding them is by luck or trial-and-error.

Whilst it is true that individual waters can be idiosyncratic, I do not accept that winter carp are entirely unpredictable. I recently did a mental audit and calculated that I have caught winter carp from approximately twenty different gravel pits; which is, I think, a sufficient number to enable me to recognise patterns where they occur.

The overwhelming impression I have gained is that winter carp like to feel secure, so they choose places where they will remain undisturbed. In big pits this may simply involve moving beyond normal casting range. In waters insufficiently large for that option, they tend whenever possible to seek areas which are inaccessible - a nature sanctuary where fishing is not allowed, for example. Alternatively they may move to places which afford cover, such as snags or dying weedbeds. Water depth is fairly irrelevant, and sometimes they move into surprisingly shallow spots.

Deep waters - which I define as those having extensive areas deeper than about 20ft - demonstrate a different pattern. During the second half of October there is a noticeable migration to deeper - but rarely the deepest - places. As an example; in a water with an average depth of 20ft, and a maximum of 30ft, I would expect to find carp in the 25ft region. If the maximum depth was 40ft, I would opt for 30-35ft.

Why carp should behave this way is difficult to understand. It is not due to deeper water being warmer, because most of the time the converse applies. All the while the water temperature remains above 4 degrees Celsius (39 degrees Fahrenheit), thermal stratification ensures that the surface layers - and consequently the shallower spots - are warmest. Only when the water temperature drops below 4 degrees Celsius, and an apparent reversal of the normal laws of thermal stratification occurs, does the surface layer become cooler than deeper areas. But some years - especially in the southern half of the country - the water never gets this cold; and even when it does happen it is likely to last for only two or three weeks and be confined to January or early February. So why do carp go deep as early as mid-October? If temperature is not the key, what is? An optimum level of dissolved oxygen, perhaps? Or maybe the pH is just right? Or could it be because deeper areas offer a more stable environment than shallower water? Or does the natural food (fly larvae, snails etc.) go deep? Or might the carp be using depth as a form of cover - in other words, do they feel safer with 20-30ft of water over their heads?

January common and tea-cosy hat!

Although I do not know why they go deep, I am convinced that the factor which triggers it is day-length because it happens irrespective of weather conditions. Which, if true, endorses the opinion first expressed, I believe, by Rod Hutchinson, that carp have their biological clocks regulated by the angle of the sun rather than temperature.

To what extent my observations are universal, I cannot say, but I have fished five winter waters with extensive 20ft plus areas, and this migration has been evident in every case.

Mid to late February the migration reverses and, again irrespective of weather, the carp gradually move back to shallower water.

The final location factor I would mention - and this applies to both deep and shallow waters - is the north-east of middle phenomenon. If I am unable to identify any promising looking "safe" areas, and depth variations are insufficient to induce slope migration, I fish north-east of the middle. As a location tactic, it is surprisingly consistent. Why it should be so, I do not know. When I first mentioned it in print - about ten years ago I would guess - I speculated that it combined distance-from-the-bank security with a degree of shelter from cold north-east winds. Additionally it offered maximum exposure to mild south-westerlies. Ten years on, it still seems like a reasonable explanation.

Application of the north-east of middle "rule" once enabled me to locate carp in a pit I had never seen! What happened was that a midlands' angler sent me a detailed depth map of a large (30 acres plus) gravel pit in which he had been very successful in summer, but had thus far had a fruitless winter. "Any suggestions where I might find them?" he asked. The water had considerable depth variation, and lots of areas qualified for the "deeper than average" guideline. I circled two such spots which were within casting distance, and were situated north-east of middle. A couple of weeks later I received another letter, and was gratified (and not a little surprised!) to read, "I managed to borrow an electronic fish finder, and the only areas where I found fish were those you picked out."

The foregoing should not be taken by readers as an invitation to send me maps of their pits in the hope that I will pinpoint winter carp hotspots. I am not unwilling to help; it is just that I would like to quit the remote location business with an unblemished 100 per cent success record!

Bait

During the course of a long, albeit erratic winter carp fishing career (involving numerous diversions for cod, pike, bream, roach and skiing!) I have caught them on:

sausage meat paste
frankfurter
luncheon meat
sweetcorn
bread crust
bread flake
maggots
worms
cockles
trout pellet paste
salmon pellet paste
trout/salmon pellet boilies
birdfood boilies
Nash S-Mix boilies
Nash readymade boilies (Peach, Strawberry and Scopex)
milk protein boilies
Nash Winter Mix (birdfood, cereals and milk proteins)

For a number of years I held the view that milk protein boilies were the most effective winter baits. But when I look back I have to acknowledge that whilst I caught plenty of fish on them, I had no basis for valid comparison because at the time I used nothing else! I even conveniently chose to forget that before being seduced by the milk protein HNV hypothesis, I caught loads of winter fish on salmon and/or trout pellet based baits.

My use of milk protein baits in winter persisted even after I underwent a sort of Saint Paul On The Road To Damascus anti milk conversion for my summer and autumn fishing - but predictably the time came when I questioned the validity of their use in winter too. My first change was a fairly gentle one in that I tried Nashbait's Winter Mix (now discontinued) which incorporated some refined milk products but consisted primarily of birdfoods including Red Factor and Carophyl Red. It also contained maize meal, wholemeal semolina and soya-based Protein Trusoy. It proved far superior to my usual 60% milk/40% semolina mix and produced a lot of carp - some multiple catches, too.

Then something happened which confused me utterly. I was talking to Nashbait boss, Gary Bayes, about winter fishing and he said, “I nearly always put a fruity-type readymade on one rod." This, remember, from the Director of one of the country's leading bait companies - a man with every imaginable bait at his disposal - yet he chose to devote one rod to readymades. To an erstwhile dyed-in-the-wool HNV-milk-protein-in-winter disciple this was tantamount to sacrilege! Yes, I knew readymades were okay for summer and autumn, but not for winter surely...

Had the advice come from anyone else I doubt if I would have heeded it, but such is my respect for Gary's opinions that I gave readymades a try on one rod. On my second rod I stuck with the Winter Mix flavoured with one of my top three winter additives: Nash Strawberry Palatant, asafoetida essential oil, or maple/butterscotch (Richworth Butt-Cracker Special). I caught fish on both rods, probably in similar numbers, but what really impressed me was that on days when only one take occurred, it was as likely to come to the readymade as to the Winter Mix. By Christmas I was happily fishing readymades on both rods.

For the two or three winters up to and including '96/'97 I continued to rely primarily on readymades, but then I decided to heed the advice I kept getting from Kevin Nash and Gary Bayes, to try their S-Mix. The version I used was Scopex/Red Liver Oil. I fished two 10mm baits on a hair, with a grain of sweetcorn sandwiched between them. Fairly tight to my hookbaits I free baited with boilies, hempseed, 2.6mm trout pellets, Micromass and sweetcorn. It sounds like a lot, but I only used a couple of pult-pouches of each. It proved to be a very effective combination and I caught consistently.

But here was a conundrum. The S-Mix contains fishmeals - and, as everyone knows, fishmeals are useless in winter. To my embarrassment I admit that I had allowed myself to be brainwashed into accepting this dogma despite, as mentioned earlier, having caught plenty of winter carp on salmon/trout pellet pastes and boilies which - depending what I added to them - had a fishmeal content of 20-30%! Brothers Rick and Martin likewise.

Proof that my '97/'98 experience with the S-Mix was not a "one off" was provided by Rick who, during the course of the '98/'99 winter, achieved absolutely astonishing results on it. From early January onwards, hardly a week went past without a telephone call which started with the words, "It continues....". There would then be a pause, followed by an account of yet another incredible catch!

Gary and Chris Williams, in various Carpworld articles (some of the best winter pieces I have read in recent years, incidentally), said that despite the widespread belief that fishmeals were ineffective in winter, they used their own Neptune fish mix to obtain some very consistent results. Simon Crow, writing in issue 45 of the Carp Society's bi-monthly magazine, Carp Fisher, described how he had achieved good winter catches on Orchid and Birch Grove while using fishmeals. Simon fished to quite heavily baited areas too (1-2kg) - but that is an issue I shall come to presently.

A diligent trawl through back issues of various carp magazines would doubtless reveal other references to the success of fishmeals in winter - but they would be vastly outnumbered by statements which express the exact opposite.

Who is correct?

The pro-fishmeal group is in the minority, but you cannot argue with the indisputable evidence of their catches. So from where did the belief come that fishmeals are ineffective in winter? It came, as has so much of our received wisdom, from that vast repository of folklore which owes its acceptance to the frequency with which it is repeated, rather than the frequency with which it proves to be correct.

The origin of the "fishmeals are rubbish in winter" tenet stemmed from the one-time all-conquering fishmeal mixes which were sold by Premier Baits. Premier did not invent fishmeals, nor even produce the first proprietary fishmeal readymixes, but they were the first to demonstrate how effective fishmeals could be when accompanied by what, at the time, were considered to be extremely high baiting levels. In addition they popularised the use of high dosages of fish oil in, and subsequently on their baits. The Premier success story gathered momentum and numerous waters - in the jargon of catch reports, articles and advertisements - were "taken apart" by anglers using fishmeals in conjunction with high baiting levels. Among the pits which fell under the Premier spell were high profile fisheries such as Darenth and Harefield. Even committed HNV milk protein devotees like Paul Selman switched their allegiance and sung Premier's praises.

The bandwagon rolled.

Leastways, it did until late autumn when results slowed dramatically. "Slowed" as in, "ground to a virtual stop," actually. A development which should have surprised no one - but amazingly it seemed to do so!

Attempts were made to revitalise the baits with so called "winterised oils" which were, in effect, oils which did not solidify or become overly viscous in low temperature. This made little difference because Premier Baits used a high level of fishmeal (50% by weight) in their mixes, so the bait's natural oil content was high anyway.

Had anglers "cut" a standard Premier fishmeal mix with a birdfood mix - thereby reducing the fishmeal component to 25% - and resisted the temptation to add extra oil; and had they radically reduced their baiting levels, I have absolutely no doubt that they would have continued to catch throughout the winter.

Fishmeal is an effective ingredient for winter baits - but not if used at very high levels. Intuition and experiment lead me to believe that the upper limit is somewhere in the region of 30% - although it will depend to an extent on the type of fishmeal(s) used, and the means by which they have been processed. The significance of that last point is that it affects the meal's oil content. On which subject, I strongly believe that no bulk oil should be added to winter fishmeal baits, from whatever source - fish or vegetable.

Particles

Fishmeals are not the only winter baits to have suffered an undeserved "bad press"; so have particles. In the many articles I have read on winter fishing, rarely have particles been mentioned other than in a negative sense. But, yet again, popular perception is not supported by empirical evidence. My first demonstration that particles could work in winter occurred many years ago when I accompanied Gerry Hughes - then Features Editor of Anglers' Mail - as a guest to the Red Spinner water at Cheshunt. I used luncheon meat, and caught five or six carp. Gerry used soya beans, and caught a similar number.

At about the same time as my trip with Gerry, Rick caught winter carp from a couple of his Essex club waters on broad beans.

At the Faversham Angling Club's famous Bysingwood Pool several anglers - Andy Spreadbury was one of them I believe - made some excellent winter catches on sweetcorn (this was back in pre hair rig days, incidentally).

Two friends of mine, Mick Nolan (Cygnet Tackle boss) and Cliff Herridge, are particle specialists. Both have used particles in winter with considerable success - but in fairness to them I will not give further information because it is not for me to disclose the fine details of their respective approaches.

Kevin Maddocks caught winter carp from Redmire on tigernuts, and the "Redmire Winter" chapter in his lovely book "In Pursuit of Carp and Catfish" (Beekay, 1986) contains this telling phrase, "I knew the carp would feed on the tigers sooner or later - they always did... ."

Rick recently told me that one of the anglers who was close to being top winter rod on one of his club waters used - as you will no doubt have guessed - particles. Like Kevin Maddocks, he chose tigernuts.

Martin Clarke has written of baiting quite heavily with hempseed - and while he used popup boilies as hookbait, he was in no doubt that carp ate the hempseed.

Particles - like fishmeals - if used in moderation and with common sense can be effective winter baits. They have fallen victim to a negative dynamic - few anglers use them, so few carp are caught on them. This in turn gives no encouragement for anglers to try them… and so it continues.

Bait Quantity

I have made several somewhat oblique references to baiting amounts. It is now time, I think, to examine the subject in more detail. Back in my milk protein days I winter fished with just hookbaits in very cold conditions, or a stringer and possibly a few freebies if it was milder. In more recent winters, while using readymades, I have used anything from twenty to fifty 15mm freebies around each stringer-rigged hookbait. After each take I topped up with another twenty or so. It worked very well - and occasionally led me to wonder if I might have benefited from increasing the baiting levels yet further. I resisted the temptation, however, because I have seen winter waters switch off suddenly and completely when too much bait has gone in. But how much is too much?

Obviously it depends on the stock density in the pit, the weather conditions, and the extent to which the carp in that water are winter feeders. It also depends what other anglers are doing. That last point is very significant - possibly the most important element in the equation. In the May 1999 issue of Carp Fisher, Phil Roots wrote about his winter experiences on Orchid Lake. After his first November session he introduced 5kg of particles and 5kg of boilies (Carp Company's Icelandic Red Base Mix, I believe). Phil continued to, in his own words, "keep a steady stream of bait going in… throughout the winter until March." His article did not make it clear whether he maintained the original quantities, nor how frequently he baited; but he left me with the distinct impression that he used a considerable amount, and put it in two or three times a month (after each trip, in fact). That his baiting policy worked was demonstrated by the consistent and excellent results he achieved. But - and here we come to the crux of the matter - in relation to his initial baitings, Phil wrote, "The other anglers on the lake must have thought that I was mad, as they were using very small amounts of bait or stringers."

Orchid is a biggish pit (19 acres), and contains a good stock of big carp. But had two, three, five or ten other anglers decided to emulate Phil's approach what, I wonder, would have been the outcome? Observation on other waters suggests to me that the fishing would have ground to a halt. Heavy winter baiting - providing the water and the carp population can sustain it - is okay all the while only one, or maybe two anglers are doing it. But there comes a threshold beyond which it stops working. Trouble is, not only does the heavy baiting approach stop working, but everything else does too. There is just too much readily available food for there to be any likelihood of it being consumed.

One of my local pits was very heavily baited three winters ago with Mainline's Grange. The anglers concerned were extremely successful; they caught more between them than did all the other regulars put together. The reason for their success did not go unnoticed, however, and the following winter a number of others adopted similar tactics. The outcome was inevitable - hardly anyone caught anything from winter's beginning right through to the season's end! Fortunately it was not one of my winter venues so the switch-off did not affect me, but early March I decided to have an investigative "dabble" to see if it was worth a few back-end trips. To my astonishment, when I retrieved my rods at dusk I found that on two out of the three I had foulhooked someone else's freebies! Incredible! The bottom must have been carpeted with putrefying boilies for that to have happened. Possibly only my swim was affected - but somehow I doubt it. Needless to say, I deleted the water from my list for the remainder of the season! In exceptional cases, excessive baiting by just one individual can ruin things. Rick told me how the fishing on one of his Essex pits - a fishery which is usually a good winter prospect - was rendered very difficult a couple of years ago by the excessively high baiting levels employed by one angler. The following year - doubtless discouraged by his lack of success on that water - the offending "master baiter" (pun intended!) went elsewhere. Winter results returned, not surprisingly, to their former level.

So, I repeat the question I asked earlier - how much is too much?

If heavy baiting results in consistent success, then clearly the water is not being over baited. On the other hand, if carp are not being caught, it makes no sense to continue with the tactic - leastways, not at the same level.

Notwithstanding the occasional successes achieved in conjunction with heavy baiting in winter, it is a high risk strategy. Good catches will very likely encourage others to bait heavily - with the probable consequence that aggregate baiting levels will be far too high and few carp will be caught by anyone.

For the last couple of winters my main feeding procedure has been the use of a scaled-down version of the multi-item system which I described in Chapter Eleven. This is particularly well suited to close range fishing where my freebie boilies can be supplemented with loose fed hempseed, Micromass, sweetcorn and mini trout pellets. On packing up I throw in whatever I have left over - it is never more than 500gm overall, and usually much less. Whether this low-level "tick over" baiting serves any useful purpose I cannot say - but I doubt that it is sufficient to do any harm.

Another tactic which shows promise is modified Method fishing. I had hitherto not associated winter fishing with the use of groundbait, but was persuaded to review my opinion when, from Christmas '98 through to the end of January, I concentrated on a seven-acre pit from which most of the carp had been removed (the controlling club wanted to develop it as their "match water"...). To be truthful I had bream in mind rather than carp, because by reputation it held fish to double figures. In the event, although I caught bream over 9lb with gratifying frequency, I did not catch my "double" - I did, however, catch six carp. They, like the bream, fell to Method tactics. During the course of my five weeks' fishing (which comprised about a dozen single day trips) I used approximately 20kg of cereal groundbait which was augmented with at least 5kg of hempseed, sweetcorn and hookbait samples. I was therefore averaging about 2kg of bait per trip! Yes, I know bream ate it too, but it nonetheless represents a lot of bait for sessions which rarely started before 9.00am, and were almost always over by teatime. But - and here I echo the point I made earlier - I was the only one fishing this way. The pit, you will recall, had been de-carped by the controlling club, and the carp anglers who previously fished there calculated that only about 30 remained. So the water was neglected. Most days, apart from a few pike anglers and the occasional float fisherman, I had it to myself. I cannot be certain, of course, but I am convinced that had others adopted similar tactics, the quantity of bait used would have been too great for the relatively small number of bream in the water and the low winter consumption rate of the carp.

Tactical Summary

After that wide ranging discussion of general issues pertaining to winter carp fishing, I would like to conclude with a summary of my current approach.

My first tactical decision concerns where to fish - and as you will have gathered from what I have already written, I generally opt for waters which receive little angling pressure. Gravel pits, by their nature, are often found in clusters. If among them is a highly rated carp water, chances are it will attract most of the carp fishing effort. Other pits in the group, where the carp may be smaller or fewer in number - or both - are likely to receive less attention. Occasionally these "Cinderella" fisheries, as I call them, are almost entirely neglected. These are my preferred waters.

By reducing the competition from other anglers I believe I increase my chances of success. The fish will be less nervous, and less likely to have become replete on someone else's baits. Additionally, I think the statistical odds in my favour are increased by the fact that although I may be fishing for fewer carp than are to be found in higher profile waters, I do not have to share them.

Then there are the purely practical issues to consider. I do not have to worry that I may be fishing a swim which someone has "filled in" with bait. And if I am the only one fishing a water - or at least, the only one in "my" few acres of it - there is no likelihood of my fishing being ruined by someone else's casting, baiting, feature finding etc.

Which reminds me - I have occasionally read advice to the effect that when winter fishing it is a good idea to use one rod as a rover. It might, for example, be cast to a different spot every couple of hours - the hoped for outcome, of course, being the discovery of a feeding carp or two. While I cannot claim to have tried this approach to any extent, it is not one which appeals to me due to the risk of fish being spooked. Only if carp are feeding hard will they tolerate a lead splashing down nearby - and feeding of that intensity is extremely rare in winter. Far better, I think, to cast out and leave it. Having chosen my quiet, hopefully neglected water, I try to chip away at it with regular visits - twice a week if possible. Within reason I will go whatever the weather - although heavy rain or bitterly cold winds might discourage me. When heavy rain and bitterly cold winds join forces and arrive together, I will wimp out for sure!

Hitherto - as previously described - I have tended to use 15mm readymades in conjunction with moderate baiting levels if fishing at medium to long range, or 10mm S-Mix and a mixed feed approach if fishing close. Both strategies have served me well, but after last winter's experience on the de-carped bream pit, I intend giving more attention to Method-style tactics. Where they are permitted, I shall try tigernuts, too.

Most times I use bottom baits - but I have also caught a lot of carp on the snowman arrangement and slow sinking critically balanced baits.

I am not a fan of popups and, in truth, rarely use them. I do, however, acknowledge the likelihood that this sometimes costs me fish because evidence suggests that there are times - in winter more than in summer - when popups offer the best chance of success. Not just conventional popups either, but baits fished 1-4ft off the bottom. High water popups, relative to their comparatively infrequent use, have a good track record. Clearly, the tactic warrants more attention than it receives - my problem, though, is that I have difficulty psyching myself up to give it a fair trial.

I almost always attach a stringer. Four is the usual number, but I may decrease it if I want to cut down on air resistance in order to achieve the required distance.

My winter trips start about breakfast time and usually see me packing up at dusk.

November mirror from 20ft plus.

Long range winter fishing in Essex.

Anglers argue whether November carp qualify as autumn or winter captures. Frankly, when they are this beautiful, I don't much care!

"Geordie" Mike and I have a winter social trip to Johnson's.

Neglected waters are my winter preference.

Midwinter common.

The exception is during November and December when many pits fish better after dark than they do in daylight, so during that period I try to extend my fishing into the evening.

Rick with a January mirror from an Essex pit.

Whenever possible I use a light lead (1.5oz or less), but I do not hesitate to go heavier if range or wind conditions require it. Most times it will be fished running, in conjunction with a 12lb Snake-Skin or 15lb Snake-Bite hooklink, and as small and light a hook as possible - usually an Owner spade-end, size 6 or 7 (8 or 9 equivalent), or a Fox Series Two, size 8.

Indicators will be as light as range and undertow allow. If it is practical to do so I fish with a drooping line. The usual pattern is that I get a "bleep" or two from the Delkim - which I am virtually certain are line brushes - followed within ten minutes or so by a run. Most are conventional "fliers", but I get a few slow trundlers, and the very occasional pull-tight-and-stop take. Very few are missed.

Warm and Dry

The fact that I use an umbrella rather than a bivvy, and have no sleeping-bag in which to cocoon myself, means I have to rely on my clothing to keep me warm and dry. After a succession of one-piece and two-piece suits from different manufacturers, I have finally opted for a top-of-the-range two-piece from Sundridge - their Igloo model. And no, cynical reader, that is not a product "plug" in gratitude for a freebie! I bought it with my own hard-earned wonder-wallet-filler from my local tackle shop. The Igloo is so warm that most times I only wear tracksuit bottoms and a sweatshirt beneath it. A zip-up fleece top is carried in my rucksack for those rare occasions when I require an extra layer. To reduce sweating when "yomping" to my swim I unzip the Igloo's bib and brace, and carry the coat. This is only practical if the weather is dry, of course.

The Igloo has a hood, but I reserve it for wind and rain, preferring to rely on a woolly hat the rest of the time. Apart from keeping my head warm, my varied selection of hats provides Maria with hours of merriment because she reckons I look like a total nerd in them. I aim to please...

Most "keeping warm" articles recommend moonboots. I find them uncomfortable for walking, so rely on oversize wellingtons worn in conjunction with two pairs of thermal ski-boot socks.

Chapter Fourteen

Equipment

Rods

For most of my gravel pit fishing I use 12ft/2.25lb Eclipses. Their action is best described as "semi fast", which makes them suitable for everything from swinging out a 1oz (28gm) margin rig, to pushing 3oz (85gm) beyond 100 yards. Where the range is not too great - say up to 40 yards - I even use them for lobbing Method balls.

Observation suggests that the majority of carp anglers prefer heavier models - usually something in the 2.5-3lb region - which is probably a consequence of their using 3-3.5oz (85-100gm) leads for most of their fishing. But if catch reports in the weeklies are anything to go by, a change is underway because an increasing proportion of anglers appear to be using leads of 1.5-2.5oz (42-70gm). If this trend continues, it will doubtless be accompanied by a gradual switch to lighter rods.

For pits over about 25 acres - where I may occasionally require leads of 3.5-4oz (98-112gm) to achieve the necessary distance - I will upgrade to 12.5ft/2.75lb Eclipses. They are also my choice for those pits which from late July through to mid-September become horrendously weedy, and where the "playing" of big carp can on occasions degenerate into a tackle-straining tug-of-war.

Only when fishing the very biggest pits do I feel the need to ratchet-up the casting weight to 4-4.5oz (112-126gm) - in which case I use 13ft/3.25lb Eclipses.

You will notice that my rods comprise 12ft, 12.5ft and 13ft models. This is not to suggest that there is anything intrinsically superior about 12.5ft or 13ft rods for distance fishing because, truth is, rod length has more to do with convention and market-led demand than optimum performance.

Most modern carp rods have six or seven rings (inclusive of the tip). Six is sufficient for 12-13ft models. Actually five would suffice, but the market is not quite ready for rods so sparsely equipped. The butt ring should be at least 30mm in diameter to reduce friction as coils of line spill from the spool during casting. If the rod is likely to be used with a wide-spool reel, a 40mm butt ring is better. It should be located approximately one metre from the reel - further in the case of a rod intended solely for long range fishing. The remaining rings should get progressively smaller, culminating in a 10-12mm tip ring (I prefer the larger size for purpose-built distance rods to allow unhindered passage of a leader knot).

Those who make their own rods, or have them custom built, might find it useful to know that the 12ft/2.25lb Eclipse is equipped with ring sizes: 30mm, 25mm, 16mm, 12mm, 10mm plus a 10mm tip ring. The 12.5ft/2.75lb and 13ft/3.25lb versions are equipped with: 40mm, 30mm, 20mm, 16mm, 12mm plus 12mm tip ring.

Do not, incidentally, worry that widely spaced rings might result in line-slap against the blank which will inhibit casting performance. When I first read about this phenomenon I tried to reproduce it, but was unable to do so. I even rigged a blank with just a tip ring - no side guides at all - and while this resulted in an alarming "bang!" as the line whacked across the blank when it recovered from compression, no line-slap occurred.

Modern ceramic-lined rings have a very low coefficient of friction, thereby enabling silky smooth casting. They are incredibly hard, too, and I have never heard of an instance where grooving has occurred. Fuji Silicone Carbide (SiC) are universally acclaimed as the best, but whether they perform discernibly better than less costly alternatives such as Aluminium Oxide or Zirconium Carbide is debatable. Overall quality differences are negligible, too - leastways, they are within the Fuji range because Fuji Aluminium Oxide rings have the same top quality stainless steel frames as their SiC models. They therefore offer the same level of protection and security to their ceramic centres, but at about one third the price.

Ceramic lined rings of whatever type share the common characteristic that they do not readily withstand sharp knocks. If a rod should fall onto or strike against a hard surface

2.25lb Eclipses, Aeros, Delkims and Chris Brown buzzer-bar/bankstick; my usual setup.

it is essential that all inserts be carefully examined because even the tiniest hairline crack, barely detectable to the naked eye, can cause serious line damage.

Frequently I see recommendations to the effect that we should use flexible rings in order to avoid the flat spots which occur when the blank is pulled into a curve.

There are times when I despair; I really do!

Flat spots belong in the same repository of nonsense as line-slap! From where such myths originate I have no idea - possibly from the same source as propounds the view that alien life forms traverse the incomprehensible vastness of space for no better reason than to make pretty patterns in cornfields!

Talking of which - the vastness of space that is - if, as we are assured, the universe is infinite, how come it is also expanding? Expanding infinity is more than a scientific paradox, it is a perfect example of an oxymoron. Which baffling conundrum I shall address to astronomer Heather Couper - she of the gorgeous voice - should I ever have the good fortune to bump into her beside one of my local pits!

As I was saying... rod rings do not cause flat spots. They do, however, add weight - and this has a significant damping effect on the action of a blank. It not only softens the overall "feel" of a rod, but creates inertia which slightly retards the speed with which it recovers from flex during casting. We cannot reduce the diameter of rings, or we increase line drag. So we keep their number to a minimum. Additionally, they should be light in weight. Single leg patterns are the lightest (which puzzlingly, despite their name, actually have two legs!), but they are rather easily deformed during transportation. I therefore prefer the more rigid tripod design of the three leg pattern. The third wire adds a little extra weight, but I think this is justified by the considerable increase in strength and rigidity which it affords.

Most production rods have the handle fitting positioned so the reel stem is 60-65cm from the extreme butt-end. Anyone who prefers a different position, or a particular fitting, or wants to break with the ergonomically unsound convention whereby DPS models are attached screw-thread downwards, should discuss their requirements with custom rod makers such as Simpsons, The Tackle Box or Bob Morris.

As regards the type of fitting, fashion plays a bigger part than practicality because the actual design makes little difference, just so long as it will securely accommodate the whole range of modern carp reels (including the large, long spool distance models). Many anglers, however, regard the cosmetic aspects as being of major importance, and I have known instances where whole sets of rods have been replaced in order to acquire the latest reel fitting! All of which is harmless enough, even though it is entirely pointless and will not put one extra carp on the bank!

Which reminds me...

Back in the '70's I went through a minimalist phase which involved dispensing with winch fittings and lashing my reels to my rods with PVC adhesive tape. One day, while I was fishing the A2 Point on Brooklands, a visitor to my swim inquired, "What's the theory behind that, Jim? Is it to retain the blank's flexibility?"

"No," I replied, "it's to stop the reels from falling off!"

I took minimalism to extremes, though, and for a couple of seasons used one-piece rods. They did not lend themselves to easy transportation, of course, and had to be carried on a roof rack. To prevent the tips from thrashing about I bent them slightly downwards and tied them to my wing mirrors, which according to Chis Ball - who remembers such things - gave my then van the appearance of an upturned sledge!

Which, via a virtually seamless link(!), brings me to the next subject - ferrules. I like overfits. Not only do I think they are stronger than spigots, but they are better able to accommodate wear. This may not be particularly relevant to session anglers who leave their rods assembled for long periods, but for those of us who fish in such a manner that our rods are assembled and dismantled frequently, ferrule wear is a significant issue.

The disadvantage of overfits is their cost. To achieve an overfit joint requires that the tip and butt sections be made separately - two separate blanks, in fact. Spigotted rods, on the other hand, are made from one blank which is simply cut in half, and the appropriate size spigot glued in place. The cost implications of having to make two blanks per rod are the reason why overfits are confined to more expensive models.

Multi modulus carbon composite blanks are immensely strong, but they are not designed to withstand overloading such as occurs when an angler hooks a snag, then tries to pull free by bending the rod over his shoulder. This strains the rod beyond its limits. If the end-tackle becomes snagged, the rod should be pointed at the obstruction, and the line subjected to a straight pull.

Reels

For most of my carp fishing I use Shimano 6010GT or 8010GT Aero Baitrunners. For close-in work I prefer the smallest of the American Series Baitrunner, the 3500. They do not have the long spool, nor the lovely line-lay of the Aeros, but the gears are beautifully smooth, and the front mounted clutch is a dream. They are not perfect, though, because their line-clip protrudes sufficiently to snag any wayward coil which comes too close. I was tempted to remove the clip, but settled for covering it with PVC adhesive tape.

When long range fishing in waters where weed requires that I use line in excess of 0.32mm I scale-up to what are generally referred to as "Big Pit Reels" which, in my case, are Daiwa PM4000's or Shimano 7000GT Biomasters. I considered

American Series Baitrunners - a much nicer clutch than on the Aeros.

having them equipped with free-spool conversions, but after trying some I concluded that it was just as easy to give the clutch adjustor knob a few turns. Another reason I decided against having them fitted was due to my concern that the protruding nature of the on/off lever had too much potential to snag the line.

Some of my reels have old-style line rollers, others have versions which, according to press releases and advertisements "eliminate an average of 40% of line twist." Some field testers, evidently, did even better and found a 90% reduction to be the norm.

Wow!

What can I say? Impressed or what?

Well, no, actually...

Line twist is an unavoidable consequence of line leaving or being wound on a spool at right angles to its axis. In an ideal world, twists imparted when casting would be removed on the retrieve. Or vice versa. We do not, alas, live in an ideal world, and the harmonious balance of this arrangement is thrown out of kilter by line being taken from the clutch or via the free-spool mechanism. Its practical outcome is that those who play fish by backwinding will suffer less line twist than those who play fish off the clutch. Furthermore, the use of the free-spool while tackling up etc. exacerbates the situation. As does allowing fish to take a lot of line from the free-spool before being struck. The shape or size of the line roller makes not one iota of difference.

Gardner Spin Doctors.

What does make a significant difference, however, is the diameter of the spool. Aero 6010 and 8010 Baitrunners spill approximately 15cm of line per coil. GT7000 Biomasters, and similar "bucket spool" models, spill

20cm. That means a twist is put in the line for every 15cm of a cast made with an Aero, and every 20cm with a Biomaster. A 100 metres Aero cast will therefore create approximately 670 twists. The same cast with the Biomaster will create 500 twists. In round figures, therefore, an Aero produces 25% more line twist than does a Biomaster.

When line twist occurs, it is easily dealt with by the simple expedient of removing the end-tackle and replacing it with a Gardner Spin Doctor. This ingenious little gadget is then cast as far as possible and retrieved rapidly. Most times, one cast will do the job; just occasionally a second cast will be required. Unlike Twist Buster and Power Roller line rollers, the Spin Doctor works brilliantly.

Line

In the autumn of 1997, Carpworld Editor, Tim Paisley, suggested to me that I might like to bench-test a batch of mono lines. My findings were subsequently published in three consecutive issues of Carpworld (Numbers 88-90) under the title, "Mono Multi Tests".

Mono 'line'-up.

Since conducting the tests, several new brands have appeared on the market, while others have become less readily available. This makes it inappropriate, I feel, to itemise my test results on a product by product basis - instead I shall make recommendations as to which monos, in my opinion, are best suited to which carp fishing situations. These recommendations will take account of tests conducted on new brands which have become available in the interim.

The characteristics I tested were:

- **Diameter**
- **Dry breaking strain**
- **Wet breaking strain (after 48 hours soak)**
- **Stress**
- **Abrasion**
- **Shear**
- **Stretch**

The pit from which this lovely linear was caught has a peculiarly fibrous type of weed which requires abrasion resistant line.

The most obvious fact to emerge from my tests was that most nominal breaking strains are underrated, making it impossible to compare one brand with another by means of label information. Only IGFA rated lines are likely to have spot-on breaking strain designations.

When fishing close in, the diameter of the line is irrelevant because air resistance and the rapidity with which line drops below the lip of the spool do not matter. For long range fishing, however, such considerations are important - we want maximum strength combined with minimum diameter. Of the brands I tested, Nash Power Plus and Trilene XL had the highest breaking strain in relation to their diameter.

Most monos, I found, lost 5-10% of their dry breaking strain after a 48 hours soak. The only brands to show no strength loss were Maxima, GR60, Sufix Supreme and Ultima Tournament.

It is widely believed that line loses a lot of its strength after it has been severely stressed - as when the terminal tackle has become snagged and we have been compelled to pull for a break. To my surprise, I found that there was only a short-term reduction, and after a period of rest most monos regained all or most of their pre-stressed strength.

If you read advertisements and promotional literature you will doubtless be confused by the number of monos which claim to be "the most abrasion resistant". Clearly, they cannot all qualify for the title! And whilst abrasion resistance is undoubtedly important, when did it suddenly become the most vital characteristic of all? Indeed, to read some advertisements you might be tempted to assume it is the only quality which matters. Truth is, it is just one of many attributes which we need to consider when choosing a line. If we are fishing a snagfree, weedfree water, the abrasion resistance qualities of our line are, within reason, irrelevant. If our water is heavily weeded, however, abrasion resistance becomes important. Most of the lines I tested would cope adequately in this situation - notably Power Plus, Big Game, Sufix Supreme, GR60, Pro Gold, Ultima Tournament and Soft Steel - although I would almost certainly choose a 15lb (or more) version for the purpose.

If we consider abrasion in a more demanding context - and in some gravel pits this will certainly apply - we are looking at the line going over, round or through such underwater obstacles as branches, wooden posts, mooring ropes or cables, underwater spoil dumps, bars, the lips of plateaux, islands, and possibly ridges and boulders. And this with a considerable poundage of powerful carp on the end. My tests indicated that the brands best able to withstand severe abrasion of this sort were Pro Gold, Ultima Tournament and Soft Steel.

Some pits, particularly new ones, have gravel bars topped with flints and other sharp stones, while bars in mature pits are often colonised by mussels. A few pits have bits of rusty metal littering the bottom. To cope with hazards of this sort, line requires a high level of resistance to shear. Unfortunately no mono is up to the job. Those who fish pits containing sharp-topped gravel bars and discarded ironmongery will not be surprised at my findings because they know what happens the moment a tight line makes contact - it severs. There is no scraping back and forth, just a sudden slackening and the fish is lost. No standard diameter mono can help in this situation, although chances of survival are increased if a long, ultra thick rubbing leader is employed - like the 60lb version described by Paul Gummer in his entertaining contribution to Rod Hutchinson's "The Carp Strikes Back". But heavy duty mono is stiff as well as being thick, which makes it awful stuff to use. A much better option is to incorporate the longest manageable length of 35lb, or even 45lb Kryston Quicksilver, which is both user friendly and resistant to shear.

All monos stretch, but they do not all do so to the same extent. Does it matter? It depends on the sort of fishing we are doing. I prefer a relatively low-stretch line for long range fishing because it enables the force of the strike to be transmitted more effectively to the hook. The brands which demonstrated the least stretch were Power Plus, GR60, Trilene XL, Ultima Tournament and Sufix Supreme.

For circumstances where I choose to use (or am compelled to use) barbless hooks I prefer a stretchy line so as to provide a "bungee" effect - the most elastic of my test batch was Maxima; others which stretched more than average were Soft Steel and Big Game.

Bench-tests, while informative, do not tell the whole story. They do not, for example, give any indication of a line's long-term durability. Nor do they reveal if it is likely to change character in use - I am thinking here of brands which are nice and supple when first loaded, but seem to stiffen after a few trips, or adopt an unacceptable level of spool-memory which makes them leap unbidden from the reel in a manner not unlike a child's Slinky toy! I therefore used the brands which emerged well from bench-tests for actual fishing; following which, these are my recommendations (in alphabetical order):

LONG RANGE:
Ande IGFA Yellow Tournament
Insight GR60
Nash Power Plus
Sufix Supreme
Trilene XL (in weedfree, snag-free waters only)
Ultima Tournament
GENERAL PURPOSE:
Ande Premium
Berkley Big Game
Daiwa Sensor
Fox Soft Steel
Gold Label Pro Gold
Insight GR60
Nash Power Plus
Sufix Supreme
Ultima Tournament
ABRASIVE WEED AND SNAGS:
All the previous group, but particularly *Pro Gold, Soft Steel and Ultima Tournament.*
BARBLESS HOOKS:
Berkley Big Game
Fox Soft Steel
Maxima

Mono is best loaded from a revolving spool in a bucket of water, but care needs be taken with spools which are filled to the brim - Soft Steel, for example - because loose coils can be thrown which have a tendency to tangle or snag.

Alarms

I bought three Delkims from the very first production batch and the only maintenance they have required has been an annual battery change. In addition to their reliability, I like their efficiency - they can be adjusted so they resist giving false bleeps in response to wind or waves and only sound when a take occurs.

A couple of years ago I acquired a set of dedicated Delkim TX2000 Transmitters which fit under the standard compacts, and operate in conjunction with the RX2000 Remote Receiver. I find this system a boon when the wind is howling and heavy rain is drumming on the canopy of my umbrella. It also enables me, when I do not want to draw attention to the fact that I am getting takes, to have the compacts set to mute and the remote sensor on low volume adjacent to my ear.

Delkim compacts fitted with TX2000 transmitters. I have taped the rat-tail aerials to the sides of my alarms.

The rat-tail aerials with which TX2000 micro transmitters are equipped looked somewhat vulnerable, I felt, so I encased them in silicone tube and taped them to the sides of my alarms. Whether this affects their transmission range I do not know - but then I do not use my remotes for the purpose of sitting in a friend's swim 100 yards away...

Prior to buying my Delkims I used a trio of Steve Neville's beautifully made mini compacts. They proved totally reliable. As did some GF1 alarms I tried which were produced by Good Fishing Ltd.

Indicators

Back in the days when we fished open-spool methods I just loved watching a "monkey" fly excitedly up and down the needle! In addition to providing a visual indication of a take, "monkeys" served the important function of preventing wind-blown coils of loose line from spilling off the spool while awaiting a run.

The advent of free-spool Baitrunner-type systems rendered monkey climbers obsolete. The most popular indicators nowadays are probably cord restrained bobbins - although fashion currently dictates that the restraining cord comprise a rather naff and not very strong sink-plug ball chain!

Bobbins work well in quiet conditions, but flap in a strong wind. To overcome this, anglers tend to fish them on a very short drop - sometimes so short that they almost touch the rod. This severely limits the amount of information they can impart and reduces their usefulness to that of registering drop backs. Nor is a bobbin suitable for use with a slack line because if it is allowed to hang straight down it can twist and cause a tangle. I also worry that a lightning fast run may cause a long-drop bobbin to flip over the rod and become jammed against the alarm. From which comments you will correctly conclude that they are not my choice.

Nash Butt Cracker Indicators with Steve Neville bracket adaptors.

Nor am I a fan of spring-arm or quiver-type indicators. They work reasonably well but are not very versatile.

My preference is for hinged swing-arm indicators. There are many good models from which to choose, but care needs be taken in selecting the right one because some embody basic design faults which detract from their efficiency. To start with, the swing-arm should be at least 15cm long. Short-arm versions (some less than 10cm) serve no useful function that I can see - other than being decorative, of course!

It is important that the indicator incorporates some sort of restraining mechanism to prevent it moving much past the horizontal, otherwise it can flip above the rod and become jammed.

It also needs to have a means by which loading can be adjusted, thereby enabling it to cope effectively with varying wind and subsurface drift conditions.

Finally, the line-release must be smooth and reliable - and function with no risk of line damage.

As I said, there are a lot of good models around - far too many to list. An indicator which is particularly well suited to my style of fishing is the Nash Wisp. This is an ultralight, extended length (26cm arm) indicator which has been developed for margin and close range fishing with light leads and/or running setups. I usually let it hang vertically and use it in conjunction with a slack or semi slack line. In summer, when a high proportion of my carp are caught close in, this is the indicator I use most often.

The Wisp is equipped with a small sliding weight on its fine wire arm which allows the tension of the indicator to be finely balanced to counteract subsurface line drag.

The Wisp is now out of production, and Kevin Nash has replaced it with the Butt Cracker which, in design as well as name, is very similar to Martin Locke's Butt Banger. Butt Crackers utilise interchangeable weights so are suitable for use at virtually any range - but that said, I doubt if they will depose my Wisps for delicate close-in fishing.

To enable me to switch from Wisps to Butt Crackers, and vice versa, I contacted Steve Neville who makes custom stainless items. He provided me with a set of adaptors which are compatible with both sets of indicators and so enable me to leave my Wisp anchor brackets attached to my buzzer bar and attach either the Wisps or Butt Crackers according to circumstances.

Brothers Rick and Martin, and my son, Peter, use Solar Quiverlocs, with which they are entirely satisfied.

While I have not used them, I recently had the opportunity to examine prototypes of the Cygnet Reflex indicator system. I like the look of them. Mick Nolan, Cygnet boss, worked as an instrument maker for the Ministry of Defence before starting his tackle manufacturing business so he has a high level of engineering expertise. I have known Mick for many years and can vouch for his commitment to quality.

Pods, Bars and Banksticks

Almost everyone I see uses a rod pod.

Why?

While readily acknowledging that pods are indispensable in some circumstances - when fishing from a wooden platform or a concrete bank, for example - I do not understand why most anglers use a pod as standard. They are incompatible with marshy, reedy swims, or where the bank is particularly steep or uneven. Yes, they can be pressed into service in most circumstances, but not very efficiently. Nor are they anywhere near as stable as bankstick setups, so are vulnerable to being blown over in a very strong wind, or pulled on their side if a very fast parallel-to-the-bank margin run occurs. Various clamps and bungee-type pod security systems are available - but if you can push pegs etc. in the ground, why not use banksticks in the first place?

I always carry a pod in the boot of my car, but I cannot recall the last occasion when I was compelled to use it - certainly upwards of two years ago.

The dam wall of this French reservoir provides a circumstance where a pod is essential.

One of the reasons I am able to dispense with a pod is because I use Chris Brown's bankstick/bar system which can be rammed into all but the very hardest banks. Chris uses wide diameter, umbrella-gauge alloy tube for his banksticks which, in addition to being robust and stable, do not twist (other than in loose sand or shingle). Additionally, the dedicated angle-steel buzzer bars are sufficiently strong to enable them to be gripped in both hands in order to force the banksticks into the ground. Only hard baked clay, especially when it contains stones, resists Chris's banksticks. On such occasions I remove the alloy outers and replace them with Nash screw-tipped Power Spikes which will grind their way into virtually anything. At the other extreme, when I encounter marshy, flooded or reedy banks I incorporate outers from Gardner extra long storm rods. All these items are compatible, and together they provide me with a versatile, secure and stable rod support system which can be used almost anywhere.

Shelters

My shelter does not have to provide the comforts of home, it merely has to protect me from the sun, wind and rain. Most trips I opt for an inexpensive (about £15) 45in Awnhaven umbrella from Argos. The nylon canopy used on lightweight brollies of this sort benefits from an application of waterproofing compound; I use Fabsil, an aerosol spray which dries within hours and loses all odour within two or three days. It provides 100 per cent waterproofing for at least a year.

When fishing a water where I know the banks are particularly hard, I replace the standard hollow ground-spike with Gardner's solid screw-tip version.

The stability of a simple, single-pole umbrella is improved if two guy cords are used. A storm pole is useful, too - especially on days when circumstances prevent the umbrella being positioned in a perfect canopy-into-the-wind configuration. I have therefore equipped a couple of ribs with swivel storm caps - I rarely use more than one pole, but the two caps enable me to choose where best to attach it.

If the weather is particularly unpleasant I upgrade to to a Nash Oval. The heavy duty ribs of the Oval will withstand a tremendous battering from the wind, and the large canopy provides plenty of shelter to both me and my kit. Again, as

Neither a dome nor a pod would be much use in this terrain.

mentioned in regard to my standard umbrella, twin guy cords add both security and stability.

Combined with Nash screw-tipped Power Spike storm poles, the Oval can be used on virtually any bank in any weather.

Bits and Bobs

In the boot of my car I carry some shears and some long-arm branch loppers. Just occasionally a bit of discreet cutting back is necessary, and these enable the job to be done quickly, quietly and efficiently. I also carry bolt croppers. They have never been used, but are there in case I get a repeat of the time when someone, who we can safely assume was not an intellectual colossus, gained amusement from Supergluing the innards of a car park padlock. On that occasion I avoided being locked in by lifting the gate off its hinges, but if it happens again and the gate is one which does not have lift-off hinges, I may have to resort to cutting the lock or chain.

In my rucksack I carry a pair of serrated edge scissors which I use for trimming back stray brambles or thorny twigs which sometimes invade the little cubby-hole swims of which I am so fond. To protect my hands when handling brambles I carry a pair of industrial gloves. Their main use, though, is provided by their PVC criss-cross surface coating which affords an excellent non-slip grip when forcing banksticks, umbrella poles, storm rods, pegs etc. into hard ground.

Daytime-only fishing enables me to keep kit to a minimum.

Like most anglers I use multi compartment boxes for my small items, and just occasionally I have had them open in my rucksack with the inevitable spillage of swivels, beads, clips, links etc. But no longer. Several years ago I hit on the idea of cutting a discarded motorcycle inner tube into thick rubber bands. These are tremendously strong and once fitted round my Raaco and Stewart tackle boxes hold them securely shut, even if their catches fail.

I always carry a basic first-aid pack in a small snap-lid plastic box. It holds Paracetamol tablets (ever had a trip ruined by a bad headache?), diarrhoea capsules, anti histamine tablets (for wasp stings etc.), some antiseptic wipes and a few adhesive plasters. The whole pack weighs next to nothing and takes up hardly any space, yet has occasionally enabled a companion or myself to continue fishing with a modicum of efficiency, and once or twice has avoided the need to pack up and return home.

Finally we come to the most indispensable ancillary items of all - my notebook and water maps. In my notebook I record depths, weedbeds, snags, hard patches, soft silt, where fish show by jumping or rolling, times at which takes occur... in fact, everything and anything which might be useful. The water maps - which are covered with Blue Peter style sticky back plastic to enable their use in the rain - contain information gleaned from countless hours plumbing and echo-sounding. Those I carry with me are photocopies; the originals are kept at home because they are too valuable to risk being damaged or lost.

Fishing a mature Kent pit.

These very dark, chestnut-flanked fish are my favourites.

An Essex gravel pit cum irrigation reservoir.

This Essex gravel pit is used for crop irrigation, hence the exposed "beach".

A stunning big tailed, big-scaled margin mirror.

Just "having an enjoy".

Chapter Fifteen

Clay Pits, Chalk Pits and Reservoirs

The title I intended using for this chapter was "Other Man-Made Waters". But then I realised that with the exception of rivers and Cumbrian lakes, virtually all English waters are man-made.

Some, like estate lakes, were created purely for ornament. Most, however, were a by-product of industry. The hammer ponds and furnace lakes of the Kent-Sussex border, for example, were formed to provide water for the smelting of iron, which was in turn used to make armaments. Some of these furnace lakes were originally quite large - 20 acres or more - although silting and reed encroachment has reduced the size of many.

Smaller impoundments, also formed by damming streams, were created by early fabric dyers.

The meres (the word "mere" being derived from the Dutch and German "meer", and Latin "mare", meaning sea) and flashes of the north-west were not created deliberately, but were an inadvertent consequence of subsidence following the 19th century mining of salt.

Even village dewponds, like the one illustrated in Constable's "Haywain" painting, are not natural but were excavated to enable wooden cartwheels to be soaked so they did not shrink and shed their metal rims.

Prior to the coming of the railways our industrial centres were linked by a network of navigable canals.

Agriculture played its part, too, with excess water from low-lying marshy areas being run off via dykes and drains (sometimes, on the Romney Marsh, disconcertingly called sewers!).

Estate lakes, like this one in Kent, were created for ornamental purposes.

I keep a watchful eye on several tons of beef beside a marshland dyke.

Elimination

For reasons of geography I have no experience of meres - they occur in the north-west, while I live in the south-east. I shall therefore omit them from the discussion. Likewise furnace lakes, estate lakes and small ponds which, for the most part, are not to my taste.

Canals and dykes I like - particularly the latter. I have caught some big carp from them, too. But they are so unlike pits that to discuss them here seems inappropriate.

Which leaves us, in considering other man-made waters, with clay pits, chalk pits and reservoirs.

Clay Pits

Clay pits - sometimes referred to as brick pits - were created, as their alternative name suggests, to serve the brick making industry. They tend to occur in clusters - as much for economic as geological reasons. Clay, like gravel and sand, is a relatively low value commodity which is expensive to transport from one place to another. So brick kilns were located near naturally occurring sources of clay. One of the most prolific groupings is between Luton and Bedford where are found such well known clay pits as Arlesey Lake, Elstow, Kempston Hardwick, Woburn Sands, the Airman Pit and, of course, Kevin Maddocks's Withy Pool. There are others certainly as far north as Yorkshire (the Tilery), down through the Midlands - notably the Peterborough area - all the way to the south coast.

In some areas, the south-west for example, very high quality china clay was extracted. This was not used for bricks, but for pottery.

Clay pits vary considerably in size, ranging from Withy Pool's 2.5 acres up to about 30 acres.

Most are deep, 20-30ft being not unusual. This is not an invariable rule, however, and some of the oldest, which were dug by hand, are quite shallow.

All get appallingly "claggy" after rain!

Generally they have fewer features than you would find in the average gravel pit. There will still be depth variation, and where unwanted spoil has been dumped there may be high rise plateaux and possibly islands; but for the most part, they are steep sided and uniformly deep.

The non-porous nature of clay restricts the ingress of nutrients from groundwater, so only those pits which receive direct run-off from agricultural land are eutrophic. This, combined with their depth, means that most clay pits are relatively weedfree.

What clay pits lack in weed they can make up for with snags. In addition to shrubs and bushes which grew before the pit filled with water, it is not unusual to find cables and defunct machinery. The remains of old kilns, too. In one of the clay pits I occasionally fish it is possible when the light is right to discern what look like small rubbish skips - they are actually open-topped railway trucks.

Being non-eutrophic, with a consequent lack of algae, the water is usually clear. I said "usually" because clay pits can "milk up" when a strong wind blows. This is the term I use to describe the discolouration which occurs when minute clay particles are stirred up by wave action and held in suspension. Depending on the configuration of the pit and the wind strength and direction, "milky" water can form a large slick which may extend a long way from the bank. The significance of this discolouration is that I have never caught a carp from an area thus affected. In clay pits, therefore, I only follow the wind so far as it enables me to fish uncoloured water.

Dyke, drain or sewer - unfortunate names for attractive waters.

Like most deep waters, clay pits respond well to margin tactics in warm sunny weather. Also a good bet are plateaux where the depth is approximately half the lake's average. In other words, if the general depth range is 20-30ft, its average is about 25ft, so I opt where possible for areas of up to 13ft or so. The "half the average"

A big, deep clay pit - and the hunting ground, if you believe such stories, of a Bodmin Beast type big cat!

guideline is not set in stone (nor even clay, for that matter!) but is merely a starting point.

As autumn approaches, carp slip down the slope and are more likely to be found in depths of 20ft plus.

Winter fishing can be productive. Most fish come from deep, but by no means the deepest areas. In a pit with a maximum depth of 30ft, for example, I would expect to find carp in the 25ft region. It pays to keep an open mind, though, as was demonstrated by my friend Dennis Holding who caught a succession of January and February fish just off some tree-hung margins where it was only about 6ft deep. Interestingly, all Dennis's fish came between 9.00pm and 11.00pm. He caught none in daylight, and despite staying on until about 1.00am some nights, never had a take after 11.00pm.

Chalk Pits

Chalk pits - or limestone quarries if we want to be pedantic in our nomenclature - are dug to serve the cement industry. By their nature they are confined to comparatively few areas of the country - one of which is my home patch, north Kent. The chalk hills which run roughly from the M25 in the west, to the River Medway in the east, comprise the North Downs. Scattered along the Downs are numerous chalk pits; most are semi-dry (one has recently been turned into Europe's largest shopping mall), but several have become flooded and a few hold carp.

My experience of chalk pit carp is confined to just one water - Blue Lake, near

Northfleet. To tell the truth, I hesitated before including chalk pits in this section, but I finally decided to do so because lessons learned on one will probably be valid on others. Also, few anglers have any experience at all of chalk pits, so I concluded that inclusion - albeit based on limited experience - would be better than omission.

Chalk pits are deep, 30ft being by no means unusual. The sides are often cliff-like, sometimes requiring a hazardous descent to reach ledges from which the water can be accessed. There was a particular spot on Blue Lake where I used to lower my gear by rope before climbing down myself. It was somewhat "hairy", and one afternoon I fell, which resulted in a badly sprained ankle. It swelled alarmingly and turned a horrible mauve colour. I carried on fishing, though...

In warm summer weather I have found chalk pit carp to be very wind oriented - they will follow even the lightest breeze. When it is calm they are likely to be found where bankside access is difficult, like the base of a high vertical cliff.

As you would expect, many chalk pit carp are caught from the margin slope, also from relatively shallow areas created by flooded ramps and roads. Most of mine, however, came from the surface. I caught them on crust or floater-cake fished on a self-rising running paternoster.

It seems improbable that carp would be hooked successfully on a setup which involved the line descending steeply down to 30ft plus, then rising vertically via a running link to the surface. But they were. Indeed, I missed very few. When a run occurred I picked up the rod, closed the bale, retrieved smoothly and steadily until the carp could be felt on the end - by which time the lead had been lifted to within a few feet of the surface - and struck.

Although I never fished Blue Lake in the winter, several friends of mine did - Paul Snepp and Mick Nolan, to name but two - and they caught consistently. From memory, most came at night.

You will notice that all my references to Blue Lake are in the past tense - this is because I stopped fishing there when a group of retards from the adjacent estate became serial car vandals. I have since lost touch with the place - which is a shame because I found it a fascinating water.

Irrigation Reservoirs

In some parts of the country, notably the south-east, farmers have been encouraged to dig reservoirs as a precaution against summer drought. To qualify as a reservoir, and thereby for EEC construction grants, such waters must be able to store at least 22500 cubic metres of water above the lowest ground level. Which is why farm

Brother Martin fishes an irrigation reservoir at low autumn level.

reservoirs are usually constructed with raised embankments rather than being simply dug out of the ground.

Many of these reservoirs have been stocked with carp and subsequently leased to clubs or syndicates. The farmer thus gets an extra income in addition to a reliable water supply, and we get new carp waters. Everyone is a winner!

An intriguing characteristic of farm reservoirs is that they produce more and bigger carp than their size (typically 2-7 acres) would lead you to expect. The best known example is Derek Ritchie's Manor Farm (aka "Dollop City") syndicate water in Essex. The main reason irrigation reservoirs can hold a high biomass and still achieve good growth rates is, I am convinced, due to their constantly fluctuating water levels. This is a consequence of their being used for irrigation in summer, then being refilled in the winter. The resulting "tidal" effect periodically exposes to the air a wide beach all round the perimeter. This enriches the lake bed and increases the water's productivity.

Few farm reservoirs can rely on receiving adequate winter top-up water directly from rainfall, so most are licensed to get supplies from an adjacent river or stream. Winter rainfall and the consequent run-off from farmland ensures that rivers at this time of the year are rich in nutrients. This nutrient-rich water is pumped directly into reservoirs, thereby creating a eutrophic environment.

Most farm reservoirs, especially those constructed in recent years, are quite deep (15-20ft plus at full level). This is sufficiently deep for reduced light penetration to inhibit weed growth in the main body of the reservoir and confine it to the margin slope. The aforementioned "tidal" effect can, however, result in the weed growing in lateral bands. You might, therefore, have weedfree water down to a depth of about 3ft, then a band of weed - probably of a variety which can withstand annual drying out - then a partially clear strip, then another band of weed.

Like most deep waters, when the weather is warm and sunny carp come right into the edge. Generally, the warmer the weather, the closer to the bank and the higher up the margin slope they will come.

From late August or early September the margin slope becomes less productive; as is also the case in high summer if the weather is cool. Under those circumstances my carp have come from what I refer to as the "anonymous middle".

This lovely, unblemished common came from an irrigation reservoir cum gravel pit - the water is on the way down, as can be seen from the exposed 'beach'.

Due to their elevation above ground level, most farm reservoirs are exposed to the wind. This has the advantage that it enables even the gentlest of breezes to have an effect. The downside, however, is that any wind much above Force 4 (moderate) blows a "hoolie"!

Strong winds have a disadvantage beyond that of mere discomfort - they tend to create a slick of "milky" muddy water (irrigation reservoirs are lined with clay). As previously mentioned when talking about clay pits, I have never caught a carp from within a "milked up" coloured area.

Large Reservoirs

Most of the country's large reservoirs supply drinking water, although some, like Startops at Tring, provide canal top-up water.

The biggest reservoir I have fished is the King George Fifth at Chingford (known while still on the secret list by its code name of K-G Five!). At a guess I would say it is in the region of 400 acres. Next largest, at about 300 acres, is the lovely Bough Beech, situated north-east of Edenbridge. At the other end of the scale are those which comprise the Walthamstow group, which range from the 12

Walthamstow's Low Maynard Reservoir is a much more attractive water than you might expect.

acres of the prosaically named Number Three to the 80 acres of the Lockwood.

Reservoirs vary as much in character as they do in size. Those created by flooding a valley - Bough Beech and Weirwood being classic examples - have meadows and copses running down to the water's edge. Were it not for the existence of a concrete dam they would look like giant estate lakes. Others, and here the Lockwood and the King George Fifth spring immediately to mind, have much of their perimeter constructed of concrete slabs.

In common with most large waters, the wind is likely to be a major factor influencing carp location. Trouble is, I am so programmed to follow the wind that I find it difficult to do otherwise even when I know I ought to - like the time a number of years ago when I opened the season on the mega difficult Lockwood. Several of us had positioned ourselves along the southern bank, towards which a cold northerly was blowing. It was obviously the wrong thing to do but I could not help myself! Predictably I blanked. As did the three or four others who fished nearby. The only carp caught that day was a near-twenty mirror taken by an elderly husband and wife duo who stalked with sweetcorn and float tackle in the calm sheltered margins of the upwind bank. Whether they fished there because they had correctly assessed the situation or because it was the most comfortable place to be, I do not know. But whatever their motive, they got it right while the rest of us got it unambiguously wrong.

Location difficulties on some reservoirs are exacerbated due to the existence of extensive out-of-bounds areas. Approximately a quarter of Bough Beech, for example, is set aside as a nature reserve; predictably it is the shallowest water and located at the end which receives the benefit of southerly and south-westerly winds! Abberton Reservoir (one of my erstwhile pike haunts) reputedly contains some colossal carp. There are stories of boats being followed by the sort of bow wave which you would not normally expect to see outside a dolphinarium! But before anyone rushes off to bang out boilies in the "Big A" (another code name!), I ought to warn them that Abberton covers approximately 1000 acres and has, I believe, 12 miles of bank - only a few hundred yards of which can be fished!

Some reservoirs, like those in the Walthamstow group, are established and known carp waters. The carp they contain are, as a consequence, boilie oriented. Reservoirs which receive little or no angling attention are better fished with particles - at least initially. Chick peas, black eyed beans, maples, maize etc. are generally more instant than are boilies. If, at the end of every trip, a couple of kilos of boilies are put out, the situation will soon change and they will become a viable option. My first choice in this situation would be high attract, sweet tasting readymades such as Scopex, Tutti Frutti or Peach.

As regards winter fishing I can say little because my experience is confined to the West Warwick. I caught most trips, and one January day in a mild westerly gale I had three. All my fish came from the deeper end of the reservoir, casting to the middle. That was when I discovered that tufties can dive down at least as far as 34ft...

The Synthetic and the Absurd

I cannot leave the subject of man-made waters without making reference to the "instant" carp fishing facilities (in my opinion they do not qualify to be called angling waters) which are springing up countrywide. They are of two main types: those into which big fish are introduced in order to target specialist carp anglers, and those which are stocked with an excessively high biomass in order to cater for matchmen.

How anyone can gain any satisfaction from fishing in such synthetic circumstances is beyond my comprehension.

Talking of synthetic fisheries - regular readers of the weeklies may have seen carp to upper-twenties reported from Capstone Park, near Maidstone. When I first spotted such reports I was somewhat mystified because despite regularly visiting

The mighty Lockwood Reservoir on a benign summer's day.

the adjacent dry-ski slope, I was unaware there was a lake in the park. So I telephoned the warden's office to make enquiries.

"You're quite correct," he said, "there wasn't a lake here. There is now, though; we made it with plastic pond-liner, landscaped it with an island and..."

"A plastic liner?" I queried, thinking I must have misheard.

"That's right," he said, "otherwise the water would leach out."

Honest. I am not making this up!

Were that the whole story, it would be preposterous enough. But there is more. Recently the saga transcended the merely absurd and moved into the realms of the surreal.

It started a couple of years ago when we had a long, hot summer here in the south-east which caused water levels to drop throughout the region. As Capstone's margins dried out, so anglers found themselves sitting where once had been water.

At which point some readers are doubtless ahead of me!

For those who have yet to make the connection I will provide a hint - banksticks, plastic liner...

Last winter we had plenty of rain and water levels rose, but Capstone's recovery was delayed by leaks. Until, that is, repairs were made to its liner!

The resulting image of earnest camo-clad carpmen sitting around a puncture-patched pond is one I shall treasure always!

Chapter sixteen

Tactics

In the accounts which follow, I have tried to show how theory is translated into practise. But carp fishing is not an exact science - so I have included details of trips which had their outcome affected by unexpected or untoward events.

They are not all big fish stories because size was not the main criterion on which I based my selection - but equally, nor was it a bar to inclusion, which is why the carp range from massive to modest.

"The crack" features nowhere in these accounts because I regard it as an entirely inappropriate adjunct to carp fishing. Others feel differently, and socialising is important to them - which is fair enough providing it does not lead to rods being left to fish unattended, or to bankside disturbance.

The narratives are written in the present tense - what media people call "actuality" or "real time".

All follow the same format - first, the heading, which refers to the angling situation, then a factfile, and finally an account of events as they occurred.

Mid Range Gravel Bank

Time of year: *late June.*
Rods: *Three, 12ft/2.25lb Eclipse.* ***Reels:*** *Aero 6010 or 8010 Baitrunner.*
Line: *Power Plus, 15lb.* ***Hooks:*** *Fox Series 2, size 6.*
Bait: *15mm Nash Amber Attractor Birdfood with Sting Oil*
Rig: *Line Aligner, Combi-Link made with 35cm of 12lb Snake-Skin, 2.5oz running Gardner Stealth Lead, no anti-tangle tube.*
Venue: *Kent coastal gravel pit, shallow and virtually weedfree.*

10.00am. Not the late start it seems. Shortly after dawn I was on a 60 acre pit, but the moderate, force four wind which was promised, increased to near-gale. It was accompanied by lashing rain, too. In addition to being uncomfortable, such winds on that pit tend to be unproductive - so I packed up and moved here. As if on cue, the rain has stopped. There are even some patches of blue showing though the clouds; I think the sun will come out.

The Shingle Point primrose coloured leather.

This pit is long and narrow, and due to the configuration of its bank, enables me to fish the downwind end but with a degree of shelter.

The swim is one of my favourites - it comprises a shingle point in the lee of a steep bank. Received wisdom has it that baits have to be tucked tight against a far bank reed promontory - a cast of about 60-70 yards. Most of my fish, though, have come from a hard gravel plateau, four or five yards short of the reeds. It is an easy target - about as big as the average dining room. The depth is 6ft, shelving to 8ft either side.

Two rods are cast to the plateau. The third - as per convention - is dropped a foot or two from the reeds.

I decide against spodding with pellets or particles due to the pit's bream population - lots of them, averaging 6-8lb. I rely on a modest scattering - about 30 to each rod - of boilies.

And here's the sun. Lovely! The wind is dropping too - more like the force four which was promised. I'm not sorry I moved, though - I like this pit.

12.00. Middle rod, fast run. Strike and ... don't think it's a carp, feels like a tench. Can't be sure because the tench in here fight tremendously hard. Yes, definitely a tench - but by heck, it's pulling! In she comes; over the net. A lovely yellow-green fish. Unhook it in the net, while still in the water, and return it immediately.

Recast another double boilie coupled with a four-bait stringer. Feather the line just before the lead lands, then trap the coils so the rig sinks on a tight line. I am not using tubing, so the feathering and line-trapping procedure is necessary to avoid a tangle. Another 30 freebies are put out.

A few quick self-takes.

12.45pm. Middle rod again, the indicator lifts tight to the rod and holds. The Baitrunner clicks just once or twice. Bet it's a bream. Strike - yes, a kiting resistance but no fight to speak of. I try to unhook it in the water without using my net, but it is a big fish and I can't grip it properly; it keeps slipping from my grasp. At the third or fourth attempt I succeed. It would have been less trouble to net it - albeit at the cost of getting slime all over the mesh.

Recast - and more freebies.

2.30pm. A take on the right-hand rod - a trundler. Previously, most of my takes on this pit were of the lift-and-hold variety, but a switch to running leads has converted them to steady, albeit slow runs. Strike. Rod stops solid. Wow! Look at it go! No doubt about this one - a carp for sure. As with others I have caught from this swim, it makes no attempt to dive into the reeds but stays in open water and runs to the right. It stops, comes to the surface and thrashes - spray flies skywards! Now it is going the other way. I backwind to keep pace with it. It stops again and wallows on a tight line. In you come; nice and steady. I loosen the clutch a tad in case there is an unexpected lunge - yes, just like that! The rod is wrenched violently down and the clutch snarls. Back you come. To and fro in the margins - up to the top - tail waving impotently in the air as it tries to gain purchase in the water. Over the net first time of trying - a pretty, primrose coloured near-leather.

In the Sling-Retainer while I set up the camera - a few quick self-takes, and returned to the water.

Rebait. Just attaching the stringer and my middle Delkim is "diddley diddleying" its little heart out! Strike - fish on, and virtually a repeat performance except that this one is a common.

More pics - then returned. What a shambles! Two rods out of the water - camera gear and attendant post-catch clutter all over the place.

Rods recast. Swim tidied.

5.00pm. I nearly always get a teatime run on this water - especially in this swim. But two carp in a day is top quota - it is unrealistic to expect a third. Oh look at that! A fish leaps completely clear of the water, just off the reed fringe. And again! I wonder why they do that?

6.30pm. A take to the left-hand rod; the one tucked close to the reeds. The teatime leaper, perhaps? In it comes; over the net - a mirror this time. First a leather, then a common, now a mirror - that makes a full set! More pics, and straight back in the water.

Three in a day - fantastic! I usually manage one; two is an event; but three...

Recast. Damn it - landed in the reeds. Retrieve; attach a new stringer. I notice the Multistrand section of Combi-Link is slightly damaged - there are a few wayward fibres sticking out. That must have happened when I pulled clear of the reeds. Looks okay, though. Besides, I have already had more than my share - there won't be any more today, that's for sure.

New stringer; recast. Oh no, it's in the reeds again! I should have harnessed-up with Power Gum. Pull and... brilliant! It's clear of the reeds and has dropped within inches of the stems. The stringer has come off, but no matter.

8.00pm. Away again on the tight-to-the-reeds rod. Strike. It's on. Feels smaller than the others. In you come - yes, as I thought, a mid double. Another mirror. It tries to get beneath a semi-submerged bush which lies to the left of the swim - oh no you don't... Damn. It's off. The hooklink has parted. My fault entirely - I should have changed the link when I noticed it was damaged. Chances are it became further frayed when it landed in the reeds the second time. Unforgivably stupid of me, and I have paid the price - so, unfortunately, has the carp because it's got a hook in its lip.

Couldn't do that with a pod... My front bankstick is pushed in the margins to make more room.

Annoyed with myself, and with a damper placed on what had otherwise been an excellent day, I pack up.

Not the Gazebo - but a similar sort of swim.

Weedy Margins

Time of year: *early July.*

Rods: *Two. 12ft/2.25lb Eclipse.* *Reels:* *Aero 6010 or 8010 Baitrunner.* *Line:* *Power Plus, 18lb, treated with Kryston Granite Juice.* *Hooks:* *Owner spade-end, size 10 (size 6 equivalent).*

Bait: *15mm own recipe birdfood/fishmeal, and 15mm Sting.*

Rig: *Line Aligner, 45cm of 20lb HPPE braid fished Concertina style, 1.5oz semi-fixed Korda "Distance" inline in conjunction with 50cm No Spook anti-tangle tube, lightly backweighted.*

Venue: *Kent gravel pit, club water, deep and extremely weedy.*

7.00am. The heatwave continues. The weather forecast has promised a hazy, humid day with little or no wind. I choose what I call "The Gazebo" - a swim which is always cool due to being shaded by a canopy of branches. It is a somewhat confined spot which forces me to sit closer to the water's edge than I like, so last time I fished here I pushed a few willow fronds in the bank to provide a screen. They are wilting somewhat, but they are still in position. I gently lower my chair and rucksack behind them.

The steep margins are very heavily weeded with Elodea and eel grass. To my left, about halfway down the slope, in approximately 9ft of water is a small clear spot. I do not need to use a marker-rod because my notebook reminds me that if I stand at the water's edge, hold my lead against the reel, and swing out on a tight line, the lead will drop directly over the clear area. Providing the line is released the moment the lead hits the surface, the end-tackle will sink vertically and hit bottom in precisely the right position. That rod is baited with two own-recipe baits on a long hair, and equipped with a four-bait stringer.

I gently tighten the line in order to straighten the anti-tangle tube, then a yard or so of slack is fed through the rings. The Baitrunner lever is flicked forward, the indicator attached, and the alarm switched on.

For the second rod I need my marker setup, comprising a smallish pike slider and a 1oz lead. I set the stop-knot at 13ft - the depth at which the weed thins out. The marker is overcast by a yard or two - then "tweaked" back until the float dimples the surface.

This rod is baited with two Sting boilies, and rigged with my usual four-bait stringer. It is cast about a foot beyond the marker float.

As quietly and unobtrusively as possible I throw a handful of boilies, a handful of boilie cubes, a couple of handfuls of mixed size trout pellets and a scattering of hempseed around each bait.

9.45am. Something makes me look up from the book I am reading; I am not sure whether I heard or sensed it. Gently undulating ripples are emanating from the margin to my left. To judge from the curvature of the ripples, whatever caused them is about 10 yards away. Has a carp broken the surface, or am I about to be visited by swans or ducks? Carefully I lean forward so as to see past the large bush which obstructs my view. There are no birds in sight! Slowly, taking care to make no sudden movement, I ease myself back in my chair. I place my book on my rucksack, and watch the water. More ripples appear - closer this time.

10.15am. The left-hand rod tip dips a fraction, the Delkim emits a couple of bleeps and the indicator lifts a few centimetres. A line bite. Until a few years ago I might have suspected skimmers, but there are none here now - cormorants have seen to that - so any sign of movement virtually guarantees a carp in the vicinity. I bet I get a take. Previous experience on the water has shown that line bites are

The pink-tinged mirror that I thought was a tuftie! (Chapter Sixteen)

The breathtakingly beautiful brass coloured common (Chapter Sixteen).

"Persistent showers" said the weather girl. See if I care!

The big, beautiful, unblemished, glistening near-leather (Chapter Sixteen).

I thought the net was snagged. . . (Chapter Sixteen).

almost always followed by a run.

10.30am. The left-hand rod stabs round, the alarm warbles a continuous note and the Baitrunner spins. I was expecting a take, but still it takes me by surprise! I pick up the rod, engage the gears and strike.

The rod is wrenched down and the clutch snarls. Good grief, this is pulling hard! A great raft of eel grass and Elodea rises to the surface. The fish stops, having burrowed deep in the weed. I maintain pressure - then increase it a bit. Nothing for a minute or two, then jag, jag - it moves. Slowly at first - then fast, parallel with the bank to my left. It is now about 30 yards away - there is a big, overhanging bush and the carp is almost beneath it. I am not too bothered about the bush, but just beyond it, at the bottom of the slope, is a snag. Not sure what it is, and I have never lost a fish on it, but I once lost a terminal tackle which became hooked up. Damn, it's in weed again.

As before, I maintain steady pressure, and once again it fights its own way free of the weed. This time, thankfully, it swings out to open, deeper water. That's better. After about ten minutes of to-ing and fro-ing it is directly in front of me. I've not yet seen it, but the fight has all the hallmarks of a big fish. Gradually it comes into view - a long, chestnut coloured leather. Draped round its head, like fairground bunting, trail green streamers of eel grass. With my eyes fixed on its mouth to reassure myself it is securely hooked, I draw it over the net and... got it!

I shut my eyes, fall to my knees and allow myself a few seconds to release the tension within me. Then with my composure restored I lift the fish from the water and place it on the unhooking mat. A big, beautiful, unblemished, glistening, near-leather.

It is transferred to the Sling-Retainer, and pegged in the margins while I set up my camera on the far side of the trees and bushes which shade my swim. A few pictures are taken - I use flash to augment the hazy flat light - and the fish is returned.

3.30pm. A fish head-and-shoulders in front of me - considerably further out than where my baits are placed, though. In the calm water I follow its subsequent progress by a horseshoe shaped trail of bubbles. It doesn't show again.

5.00pm. No more takes have occurred. I'll give it another hour - if I see a carp, I'll hang on for a while. If not, I'll pack up.

6.00pm. I pour the last of my coffee. Disgusting! Not only is it lukewarm, but it has acquired a sort of khaki colour. After a couple of sips, I throw it away. Time to go.

Static Stalking

Time of year: mid July.

***Rods:** Three, 12ft/2.25lb Eclipse. **Reels:** 3500 Sea-Series Baitrunner. **Line:** Power Plus, 18lb. **Hooks:** Nash Fang, size 6.*

***Bait:** 15mm own recipe unflavoured birdfood/fishmeal.*

***Rig:** Line Aligner, 45cm of 20lb HPPE braid fished Concertina style, 1.5oz semi-fixed Korda "Distance" inline in conjunction with 50cm No Spook anti-tangle tube, lightly backweighted.*

***Venue:** Kent gravel pit, hard fished club water.*

8.15am. Arrive at the gate - later than intended as prior to leaving home I had to deal with a blocked rainwater downpipe which overflowed during yesterday evening's storms. I put on garden gloves to protect my hands against oil contamination from the padlock - drive through the gate and down the track.

Only three anglers on the water - I am surprised but delighted! I stop to talk to one of them, "Very dour," he says, "the weather is too hot - they're just cruising on top, nothing is coming out, not even at night. I've been down all week and haven't had a touch."

I park the car, put on my Polaroids, and look for fish. In one of my erstwhile favourite "cubby hole" swims (unfortunately now enlarged to accommodate a double bivvy!) I find several mid-double commons swimming aimlessly a foot or two below the surface. As I stand watching, a big mirror comes within a yard of the bank, pauses for a moment, then unhurriedly swims off.

I collect my tackle and deposit it behind the bushes which those who enlarged the swim - to their credit - left in place.

The right-hand rod is lowered close to the edge, near where I saw the big mirror. The water is very clear, and less than 3ft deep, so I can see the bait lying on the bottom.

The middle and left-hand rods are both gently swung out five or six yards to where the depth is about 9ft. There is patchy weed out there, but I am confident that one, if not both of the end-rigs will be in a clear spot. I could have checked with a few bottom-probing trial casts, of course, but I chose not to do so for fear of spooking those fish I saw.

Whole boilies, chopped boilies, boilie cubes, 5mm and 8mm Nash Scopex carp pellets (trout pellets are banned) and hempseed are discreetly scattered in the vicinity of all three baits.

I tuck myself behind the screen of bushes, as far back as the swim allows. Coffee time.

10.00am. A splash just beyond the left-hand bait. That's a good sign - splashers are sometimes feeders.

10.15am. Line bite to left-hand rod - and almost immediately it is away! Strike - it's on, and moving strongly to my left - through a sparse lily bed, under an overhanging tree and - oh no! It's gone! I watch as big, deep, oily ripples rock the surface. Damn, damn, damn - it was a powerful fish. The big mirror I saw earlier, perhaps? I examine the hook - the point has turned over. That explains it! Probably it came into contact with gravel which the carp had sucked up along with the bait. Oh damn!

The point has turned over... (this is not a mock-up, incidentally, but the actual hook from the incident described).

Recast - and some more feed.

Carp in the immediate vicinity will now be well and truly spooked. I doubt if they will return. My best hope lies with new fish which, hopefully, will wander my way during the course of the day.

11.00am. Middle rod - another flier! No line bite - no warning at all. Strike, and it's on. I play the fish quite hard in the relatively confined swim, but it is only a low-double so presents no problems. Over the net - a lovely dark coloured mirror. It is unhooked and released immediately.

Two runs in less than an hour - and from a water that is "not fishing". I am feeling somewhat smug!

11.30am. Two cars pass along the track behind me - they stop just 20 yards to my right, adjacent to a big double swim. I know what is coming, but I cling to the vain hope that I might be wrong. Bang! Bang! Bang! There ensues 15 minutes of banging doors - reminiscent of a train station. How many doors have those cars got, for heaven's sake? The cars leave. I conclude that a couple of youngsters have been dropped off by their parents.

More banging - the distinctive thud of mallets on banksticks and bivvy pegs. I sigh, and marvel at how some anglers are so mind-numbingly stupid that they remain oblivious to the ease with which carp can be frightened. I wouldn't care if they only ruined their own chances, but they ruin everyone else's, too. Or more specifically, and in this instance, mine!

Spudoosh! A marker float lands immediately in front of me, 30-40yd out. It is well beyond where I have my baits but the new arrivals do not know that. Not only stupid, but ignorant and discourteous, too.

The marker float disappears. Obviously it landed in the wrong place. Maybe I misjudged them? They probably realised it was in front of me and plan to reposition it further round. Spudoosh! Ye Gods - it's even closer to me than it was before!

No matter how hard I try, I can't love 'em.

12.00. Enough! The din from next-door has continued unabated since their arrival. Time to go. A red T-shirted teenager with dyed yellow hair appears behind me, "Done any good?" he asks.

"No," I reply - imbuing that one word with as much venom as I can muster.

Is it my imagination, or are noisy anglers on the increase? Certainly I have more trips blighted by angler-related disturbance than used to be the case. Sullenly, and with undiluted hatred of yellow haired, red T-shirted teenagers, I load my car. I make damn sure I slam my boot-lid and doors, too!

Hole in the Weed

Time of year: *mid July*

Rods: *Two, 12.5ft/2.75lb Eclipse.* ***Reels:*** *Aero 6010 or 8010 Baitrunner.* ***Line:*** *Power Plus, 18lb, treated with Kryston Granite Juice.* ***Hooks:*** *Owner spade-end, size 10 (size 6 equivalent).*

Bait: *15mm own recipe unflavoured birdfood/fishmeal.*

Rig: *Line Aligner. 45cm of 20lb HPPE braid fished Concertina style, 1.5oz semi-fixed Korda "Distance" inline in conjunction with 50cm No Spook anti-tangle tube, lightly backweighted.*

Venue: *Kent gravel pit, club water, extremely weedy.*

7.00am. Just as the forecasters promised, a brisk north-west wind is blowing. It is the first significant wind for almost a week. My instinct is to fish the downwind end, but it is a Friday and the weekend session-men will start arriving soon. They will see the significance of the new wind, too. I hate being sandwiched between other anglers, especially on this water where most of my fish are caught close in, so I make the seemingly aberrant decision to fish the upwind end.

7.30am. The swim is one of my favourites. Most anglers ignore it because it is very confined so cannot accommodate a bivvy and all the accompanying accoutrements. I can just about squeeze in with a folding chair and a small umbrella. I make more room by substituting a Gardner long storm pole for the standard-length version on my front buzzer-bar. This enables me to push it in the margin mud where the water is a couple of feet deep, thereby moving my whole rod setup forward by a foot or two. Couldn't do that with a pod...

The swim has a weed covered sandbank to my left, and drops away to about 15ft to my right. Due to the clarity of the water it is exceptionally weedy even at

15ft. There is, however, approximately 10 yards out, a small semi-clear patch. It lies at an awkward angle for casting, but is the only spot in the swim which enables decent presentation.

...and a scattering of mini-cubes.

I stand to cast and - wait a moment - I notice what looks like a kink in the mono about a foot above my anti-tangle tube. It's not a kink - the line is damaged! Probably nicked by a thorn as I pushed through vegetation to reach my swim (one of the hazards of carrying rods ready-tackled and unprotected). Relieved to have noticed it, I strip off several yards of line and retackle. To play safe, I do the same with the second rod.

Both rods are baited with twin boilies and a four-bait stringer. They are cast to the semi-clear spot; one to its right-hand edge, the other to its left. They are less than a yard apart.

Whole boilies, half boilies and mini-cubes are lightly scattered in the vicinity of my baits, along with some Micromass, a few ball pellets, a couple of handfuls of mixed-size trout pellets and some hemp. A second bag of hempseed, still frozen, is in a chilly-bag. I'll put that in the clear spot when I pack up. Browsing carp will hopefully prevent new weed growth, and thereby keep it clear. It's a good policy, and one I use in several swims here. I deliberately keep the baiting tight - I don't want my clear spots to become enlarged or they may be found by other anglers.

8.00am. My chair is tucked invisibly behind a screen of vegetation. I arrange my coffee flask and library book close to hand, and attach a mini-radio to a bankstick adjacent to my ear (with the volume so low that only I will be able to hear it). I tune to Radio Four and listen to the Today programme.

9.00am. Sue Lawley is just about to tell me who her desert island castaway is to be, when she is interrupted by the high-pitched, urgent warble of my left-hand Delkim! It is the sort of run Rick calls a "spool melter"! I strike; the rod is wrenched violently down and the clutch gives a pained screech. The ferocity and power of this fish is incredible - I offer thanks to whichever deity is overseeing events that I noticed the damaged line! It grinds to a stop - the fish has buried itself in weed. I increase the pressure and, yes, I can discern movement. Oh no, that awful, nerve-jarring, grating sensation can mean only one thing - line is rubbing

Rick and I have a rare social trip. We sit behind a bush while our rods fish Aveley's adjacent margins (we shared a 12 fish catch).

along something other than weed. I know this swim well - it is snag-free, so the juddering is probably caused by someone's lost tackle. Why oh why do anglers use inadequate tackle in weed? Once the first loss occurs, another follows. And so it goes on, getting progressively worse until a lethal cats-cradle of mono builds up. I curse whoever is responsible. Then the inevitable happens - the combination of weed and lost tackle results in the carp grinding to a halt. I increase pressure, more in hope than expectation that the fish will come free. And it does! Unbelievable! A moment ago everything was locked solid, and now it is moving again. And how! My God, this fish has attitude! It runs fast to the left of the swim - but amazingly, away from the snaring lost mono!

More runs - every one of which has me gritting my teeth and wincing with anxiety. I'm not enjoying this at all. That cats-cradle snag is worrying me too. Please don't let it become snarled up again. And don't let the hook fall out. Oh please don't let the hook fall out. It's coming up, through the weed; the fronds are gradually parting and, I can see it. Oh my God, it's massive! Here it comes - keep coming, keep coming - over the drawstring and Yes! Yes! Yes!

I reach for the meshes and try to lift - it won't budge - it must be stuck on a root or something... No it isn't. It's not snagged at all - just too damned heavy to lift! I brace myself, grip the mesh with both hands and heave! I lay it on the unhooking mat. Big, deep bodied, and immensely wide across the back. It is dark mahogany brown on the sides, and almost black on top. Huge scales too. Oh it's beautiful! I gently caress its flanks, wiping away some wayward strands of weed as I do so. I take a deep breath and try to shake off my dazed, dreamlike mood while I think what to do next. Sling-Retainer; that's it, put it in the Sling-Retainer while I set up the camera for a few self-take shots.

With photos taken and the fish returned I sit to compose myself. Sue Lawley's voice comes within earshot, "With thanks to my guest, I will say goodbye."

I wonder who it was?

Down the Slope

Time of year: *mid September.*
Rods: *Three, 12.5ft/2.75lb Eclipse.* ***Reels:*** *Aero 6010 or 8010 Baitrunner.*
Line: *Power Plus, 18lb.* ***Hooks:*** *Nash Fang, size 6.*
Bait: *15mm Sting .*
Rig: *Line Aligner, 45cm of 20lb HPPE braid fished Concertina style, 1.5 oz semi-fixed Korda "Distance" inline in conjunction with 50cm No Spook anti-tangle tube, lightly backweighted.*
Venue: *Kent gravel pit, club water, very deep.*

8.30am. "South-east England will be warm and sunny, but with the risk of heavy showers during the afternoon."

I switch off the radio, pull into the car park, and have a wander along the bank. Four... no five people fishing. All bivvied-up. Only three swims are occupied though, on account of anglers doubling-up. I wonder, not for the first time, why they fish this way - by sharing a pitch they increase their chances of being detected by carp, and significantly reduce their chances of catching. Not that I am complaining, you understand - it leaves more swims from which to choose.

On the west bank there is a 100 yards plus stretch with no one fishing. I sit on the grass, halfway along, and watch the water while I ponder the situation. There is a gentle south-west breeze, but we are approaching the time of year when wind direction becomes progressively less important. I decide to disregard it. Near one end of the unoccupied stretch is a big double swim; just 10-15 yards to one side of it is a lovely little "cubby hole" pitch. The "cubby hole" is my first choice - but there is a high risk that if the double swim is left unoccupied, someone will move into it. If, on the other hand, I occupy the double swim myself, I will probably remain undisturbed because the "cubby hole" is unsuitable for a dome. Decision made. I set up in the double swim.

9.30am. The stop-knot on my marker rod is adjusted to 12ft. A gentle underarm cast results in the slider being pulled under by the 1oz lead. Gradually I pull back until the float appears on the surface. The first rod, baited with double 15mm boilies and a four-bait stringer, is cast alongside. A few freebie boilies, some mixed-size cubes from the same mix, 4mm and 8mm trout pellets, sweetcorn and hempseed are catapulted in a dining-table size patch around the hookbait.

I repeat the process with rods to 15ft and 18ft. It is a very deep water - 30ft in places - consequently the margin slope is steep. Even the furthest rod - the one in 18ft - only requires a gentle underarm lob.

Most of my takes recently have come from 15ft, but mid-September is a cusp period when weather conditions can persuade fish to move shallower or deeper, so I like to bracket the taking depth.

1.00pm. A big, dark looking fish head-and-shoulders over my 18ft bait. I think it's a mirror. That's a promising sign.

1.30pm. One of the weather girl's "heavy showers" is falling. It is absolutely sheeting down. The water is dancing with tall spires, and a big puddle is forming in the canopy of my umbrella.

3.00pm. The lunchtime deluge only lasted for about 15 minutes. The sun appeared immediately after, and it has remained out since. It is surprisingly warm for September, too. No activity yet. The brief adrenalin buzz I got from the earlier sighting has passed. Not seen anything since. The mallards are being a pain and I am worried that they will swim into my lines. If they do, they'll panic and drag my leads out of position. Oh no, they are coming out of the water - they've spotted my hemp and trout pellet spillage. If I ignore them they'll waddle beneath my rods and blunder into my slack lines and low-slung indicators... Oh, go away you stupid animals! I throw a pebble in their direction - they think it's food and scuttle after it! There's no choice, I've got to chase them off.

3.45pm. Right-hand rod is away! It's very, very fast - so fast that the indicator has dropped free of the line. Strike and, yes - it's on. The Aero clutch snarls - it's not a nice purr like you get with the American Series, but it's a lovely sound, nonetheless! The deep water is weedfree, and in the vicinity of this swim free of snags, too. The margins are heavily overgrown with Elodea, but at this time of year it presents few problems because it is breaking up.

In she comes, a gorgeous dark-toned common. I don't know if it is due to the clarity of the water but the carp in here have lovely rich colours. Safely in the net and I pause for a moment as I consider whether to unhook it in the margins; but no, on reflection I reckon it warrants being weighed and photographed. A few quick self-takes, and back in the water.

Recast to 15ft - and more loose feed.

6.30pm. Same rod! Another one-noter. Strike. It's on and, oh yes, this feels heavy. No histrionics, just a rhythmic surge of power travelling up the line. Now it's moving straight out, heading for the centre of the pit in a slow, steady, unstoppable run. A long length of mono is above the surface - an unusual occurrence in this deep water - and is glistening in the fading sunlight. The fish has run at least 60 yards and is still plodding inexorably on. It's stopped. Now we are in the sandbag thump stage. I hate that. I presume it is caused when the line is struck by the carp's tail. I don't recall it ever costing me a fish, but it always unnerves me. It kites slowly to the right, which should be okay unless it swings all the way in and gets beneath the trailing branches of those overhanging bushes. That's better, it's moving out to open water again. In she comes; slowly, don't rush it James. Now it's beneath the rod top and swimming slowly back and forth. Good grief! Look at that vortex, and that despite the fish being too deep to see! Up she comes; it's a common. And what a common! Over the net - don't rush, don't rush. Yes! Oh just look at it! Not only is it a stunning brass gold colour, but it is fin perfect, scale perfect and shape perfect. Absolutely breathtakingly beautiful.

7.30pm. Photos have been taken. My magnificent common has been returned, and I am sitting here "having an enjoy". I haven't recast yet. Not sure if I shall. No, I don't think I will. I'll give the euphoria time to leach out of my system, then I'll pack up.

Postscript

A couple of months later one of the pit's session-men said, "I know you don't like saying too much about your fish, Jim, but did you catch the big common?"

"I did," I replied, "back in September. Why do you ask?"

"It's the one everyone wants; but it comes out so rarely that if they'd realised it had been caught, some of the regulars would have stopped fishing here."

I wish I had known that earlier!

Winter Close-In

Time of year: *early December.*
Rods: *Two, 12ft/2.25lb Eclipse.* ***Reels:*** *Aero 6010 or 8010 Baitrunner.* ***Line:*** *Power Plus, 12lb.* ***Hooks:*** *Fox Series 2, size 8.*
Bait: *10mm Scopex Squid and sweetcorn.*
Rig: *Line Aligner, Combi-link made with 35cm of 12lb Snake-Skin, 1oz running plain pear lead on split-lug leger bead, no anti-tangle tube.*
Venue: *Small Kent gravel pit, club water.*

8.30am. As usual, there is no one fishing. There are several pits in this complex - a couple of them are high profile waters and subjected to a lot of pressure, but hardly anyone bothers with this one. Recently I have been catching from the deeper water at what looks like the pit's dam end - only it isn't a dam, of course. I choose a swim halfway along. It is not particularly comfortable because it comprises a sort of mini dugout created for a matchman's seat-box. I can only make room for my chair if I fold the back legs under and wedge the rear of the seat against the steep bank behind me. A groundsheet keeps the chair's ratchet-wheels free of mud and stops damp seeping through the fabric.

To prevent my rucksack toppling over on the sloping bank I peg its grab-handle with a bivvy-peg.

My small umbrella takes up more space than is ideal, but showers are forecast so I don't want to do without it.

Directly in front of me is a wide reed margin. Back in November I cleared a gap for my lines. Someone has since enlarged it, but not too drastically.

A couple of rod-lengths straight out, the depth is 12ft. A few yards to the left it is a foot or so shallower; and conversely it deepens slightly to the right. I splay the rods so I have baits in depths of 11ft and 13ft. Lines are fished semi-slack; "droopy" is my preferred term.

Bait comprises two 10mm boilies with a grain of sweetcorn sandwiched between them. A four-bait stringer is attached - the PVA tape must not be permitted to come in contact with the moist sweetcorn or it will dissolve before I cast. Feed consists of a dozen boilies around each hookbait, plus a pouch of Micromass and a pouch of sweetcorn. Even though I am fishing quite close, the onshore breeze makes baiting with the sweetcorn somewhat difficult.

8.45am. Way over to my left a fish has just jumped. It is nowhere near my swim, but still succeeds in boosting my confidence. On my previous winter trips here, if I have seen a carp roll or jump, I have caught. Only on the couple of occasions when I have seen nothing have I blanked. And again! It jumps again in almost the

The larger of the two December commons.

same place. I'll catch today for sure!

9.30am. Left-hand rod; the swing-arm Wisp flies up to the horizontal, then falls slowly back down again. Startled me, did that! For a moment, I thought it was away! It was a fierce line bite - I hope the hook has not been dragged along the bottom and become fouled with dead weed debris? That's one of the debits of using a light lead. Recent trips, a run has come within 10 minutes of a line bite, so I'll give it 15, maybe 20 minutes, and if no take has occurred I'll check it out.

My worries are groundless - it's away! No winter twitcher this, but a run which would do credit to high summer! Strike; pause to evaluate the situation. Fast and lively - almost certainly a low double. Several short runs then, yes, here it comes. Over the net - unhook it in the landing net while still in the water, and gently tip it straight back. A deep-bodied common.

Rebait - recast - more feed.

2.30pm. Left-hand rod again; another line bite. The weather is mild and drizzly; perhaps that is why they are in 11ft rather than 13ft? I cannot think of any logical reason why it should be so, but it often seems to work that way. Here we go - that lovely "diddley diddley" Delkim note! Strike and - yes, this one feels heavier. It swings to the right and enters the outer fringe of the dead margin reeds. Lay the rod down low, apply sidestrain - the tall stems rock back and forth... pull firmly and, that's it, out it comes. Running to open water now - slowing too. I can feel it tiring - gently does it, sink the net and, lovely! In first time. Another common - substantially larger than the first.

4.00pm. It is getting gloomy. I'll pack up slowly so my baits remain in the water until the last vestige of daylight. Before I leave, I'll throw in my leftover bait to give a few fish a "taster" before my next trip.

It's been an enjoyable day - a water to myself, and two beautiful commons which, in all probability, have never seen a hook before.

Cold Water Method Style

Time of year: mid-February.
Rods: *Three, 12ft/2.25lb Eclipse.* **Reels:** *Aero 6010 or 8010 Baitrunner.*
Line: *Sufix Supreme, 12lb.* **Hooks:** *Owner spade-end, size 7 (size 8 or 9 equivalent).*
Bait: *Cockles.*
Rig: *Line Aligner, 45cm of 12lb HPPE braid, 1.5oz semi-fixed Korda "Distance" inline in conjunction with 50cm No Spook anti-tangle tube, lightly backweighted.*
Venue: *Deep Kent gravel pit, club water.*

8.30am. That's a nuisance. Two pike anglers are in the swim I planned to fish. It's a good winter spot because there is a 12ft plateau which gently slopes down to 20ft, thereby enabling baits to be placed at differing depths. The only other pitch I fancy is also occupied. So where to go? Back in November I had some success in the next pit along but it became a bit pressured for my taste so I decided to leave it alone. Not much encouragement to return, either, because word on the grapevine is that it has produced nothing for the past four or five weeks. One of the long-stay session men had a fortnight's blank, I hear. Oh, go on James, don't be a wimp - give it a go!

9.00am. Dank, damp and dour - what a miserable day! Not too cold, though. No one here - a sure sign it is fishing badly. I am undecided about which swim to choose - halfway along the south-facing bank looks as good as anywhere.

Middle rod baited with two cockles. The link is folded back Concertina style inside the freebie-packed Method ball.

The unwieldy assembly is lobbed out about 30 yards into a depth of 24 feet.

Right-hand rod rigged likewise; cast about 25 yards. Left-hand rod just 20 yards.

11.00am. Nine million tufties have just landed on the water. Okay, nine million is an exaggeration, but not by much! No sign of carp.

1.30pm. They have found me! Oh, I so hate tufties. About a dozen are diving over my furthest rod. The Delkim gives a single "bleep" and the indicator twitches. What to do? If I cast near them with my marker rod I'll scare any carp which might be in the vicinity. If I ignore them they'll clear my feed and perhaps tangle my end-rigs. I lift my landing net high in the air and wave it. They watch with rapt attention, then become bored and ignore me.

2.30pm. Having acquired confidence, the tufties move in closer; they are now over the 25 yards rod. "Bleep." I fantasise about what I would do with a 12-bore; in my mind's eye I see feathers flying everywhere...

3.00pm. Now they are over the closest rod. "Bleep." I can take just so much, as

I am not allowed (club rules) to show some of the swims featured, so this attractive alternative will have to suffice.

Popeye would say, but I can't take any more (Popeye actually says "no more", but I cannot bring myself to use a double negative!) "Bleep." Right, that's it, I'm going to pull your stupid face off. Strike and - what the..? I don't believe it. It's a carp! The clutch is doing its snarling bit, the tufties are looking puzzled, and I am astonished! A similar thing happened here in November; I thought it was a freak occurrence, but now I am beginning to wonder if there's more to it.

Typical of winter carp, it makes a few slow runs, but the fight is an unspectacular affair. In it comes - nice looking fish, a mirror. A distinct pink tint to the flanks. I used to think this was evidence that someone was incorporating Robin Red in their baits, but "pinking" occurs in so many waters from November onwards that I now suspect it is normal winter colouration.

After a few self-take flash pictures, I mull over whether to recast. It is getting very gloomy and looks like it might rain. There has been drizzle on and off for most of the day, but the last hour has been dry. I debate whether it's worth getting my gear wet again in order to hang on for an hour or two.

I look at the tufties. They are milling around just 20 yards from the bank, waiting for me to recast. I menace them with my most hateful glare. They return my gaze with expressionless indifference.

I decide to quit!

Chapter Seventeen

Carp Care

The respect, admiration - love even - that we feel for carp prompts us to treat them with the utmost care. There is a financial incentive, too - they are a valuable resource, and it would cost upwards of £600 to replace a twenty pounder.

Unhooking Mat

I may be wrong, but I think Kevin Nash produced the first custom made unhooking-mat; it was oval in shape and cost, if I remember correctly, about £12.

Unhooking mat and Nash Sling-Retainer.

Now, there are numerous models available - prices range from the region of £20 to over £50. Most incorporate a foam inner, but at least one contains polyballs which enable it to function on a sort of beanbag principle. There have been a few inflatable designs, but these proved impractical due to the ease with which they could be punctured by thorns.

Some incorporate a Velcro flap to restrain a fish from struggling. Others are combination products and serve as both weigh-sling and mat. All perform the same function - they minimise the risk of a carp sustaining impact injury to its eyes, scales/skin, fins or internal organs.

Whichever mat is chosen, it should be kept shaded from summer sun or it may become sufficiently hot to cause damage to a carp. If no shade is available, I suggest the mat be placed face-side down when not in use; and as an added precaution it should be doused in water before a carp is laid upon it.

Most of my fishing is done alone, so I cannot rely on someone else being on hand to help restrain a struggling fish. The majority of my carp, therefore, are unhooked in the landing net while still in the water, and released immediately. If the configuration of the bank makes this impossible, or if I want to weigh and photograph the fish, I lift it onto the unhooking mat, and straightaway transfer it to a Nash Sling-Retainer. It is then pegged in the margins while I set up my camera. I shall have more to say on the subject of photography, presently.

Weighing the catch

Large diameter dial scales are popular with carp anglers because they are extremely accurate. I have never owned a set because they are too bulky and heavy to carry around; also, I have no requirement for spot-on ounce-perfect precision. I use a brass tubular balance made by Salter which is sufficiently accurate for read-outs to the nearest quarter pound which, frankly, is close enough for my purposes. What those purposes are, I am not quite sure because truth is - and you can believe this or not, as you choose - I do not have that much interest in what a carp weighs. I weigh those which look 20lb or more, but only rarely does the figure stick in my mind for very long.

The nearest quarter pound is close enough.

But whatever our attitude to a carp's weight, there can be no arguing that what matters most is its wellbeing. The weigh-sling should be pre-wetted, and care taken to ensure that fins are not bent the wrong way or it may result in rays being broken. The whole process should be undertaken quickly, too, especially in warm weather.

Retention

I no longer carry a keepsack. I used to, in fact I always carried several in case I had a multiple catch, but nowadays I either return my carp immediately, or keep them in a Sling-Retainer for just long enough to set up a camera. My change of heart is due to my concluding that their welfare is best served by releasing them as soon as possible.

Why retain carp, anyway?

Some do it because they maintain that pictures taken in the daytime are usually better than those taken in darkness. I would not quarrel with such an assertion - but what is more important, photo quality or a carp's welfare?

Others justify retaining carp for several hours by claiming that it gives them a chance to recover.

Excuse me?

Run that past me again...

What complete and utter nonsense! The best place for a carp to recover is back in its natural environment where it feels secure - tucked in a weedbed, perhaps.

Long-term retention is potentially harmful and a number of big fish have died as a consequence. "But I've never lost one," people will claim. No, nor have I - but I know several who have.

Retention is particularly dangerous during periods of high water temperature when the margins can become seriously depleted of dissolved oxygen.

If short-term retention is deemed necessary in order that a fish be witnessed or photographed, the time span should be measured in minutes, not hours. Sad to say, many anglers cannot be trusted to use good judgment in this regard, so rules have to be unambiguously clear. Imprecise wording such as, "Carp may be retained for sufficient time to enable photographs to be taken," will lead to fish being kept for far too long. Like the member of a syndicate to which I once belonged, who caught a 24lb common at dusk and kept it in a sack until sunrise the following day. It died overnight. Better to have a clear-cut, inflexible rule which states the maximum time which fish may be retained - I suggest 30 minutes.

Not sure what is going on here. Perhaps I am offering up a prayer that this lovely fish is not put at risk by new introductions...

Brother Rick doing what Brother Rick does!

Almost perfect leather.

Number Two son, Peter, with a magnificent Kent pit mirror.

Rick demonstrates good carp care.

I love the "freshly minted" look of this beautiful Kent mirror.

Just being there!

Hold firm... but no wristwatch or metal badges etc. which could cause injury.

Unhooking

Modern hooks have small barbs so they are more easily removed than were the crude rank-barbed models that used to be available. Generally they can be extracted with the fingers, but just occasionally one is so securely embedded that a firmer grip is required. The best tool for the job is a pair of small to medium artery forceps.

As long as 30 years ago, friends and I carried TCP liquid or Germolene cream which we dabbed on hook wounds, bruises, cuts or torn fins. We never knew if it helped healing, but we rationalised our actions with the view that even if it did no good, it certainly did no harm. Nowadays we have custom-made products in the form of Kryston's Klinik and Solar's Remedy - both of which are based on formulations used by koi rearers. I use Klinik, which I apply whenever I think it might be beneficial. Water is a perfect medium for bacteria, which means that even small injuries - hook damage for example - can lead to bacterial infection. Klinik and Remedy provide no guarantee that infection will not occur, but probably reduce its likelihood.

In spring, it is not unusual to catch carp which are heavily infested with leeches. I am undecided about whether these are best removed or left in place - if fish are in good condition they successfully shed them when the water warms up, anyway. But leeches are such offensive things that my instinct is to remove them. A drop of Klinik or Remedy causes them to shrivel and drop off, and at the same time treats the tiny puncture hole which is left in the carp's skin.

It may not be apparent in black-and-white, but this carp had a number of small injuries (probably incurred while spawning) - Klinik was applied before its release.

Net dips

Some clubs, syndicates and fishery owners install disinfectant net-dips. Whilst this practice is well intentioned, I am far from convinced as to its effectiveness. Iodine based dips - the most common in use - degrade so quickly that they should be replaced daily, or at the very least, weekly. Clearly, this does not happen. The dips on most fisheries are left unchanged for several months, and for a whole year in some instances!

To refer to them as "dips" is misleading, too - they should more properly be called "soaks". Nets, weigh-slings and mats (no point confining the treatment to nets) need to be submerged in fresh idophor disinfectant such as Fam 30 for at least 10 minutes. Contamination and oxidation renders the solution progressively less potent, and by the end of a week the necessary "dip" time has extended to about half an hour.

Short of having someone on 24 hour "dunk-duty", it is not going to happen, is it?

But let us indulge a fantasy. Suppose a club installs a dip, replaces the disinfectant solution every few days, and all visitors to the water conscientiously soak their nets etc. for half an hour before commencing fishing (yes, I believe in Santa Claus and the Tooth Fairy, too!) - will the measure prove effective?

Truth is, we do not know, because no one has yet proved that bacteria, viruses or parasites can be carried on angling equipment. But that said, I think it makes sense to assume they can, and act accordingly. Pathogenic "nasties" thrive best in damp and dark conditions - so all we need do in order to render gear safe is to hang it out to dry, preferably in sunshine. Viruses are particularly vulnerable to this treatment because they are eliminated by even relatively short exposure to ultraviolet.

This is the best way of rendering nets, slings etc. free of pathogenic bacteria and viruses.

Springtime carp deaths syndrome

This talk of disease brings us, inevitably and depressingly, to Springtime Carp Deaths Syndrome. For the last few years, late spring has been accompanied by major carp losses. In the worst cases, waters have suffered virtually a 100 per cent wipeout.

Why is it happening?

Many, if not most incidents can be attributed to diseased imports. It is difficult to prove the link - and we should always beware of adding two and two, and coming up with five - but empirical evidence leaves little room for doubt.

But significant losses have also occurred in waters where the only introductions have been of U.K. bred fish. And they should be okay, surely?

Not necessarily.

To start with, the provenance of some "U.K. bred carp" is dubious because not everyone engaged in the business of supplying carp is, shall we say, on the side of the angels...

Not that "U.K. bred", even when the term is accurately applied, guarantees the fish are free from contagions because they might have been stored alongside imported fish, or transported in the same containers.

But while imported fish have doubtless been the direct or indirect cause of most of the mass mortalities we have suffered, it must be borne in mind that the introduction of any stock fish, whatever their source, carries with it an element of risk. And anglers should not delude themselves that a health check will eliminate that risk, because fish can be carriers of disease, and yet exhibit no symptoms - this applies to bacteria, viruses and, although not technically a disease, parasites. Following the stocking there may be no immediate effect - indeed nothing untoward may reveal itself for many months, even years - but problems may develop when the population is put under stress.

Every club, syndicate or fishery owner who introduces stock fish is taking a gamble. Before doing so, therefore, they should weigh up the risk/return equation very, very carefully.

If a club concludes that they absolutely must introduce stock fish, they should do so only via a dealer who comes recommended by other clubs in the area. The Environment Agency can help in this regard, too.

But I repeat - all stocking carries a risk.

Now we come to the real conundrum - the waters which have received no new stock fish for several years, either from abroad or the U.K., yet have suffered heavy carp losses.

What happened in those instances?

The honest answer is that we do not know. But we can look at a few facts and make some reasonable deductions.

To start with, no fishery owner can be one hundred per cent certain that unofficial, illegal introductions of stolen or smuggled fish have not occurred. Unfortunately, a lot of this sort of thing goes on, and short of making a water like Fort Knox, it is impossible to control.

But if we assume that no new fish have been introduced - officially or otherwise - what then? Does that not protect a water from losses?

Sadly, it does not. Fish can suffer from disease or parasite infestation which remains at a level with which they can cope. Take gill fluke, for example. This is quite common in the south-east, but few afflicted fish die as a result of it. Leastways, not until low dissolved oxygen levels - perhaps as a consequence of very high temperatures or an algal bloom - place excessive demands on gills which are operating at reduced efficiency.

Then there are diseases which are endemic in a water. They can lay dormant for many years, but may become activated by a factor such as stress.

Parasites, likewise. It is not in a parasite's best interests to kill its host, so most of the time fish can cope with parasite infestation. But there may come a point when the level of infestation creates problems. A subject raised by Neville Fickling in an interesting article entitled, "Mugs" (Carpworld, Issue 57), in which he suggested that extra demands placed on carp as a result of heavy parasite infestation might result in them becoming mug fish. This intriguing hypothesis set bells jangling in my brain because I recalled my friend Ken Crow (who breeds and rears carp professionally) expressing his concern that mild winters result in abnormally high levels of parasite survival. In addition, Ken believes mild winters compel carp to maintain a metabolic rate which they cannot readily sustain by feeding. Yes, they eat in winter, but their ability to utilise that food efficiently is seriously impaired. Ken is concerned that this leads to a significant deterioration in their condition, which combined with the aforementioned high level of parasite survival may put them under considerable stress - a circumstance which can only be exacerbated if they then have to cope with frequent capture.

The '98/'99 winter, in addition to being exceptionally mild - especially the period from late December through to early February - was also extremely wet. Likewise the winter of '94/'95 which, according to statisticians, was the wettest for 55 years. Such winters lead to high levels of agro-chemicals and pollutants getting into fisheries via run-off or seepage. It is reasonable to speculate, therefore, that in spring '95 and '99 stressed carp populations may have had to contend with the further problem of poor water quality.

Unfortunately, there is more. Spring weather in the U.K. is rarely a nice, even process of steadily increasing temperatures. We might get a mini heatwave - something which often happens in May - which causes water temperatures to soar. Carp respond to this by exhibiting pre-spawning chasing behaviour. But after a few days of sweltering heat, the situation changes and we often get cold north-easterlies sweeping across the country. This can cause water temperatures to plummet by as much as 10 degrees Fahrenheit (about 6 degrees Celsius) in less than a week which, as you can imagine, results in carp putting their spawning "on hold". The possible consequence of such an occurrence was detailed in Chris Seagrove's fascinating feature, "Carp Deaths - An Authoritative View" (Carpworld 54), in which he explained how during the pre-spawning period when the males chase the females through the shallows, the fine network of tissue which holds the eggs in the ovary breaks down. He then continued, "If the spawning ritual is interrupted, ie. male swims off halfway through..., the process of egg release is halted. The eggs have now gone past the point of no return and will die in the ovaries. Under certain circumstances, these eggs can become infected and the fish can die of a bacterial infection."

All of the foregoing is made worse by the fact that a carp's natural immune system does not function effectively until the water temperature reaches about 60 degrees Fahrenheit (15+ degrees Celsius). This becomes particularly pertinent when we have a prolonged and relatively cold spring, and water temperatures remain below the immune system switch-on level for a long while. Under these circumstances, even a relatively minor infection might so debilitate a fish that it results in its death.

This problem is most serious, I feel, on big, deep waters which take much longer to warm up than do small, shallow ones - thereby extending the period when the immune system does not function.

All of which might satisfactorily explain why we occasionally witness heavy springtime mortalities in established waters which have received no new stock fish. It does not, however, address the issue of why it seems to be a relatively recent phenomenon.

One clue to this apparent paradox is that poor water quality resulting from agro-chemicals is also a relatively recent phenomenon. Added to which, carp are more pressured now than they used to be, and are caught more frequently. And could it be that the strains of carp with which we now stock - Dinkelsbühlers, for example - do not have the genetic makeup required for long life? They are table-fish which are bred for rapid early-years growth to enable them to reach eating size in the fastest possible time. I wonder, too, about their resistance to disease, and their ability to spawn unaided.

That last point could be significant because in commercial carp farms spawning is precipitated by a hormone injection and fish are hand-stripped. If, as I suspect, some strains are ill equipped to spawn unassisted, it is hardly surprising if problems occur.

So, let us summarise the risk factors:

- **foreign introductions**
- **illegal introductions**
- **any introductions**
- **endemic disease (possibly dormant)**
- **heavy parasite infestation**
- **a mild winter**
- **a wet winter**
- **a long, cold spring (non functioning immune system)**
- **deep water (ditto as above)**
- **spring heatwave, followed by cold weather**
- **poor water quality (agro-chemicals and pollutants)**

- **low oxygen level (high temperature, algae, ammonia)**
- **stress as a result of angling pressure**
- **strains of carp with short life expectancy, and which are insufficiently robust to cope with stress, disease and spawning**

Any one of those factors poses a threat to carp welfare - but when they occur in combination I think there is a high likelihood of an unstoppable lethal dynamic becoming established.

If I am correct, we cannot hold an as yet unidentified "mystery disease" responsible for the U.K.'s annual crop of carp deaths, but rather a combination of factors. And crazy stocking policies apart - they are factors over which we have absolutely no control. So each year, especially in late spring, all we can do is keep our fingers crossed.

Which is a sobering thought, is it not?

Self take photography

I have included photography in the "Carp Care" section because picture-taking in general, and self-take photography in particular, can be the cause of carp suffering injury. It can even, when over-long retention is involved, result in them dying.

Many of the problems which arise would be avoided if anglers acquired equipment which enabled them to be independent of others, and learned how to use it.

The first requirement is a camera which enables self-take shots. Most have a 10-12 seconds delayed action shutter release - but this is unsuitable because it requires that the carp be picked up and put down between shots; additionally, the angler has no control over the fish when it is left on the mat while the self-timer is activated. Far better is some sort of off-camera remote facility. The systems available are pneumatic, electronic and infra-red. I have used all three, and all are extremely efficient, but for simplicity and ease of use my vote goes to infra-red. This utilises a mini remote control, about half the size of a credit card. If you look at the trophy pictures which appear throughout this book, you will doubtless spot it. To protect its circuitry from water and carp slime, I put it in a mini press-closure poly-bag.

At this juncture I should make the point that infra-red remote releases only function with dedicated cameras - you cannot use one to trigger the shutter mechanism of a non-dedicated model.

I have both SLR and compact 35mm cameras which function via infra-red

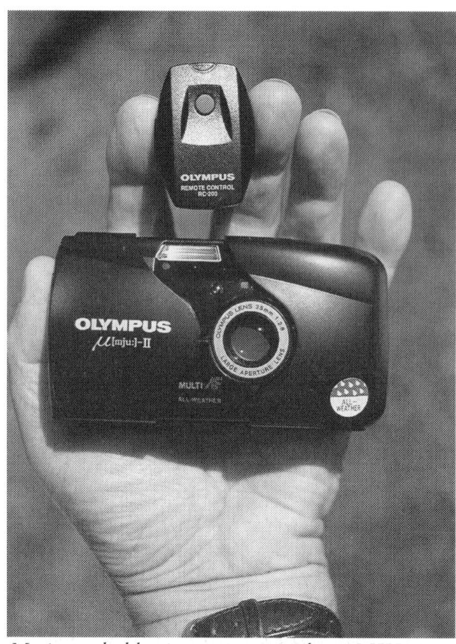

My improbably tiny auto-everything MJU11 with infra-red remote release.

remote systems. The SLR (Canon EOS 100) produces the best results, but for convenience I generally use one of my auto-everything compacts. Most modern compacts offer a range of flash options. Some offer a choice of metering systems, too. But all that is really needed is automatic exposure, focus and flash, plus a fill-in (sometimes called daylight) flash facility.

This is not the place to discuss camera operation in detail - instead, I recommend diligent study of the camera's instruction booklet. Initially it might appear confusing, especially for anyone unfamiliar with photography and its terminology, but on second or third readings it will start to make sense. Most people have an inexplicable reluctance to read instruction books - and not just those which apply to cameras - they prefer to fiddle with knobs and dials, and see what happens! An American domestic appliance manufacturer, fully aware of this tendency, tried putting a sticker on all their products which said, "If all else fails, read the instructions."

I like that!

Having mastered the camera's functions, the next skill to be acquired is framing of the picture in such a manner that the angler and catch are displayed to best advantage.

First, and most important, I recommend the use of a tripod. Bankstick camera adaptors are unsuitable because they are insufficiently stable. A tripod should have a pan and tilt head which enables the camera to be used both horizontally and vertically. For self-take trophy shots, vertical format is the safest bet because close-framing of a horizontal picture is somewhat difficult. In vertical format, if the unhooking mat is enclosed within the bottom of the viewfinder, the fish will be shown in its entirety and the angler will avoid being pictorially decapitated! All this preparation, of course, is undertaken with the carp in the water.

If the fish is to be photographed in darkness, a torch should be placed near the camera and positioned so it will shine on the subject - I use a bankstick mounted

John Roberts rubber Butt Grip to hold the torch. This is because auto-focus systems require light in order to function (some cameras project their own beam when auto-flash is activated, in which case a torch is unnecessary).

When everything is ready, the angler poses with the fish, and the remote release activated - modern autowind cameras enable several pictures to be rattled off in just a few seconds. All the while, the carp should be held over the mat so, if the worst comes to the worst, and the fish falls, it lands on the mat. If, as is advisable,

Self-take auto-flash picture. The remote release is in my hand near the carp's anal fin.

Picture quality would doubtless have benefited by waiting until morning - but would that have served the carp's welfare?

the angler is kneeling, it has only a few inches to fall, anyway.

On no account, incidentally, should a carp be supported by placing a knee beneath it because this applies a dangerous level of pressure to a small area with a consequent risk of injury to internal organs.

If a watch or bracelet is being worn, it should be removed lest it scratch the carp's skin or dislodge a scale.

Occasionally, when we need to control a carp's struggles, we clasp it to our chest - which hopefully will be free of metal badges or other sharp edged objects which could cause injury. Better still, the fish should be laid on the mat and its eyes covered with a wet weigh-sling or similar.

Some anglers stick a thumb or finger inside the carp's mouth in the belief that this will subdue it. It is a fallacy, and has the disadvantage that it requires one hand be placed too far forward to properly support the fish.

When photos are completed the carp should be replaced in the sling - taking care to ensure that no fins are bent the wrong way - and carried back to the water's edge for release. I cringe when I see anglers carrying a fish in their arms because an unexpected struggle can so easily result in it falling to the ground.

Which brings to mind the subject of multi-catch pictures. In my "bad old days" I took some of these, but not now - in fact, not since the mid '80's. Restraining just one carp can sometimes be difficult; controlling two or more is impossible.

Film choice

Films which have "color" in their name - Fujicolor and Kodacolor, for example - are for prints. Those which include "chrome" - Fujichrome, Kodachrome etc. - are for transparencies (slides).

If pictures are required solely for an album, print film is satisfactory; but those who aspire to write articles or give slide shows require transparencies. I recommend 100ASA process-paid Fujichrome Sensia which utilises Fuji's own processing laboratory.

Chapter Eighteen

The Future

The demand for aggregates currently runs at 250 million tonnes per annum, and there are no signs that this figure will decrease. This will not, alas, lead to an ever increasing number of pits being dug because public feeling against gravel extraction runs high; so high in the south-east that pressure from vociferous lobbies such as RAGE (Residents Against Gravel Extraction) reduces the likelihood of new developments being permitted.

The other primary source of aggregates is the Mendips - and likewise, NIMBY (Not In My Back Yard) protest groups are becoming both organised and vocal.

So if not in the south-east or the Mendips, where will new pits be dug?

Gravel is a low value resource with profit margins pared to the bone by transport and crushing costs, so it is not a viable commercial proposition to dig pits very far from where the aggregates are required which, again, is in the south-east. So the probable answer to the question, "Where will new pits be dug?" is, nowhere - well, nowhere in England, at any rate. Aggregate production will shift, I suspect, to Scotland - or to be more precise, the outskirts of Glencoe. This is surprising on two counts: first, geological, in that Scotland is not overly endowed with gravel seams; and second, economic, in that it is about as far away from south-east England as it is possible to get!

The canny Scots have not allowed a small matter like geology to stand in their way because what they lack in gravel, they make up for in granite. And granite, as every student of physical geography knows, does not extend down to a depth which is measured in feet, but miles! In the Glencoe region, for example, it is 5-6 miles deep. For all practical purposes, therefore, it is an inexhaustible resource.

Transport costs have been reduced by moving the aggregate in bulk. This has been achieved by siting the super-quarries, as they are called, adjacent to deep water sea lochs. Automated conveyor systems carry the crushed granite from the quarries direct to enormous ballast ships which, after a two-day sea journey, unload at Sheerness, in Kent.

A single super-quarry can produce 10-15 million tonnes of granite per annum - twenty such quarries could, therefore, satisfy the U.K.'s entire requirement for aggregates.

...join forces with other water users.

As a lover of pits, I am disappointed that we are unlikely to see the creation of many new ones. Worse, though, some of those we already have will undoubtedly be lost due to backfilling and waste dumping. Currently, we incinerate or recycle a very small proportion of our industrial and domestic waste - most of it is deposited in what Joe Public regards as mere holes in the ground. Albeit water-filled holes in many cases.

So what do we do? There is no point shouting, screaming and throwing tantrums because it will achieve nothing - well, not if we do it in isolation. If, however, we join forces with other water users - yes, even jet-skiers, God help us - we become an influential body. Add occasional users like dog walkers, bird watchers and picnickers, and we become more powerful still. Finally, and most important of all, we must enlist the sympathy and co-operation of conservation groups. If they discover the nest site of some obscure bird, or detect the presence of an unprepossessing but rare spider, or butterfly, or newt, or snake, or flower... anything; they mobilise their media machine to highlight the plight of the endangered species. They are very good at it, too.

On a more insular level we can help our case by portraying ourselves as responsible custodians of the countryside. And that means not leaving litter, ensuring built-swims are aesthetic and in harmony with the environment, not defecating on the banks - all that sort of thing. That, unfortunately, will require draconian enforcement by clubs because too many of our number are irresponsible in this regard.

Then there is money. According to cliché it will buy neither love nor happiness

- but those debatable assertions aside, it certainly can buy security. The best means by which pits can be protected is for clubs and syndicates to buy them outright - as the Carp Society has done with Horseshoe, for example. Obviously this is beyond the financial means of most small clubs, which makes it likely that when waters come up for sale, they will be outbid by large associations and commercial concerns. Leases likewise - the days of peppercorn rents and a bottle of malt whisky at Christmas are long gone!

Even water-skiers are potential allies!

Character Change

The character of much of our carp fishing will change radically - indeed, it is already doing so. Active management is the name of the game these days, with few waters being allowed to "do their thing" at nature's preferred pace. Stock monitoring and landscaping are the two main areas of intervention - both of which, I fear, are euphemisms for piling in fish and urbanising the banks! But it is the way of things, and clubs as well as commercial fisheries are competing for custom so they have to give the punter what he or she wants.

Most specialist anglers want big carp, and match anglers want loads of easy-to-catch small carp. As a consequence, an ever increasing number of waters are stocked with imported big fish - despite the attendant risks to existing populations - or overstocked with an excessive biomass of small ones. The fishing is synthetic, and invariably crowded. And to many of us, it is the very antithesis of real carp fishing. But whether we like it or not, the number of such fisheries is set to increase.

Fortunately, not all clubs and syndicates follow this trend - nor, perhaps surprisingly, do all commercial fisheries. Some of those who manage waters recognise that there are sufficient aesthetes around to warrant the creation and preservation of waters with a more natural atmosphere. Worthy of particular mention in this regard is RMC Angling who, under the guiding hand of Ian Welch, their Angling Manager, control the fishing on some lovely, unspoiled pits. At a bargain price, too. No, that is not a vested interest "plug" - I have no connection with RMC Angling beyond being an appreciative member.

Many carp of similar size to this one are likely to become available for stocking purposes.

New Waters

The market will shortly see a glut of low-doubles which are due to be removed from match oriented fishing facilities to make way for smaller specimens. As a consequence of there being an over-supply of such fish, they will be relatively cheap which, in turn, means they will be snapped up by clubs, syndicates and the owners of commercial fisheries. Many will be released into pits which, at present, contain no carp - or at most, very few. Initially these newly created "instant" fisheries will have a somewhat artificial feel about them, but that will soon pass and within three or four years the stock fish will settle down and the waters will acquire character and maturity. Some, undoubtedly, will go on to produce very large carp.

The pace at which low-doubles are relocated from match waters to relatively virgin pits is unlikely to slow down - rather, it will gather momentum because new match facilities are being created all the time. The probable outcome of this is that within ten to fifteen years, carp will become the dominant stillwater species.

Uncertain Future

In this chapter I have discussed the outlook for gravel pit carp fishing in a somewhat introspective manner. But if we look at the broader picture it seems clear that angling as a whole faces an uncertain future. The threats we are accustomed to - abstraction, pollution and backfilling - will continue to endanger our waters; while cormorants will continue to plunder stocks of small fish and render natural recruitment impossible. But those problems, serious though they are, pale into insignificance when compared with the prospect of angling being banned.

For the medium term I see little danger. The current Labour Government is decidedly populist in its outlook, and I cannot envisage them embarking on a policy which would antagonise the country's estimated 2.5 million anglers. And when we eventually get another Conservative Government, I think it unlikely we will have much to fear from them because they have a traditional empathy with field sports. But the public's mood is changing. The animal welfare lobby with its direct action liberation movement at one end of the scale, and the sentimentalised attitude symbolised by the plethora of television vets programmes at the other, could so easily target angling. At present they are preoccupied with fox hunting. When, as seems probable, it is banned, they will turn their attention to shooting. Should that campaign prove successful, I have absolutely no doubt that angling will be next in line.

Most people are somewhat ambivalent about angling. If pushed they might proffer the opinion that it is cruel, "How would you like to have a hook stuck in your lip?" that sort of thing - but only rarely does it evoke anything like the same level of feeling as does hunting with hounds or shooting. But that could change. I recall the swans and lead shot debate which saw the well managed publicity machine of the anti-angling group set against the embarrassingly ineffective defence put up by our self-appointed spokesmen. The public, very noticeably, turned against us. That antagonism has dissipated to a large degree - although it has by no means disappeared completely - but the ease with which it was generated should act as a warning.

So whilst I do not believe angling faces an immediate threat, we would be foolish to discount the possibility. We must, in short, remain vigilant. Fortunately there is a small group of articulate, well informed, politically aware anglers who are acting as watchdogs on our behalf. I am referring to the Specialist Anglers Conservation Group (SACG). I shall therefore end by asking every carp angler to give serious consideration to lending numerical and financial support to the SACG by joining as an individual member. The annual subscription is £5; it should be sent to:

Mr Chris Burt (SACG), 3 Great Cob, Springfield, Chelmsford, Essex CM1 6LA.

The future of angling depends on our vigilance.

Useful Contact Numbers

General

The Carp Society .... Tel: 01367 253959

Environment Agency
Emergency Hotline (Pollution etc.) .... Tel: 0800 80 70 60
General enquiries .... Tel: 0545 333 111

Custom Rods

Bob Morris Tackle .... Tel: 01322 278519
Fax: 01322 284590
e.mail: bmt@eurosoec.freserve.co.uk

Simpson's of Turnford........ Tel: 01992 468799
Fax: 01992 466227

The Tackle Box .... Tel: 01322 292400
Fax: 01322 292411
Web: www.tacklebox.co.uk

Ande Line

Bait 'N' Tackle Centre .... Tel: 01702 617764
Fax: 01702 602558
e.mail: sales@bandtc.co.uk
Web: www.BandTC.co.uk

Season Permits

RMC Angling .... Tel: 01276 453300
Fax: 01276 456611
e.mail: info@rmcangling.co.uk

Specialist Metalware

Chris Brown .... Tel: 01892 72 4298
Fax: 01982 72 4460

Cygnet Tackle .... Tel/Fax: 01474 355575

Steve Neville .... Tel: 0831 655583

Compressed air bait guns, laminated rollers etc.

Melton Interiors .... Tel: 01283 543482
Fax: 01283 511755

Magazines

Carp Fisher .... Tel/Fax: 01925 763572
e.mail: selmanp@globalnet.co.uk

Advanced Carp Fishing .... Tel: 01788 535218
Fax: 01788 541845
e.mail: catch@davidhall.co.uk

Carp-Talk .... Tel: 01430 440624
Fax: 01430 441319
e.mail: carptalk@carper.globalnet.co.uk

Carpworld .... Tel: 0114 258 0812
Fax: 0114 258 2728
e.mail: carp.world@virgin.net
Web: www.completeangler.co.uk/angpub.htm

Total Carp .... Tel: 01788 535218
Fax: 01788 541845
e.mail: catch@davidhall.co.uk

Crafty Carper .... Tel: 0114 258 0812
Fax: 0114 258 2728
e.mail: crafty@carper.globalnet.co.uk

Coarse Fisherman .... Tel: 0116 2511277
Fax: 0116 2511335
e.mail: concptleic@aol.com